Revolution and the State

Anarchism in the Spanish Civil War, 1936–1939

Danny Evans

AK PRESS
Chico / Edinburgh

Revolution and the State: Anarchism in the Spanish Civil War, 1936–1939

© 2020 Danny Evans

This edition © 2020 AK Press

All Rights Reserved. Published by arrangement with Routledge, an imprint of the Taylor & Francis Group, an Informa Business

ISBN: 978-1-84935-365-6
Library of Congress Control Number: 2019933785

AK Press
370 Ryan Ave. #100
Chico, CA 95973
www.akpress.org
akpress@akpress.org

AK Press
33 Tower St.
Edinburgh EH6 7BN
Scotland
www.akuk.com
ak@akedin.demon.co.uk

The above addresses would be delighted to provide you with the latest AK Press distribution catalog, which features books, pamphlets, zines, and stylish apparel published and/or distributed by AK Press. Alternatively, visit our websites for the complete catalog, latest news, and secure ordering.

Cover design by John Yates | stealworks.com
Printed in the United States

DEDICATION

At the beginning of my research I had the pleasure of corresponding with the late Antonia Fontanillas, a former member of the Juventudes Libertarias, whose commitment to preserving the memory of her generation and its struggle for a better world belied her years and serves as an inspiration. This book is dedicated to her.

CONTENTS

Acknowlegments

This book began life as a PhD thesis made possible by an Arts and Humanities Research Council studentship. Research trips were partly funded by the school of Languages, Cultures and Societies at the University of Leeds, the AHRC Research Training Support Grant Funding scheme and the Leeds Humanities Research Institute.

The notion of undertaking original research into Spanish anarchism did not occur to me until I had lived in Spain for a couple of years. I owe a great deal to the friends whose patience and generosity made learning Spanish so pleasurable, and to the enormous good fortune I had in meeting Uta, Marc, Gustavo, Alfredo, Vanesa, David, Patricia, the Garcia Anguita family, Oscar, Mara, Helena, Jordi and many others, particularly the stalwarts of the Spanish soul scene. Any difficulty that might have been caused by leaving Spain was alleviated by the presence in Leeds of old friends who made me feel at home again: Carl, Mallie, Mark, Karen, Juan, Maria and others; and new friends made through political and cultural activities, in particular those I met through the Critical Cinema group and Leeds No Borders.

Richard Cleminson and Angel Smith were extremely supportive supervisors of my PhD thesis and their guidance has been enormously helpful in shaping the present work. I am also grateful to the editorial team at Routledge and to the anonymous reviewers whose comments helped to improve this book. Many other friends, colleagues and historians have provided support and advice over the past four years and I would like to thank David Goodway, Jim Yeoman, Chris Ealham, Dolors Marín, Peter Anderson, Mercè Lázaro García, Claudio Hernández, Kees Rodenburg, Gregorio Alonso, Rafael Tapia, Joey Whitfield, Miguel Ángel del Arco Blanco, Diana Battaglia, Josep Antoni Pozo González, Daniel Mourenza, Francisco de Paula, Christian Høgsberg, and in particular Agustín Guillamón. I am also grateful to Edu, Javi, Silvia, Ruth, Quinnie, Colin, Ana, Arantxa and Andy for providing a bed and/or warm welcome on research trips to Barcelona, Madrid and London, and especially to Paz and Iu, who very kindly put me up for a week when conducting last-minute research for the book.

I am very lucky to have a network of loving, intelligent and funny family members that I can rely on for support and encouragement. I would like to thank in particular my parents, Helen, Rach, Phil, Peter and my much-missed grandmother. Finally, I am grateful for the love and companionship of my partner Liz. Her empathy and encouragement have been a constant source of reassurance and support, and her insight has sharpened many of the ideas contained in this work.

Acknowledgements (AK Press edition)

I am very pleased that a paperback version of my book has been made available so quickly and would like to thank those at Routledge, AK Press and the Kate Sharpley Library who have made this edition possible. In particular I'd like to acknowledge the efforts of Charles Weigl and Zach Blue at AK.

Apart from the correction of a few errors and typos, new work contained in this edition is based chiefly on material made available to me by Nereida Xena and Mar y Sol Gracia. I am very grateful for their generosity and kindness. The present edition has also been improved by the addition of images. The reproduction of engravings by the anarchist artist Gustavo Cochet is especially pleasing and is due to the co-operation and support of his granddaughter, Silvia Cochet, who runs the Museo Gustavo Cochet in Funes, Argentina, and Agustín Alzari at the Ministerio de Innovación y Cultura de Santa Fe.

Abbreviations

AAB	Agrupación Anarquista de Barcelona – Barcelona Anarchist Grouping
AAD	Agrupación Amigos de Durruti – Friends of Durruti Grouping
AJA	Alianza Juvenil Antifascista – Anti-fascist Youth Alliance
CAP	Comisión Asesora Política – Political Advisory Commision
CCMA	Comité Central de Milicias Antifascistas – Central Committee of Antifascist Militia
CGT	Confédération Générale du Travail – General Confederation of Labor
CGT-SR	Confédération Générale du Travail–Syndicaliste Révolutionnaire – General Confederation of Labor–Revolutionary Syndicalist
CNT	Confederación Nacional del Trabajo – National Confederation of Labor
DAS	Gruppe Deutsche Anarcho-Syndikalisten im Ausland – Group of German Anarcho-Syndicalists in Exile
ERC	Esquerra Republicana de Catalunya – Republican Left of Cataluña
FAI	Federación Anarquista Ibérica – Iberian Anarchist Federation
FECL	Federación Estudiantil de Conciencias Libres – Student Federation of Freethinkers
FIJL	Federación Iberica de Juventudes Libertarias – Iberian Federation of Libertarian Youth
FJR	Frente de la Juventud Revolucionaria – Revolutionary Youth Front
FRE	Federación Regional Española – Spanish Regional Federation
GEPCI	Gremis i Entitats de Petits Comerciants i Industrials – Associations and Bodies of Small Traders and Industrialists
IFTU	International Federation of Trade Unions
IWMA	International Working Men's Association
JCI	Juventud Comunista Ibérica – Iberian Communist Youth
JDM	Junta de Defensa de Madrid – Madrid Defence Council
JJLL	Juventudes Libertarias – Libertarian Youth
JSI	Junta de Seguridad Interior – Council of Internal Security

JSU   Juventudes Socialistas Unificadas – Unified Socialist Youth
MMLL   Mujeres Libres – Free Women
PCE   Partido Comunista de España – Communist Party of Spain
POUM   Partido Obrero de Unificación Marxista – Party of Marxist Unification
PSOE   Partido Socialista Obrero Español – Spanish Socialist Workers' Party
PSUC   Partit Socialista Unificat de Catalunya – Unified Socialist Party of Cataluña
UGT   Unión General de Trabajadores – General Union of Workers

Notes

Regions and cities within Spain are given their Spanish spelling, with the exception of the Basque Country, presented in its English form, and the areas and insitutions within Cataluña, which are rendered in their Catalan spelling. All translations are the author's.

Introduction

The revolution that accompanied the outbreak of the Spanish civil war (1936–1939) was one of few occasions in world history when a conscious attempt to change the fundamental relations of a society has been undertaken by masses of people. During this period, relations of production in the town and country, gender relations, and the physical and cultural expressions of a class-bound and Catholic country were profoundly, if only temporarily, altered for many of the millions of people caught up in the revolutionary experience in the Republican zone. The way people dressed, spoke and carried themselves changed overnight, as working-class people seized the opportunity to live differently. At the forefront of this process were the organisations that, in several Spanish cities, had taken the lead in opposing the attempted coup launched on 17 July 1936 by officers in the Spanish army: the anarcho-syndicalist Confederación Nacional del Trabajo (National Confederation of Labour – CNT) and the anarchist Federación Anarquista Ibérica (Iberian Anarchist Federation – FAI).

Such was the role of the anarchist organisations in suppressing the Nationalist mutineers that, on 21 July in Barcelona, they appeared to be the masters of the city. With the smell of gunpowder still lingering in the air, several of the CNT and the FAI's most prominent members met in the newly expropriated offices of an employers' association in the "Casa Cambó," an imposing building in the heart of Barcelona soon to be renamed the "Casa CNT-FAI," to discuss the question of whether to proceed immediately to their shared objective of libertarian communism. There it was decided, on a provisional basis, that no such attempt would be made, and that the Spanish libertarian movement would collaborate with other political tendencies, such as communists, socialists, liberals and Catalan and Basque nationalists, in fighting the common fascist threat.

This commitment to collaboration did not prevent the acceleration and expansion of the revolutionary process in the weeks that followed. CNT members took the lead in organisational efforts that saw militia columns established, workplaces taken over and land collectivised in the summer of 1936. The government, thrown into chaos by the upheaval of July, was marginal to these developments. However, in the absence of any attempt

I

to dissolve governmental and administrative bodies, and in a spirit of coop-eration that was variously described by anarchists as pragmatic, magnan-imous and indicative of a new era of social harmony, many revolutionary phenomena were, from the first, formally subordinate to the national or regional organs of state, in spite of being self-managed or union-controlled in their day-to-day functioning. The collaboration of the libertarian move-ment in Spain with the state can therefore be understood to have begun months before this process was accelerated and formally consummated in late October 1936 by the unprecedented acceptance of ministerial roles in the central government by four Spanish anarchists.

This book is about the interrelated and opposed processes of revolution and state reconstruction as they unfolded in the Republican zone during the Spanish civil war. Its focus is on what are here referred to as "radical anar-chists": those members of the movement committed to pushing the revolution forward and resisting the encroachments of the state. A revolution, as James C. Scott has pointed out, is an interregnum. Between the collapse of one regime and the consolidation of another there is a period in which the experience of the state – the experience of being governed – is no longer a feature of daily life.[1] In Spain, the interregnum of 1936 has been termed the "short summer of anarchy."[2] During this period, the Republican state was challenged, not only by the emergence of phenomena that bypassed the authority of its political and police bodies, but also by the rupture in the nationalist and patriarchal "common sense" on which these structures rested. By studying the ways in which a reimposition of governance was resisted over the following months, this book sheds light on the perennial question of how states are (re)consti-tuted, in ideological and cultural as well as administrative terms.

Students of Spanish anarchism are indebted to the activists who, hav-ing survived the war and escaped Francoist repression, wrote about their experiences in memoirs or historical works. The extraordinary efforts of Abel Paz and, in particular, José Peirats, to document the movement have provided the building blocks for all subsequent endeavour.[3] Much research has added to this foundational labour. In a recent article, Barry Pateman

---

1   James C. Scott, "Foreword," in *Everyday Forms of State Formation: Revolution and the Negotiation of Rule in Modern Mexico*, ed. by Gilbert M. Joseph and Daniel Nugent (Durham and London: Duke University Press, 1994), ix.

2   Hans Magnus Enzensberger, *El corto verano de la anarquía. Vida y muerte de Durruti*, trans. by Julio Forcat and Ulrike Hartmann (Barcelona: Editorial Anagrama, 2010).

3   Especially José Peirats, *The CNT in the Spanish Revolution, Volume 1*, trans. by Chris Ealham (Hastings: PM Press, 2011) and subsequent volumes; and Abel Paz, *Durruti in the Spanish Revolution*, trans. by Chuck Morse (Oakland: AK Press, 2007). An early English-language contribution to the historiography, first published in 1953, is Vernon Richards, *Lessons of the Spanish Revolution (1936–1939)* (London: Freedom Press, 1995).

has affirmed that, in the last twenty years, the state of anarchist historiography has "changed beyond recognition" in qualitative and quantitative terms.[4] This is in no small measure due to work on the movement in Spain, which reached its apogee during the civil war. Pateman mentions Chris Ealham and Agustín Guillamón, whose work on the CNT is fundamental to understanding the social and cultural universe of Spanish anarchism and the internal mechanisms and divisions within the organisation.[5] The present book builds on their research, and expands on recent historical work on the Spanish revolution and its political opponents.[6] I am further indebted to the labour of committed historians, translators and websites who, often without institutional support, have recovered the stories of little-known activists, events and groups.[7] The hypotheses presented here also depend to a great extent on work that has foregrounded the role of women anarchists.[8]

This brief and not exhaustive survey suggests that Stanley Payne's observation that "there has been little effort to account for Spanish

4   Barry Pateman, "Anarchist History: Confessions of an awkward pupil," *Bulletin of the Kate Sharpley Library*, 84 (2015): 1.

5   Chris Ealham, *Anarchism and the City: Revolution and Counter-revolution in Barcelona, 1898–1937* (Oakland: AK Press, 2010), *Living Anarchism: José Peirats and the Spanish Anarcho-Syndicalist Movement* (Chico, CA: AK Press, 2015); Agustín Guillamón, *Los Comités de Defensa de la CNT en Barcelona, 1933–1938* (Barcelona: Aldarull, 2013).

6   In particular, that carried out by: Josep Antoni Pozo González, *Poder legal y poder real en la Cataluña revolucionaria de 1936* (Sevilla: Espuela de Plata, 2012), *La Catalunya antifeixista, El govern Tarradellas enfront de la crisi política i el conflicte social (setembre de 1936 – abril de 1937)* (Barcelona: Edicions DAU, 2012); François Godicheau, *La Guerre d'Espagne. République et révolution en Catalogne (1936–1939)* (Paris: Odile Jacob, 2004); Agustín Guillamón, *Barricadas en Barcelona. La CNT de la victoria de Julio de 1936 a la necesaria derrota de Mayo de 1937* (Barcelona: Ediciones Espartaco Internacional, 2007), *La Guerra del pan. Hambre y violencia en la Barcelona revolucionaria. De diciembre de 1936 a mayo de 1937* (Barcelona: Aldarull and Dskntrl-ed, 2014).

7   D. Nelles et al., *Antifascistas alemanes en Barcelona (1933–1939). El Grupo DAS: sus actividades contra la red nazi y en el frente de Aragón* (Barcelona: Editorial Sintra, 2010); Los Gimenólogos, *En busca de los Hijos de la Noche. Notas sobre los Recuerdos de la guerra de España de Antoine Gimenez*, trans. by Francisco Madrid Santos, Carlos García Velasco and Los Gimenólogos (Logroño: Pepitas de calabaza ed., 2009); Miquel Amorós, *La Revolución Traicionada: La verdadera historia de Balius y Los Amigos de Durruti* (Barcelona: Virus, 2003), *José Pellicer: El Anarquista Íntegro* (Barcelona: Virus, 2009), *Maroto, el héroe: Una biografía del anarquismo andaluz* (Barcelona: Virus, 2011), *Los Incontrolados de 1937. Memorias militantes de los Amigos de Durruti* (Barcelona: Aldarull, 2014); Agustín Guillamón, *Los Amigos de Durruti. Historia y antología de textos* (Barcelona: Aldarull and Dskntrl-ed, 2013); Frank Mintz, *Anarchism and Workers' Self-Management in Revolutionary Spain*, trans. by Paul Sharkey (Oakland: AK Press, 2013); see also the websites cedall.org, christiebooks.com, estelnegre.org, libcom.org, militants-anarchistes.info and that of the CNT in Puerto Real, puertorealcnt.es.

8   Martha A. Ackelsberg, *Free Women of Spain: Anarchism and the Struggle for the Emancipation of Women* (Oakland: AK Press, 2005); Eulàlia Vega, *Pioneras y revolucionarias. Mujeres libertarias durante la República, la Guerra Civil y el Franquismo* (Barcelona: Icaria, 2010).

anarcho-syndicalism in analytic and theoretical terms" in the last forty years is somewhat misplaced.[9] Nevertheless, this book seeks to counter certain tendencies that have persisted in the historiography in spite of such efforts. First, it considers the "counterrevolution" in Republican Spain to be synonymous with the process of state reconstruction, rather than a political project carried out chiefly by the Partido Comunista de España (Communist Party of Spain – PCE). In this sense it builds on the work of Helen Graham, who contends that the reconstruction of the Republican state was a cross-class, multi-party process that was not driven primarily by the ideological priorities of the PCE.[10] The participation of Stalinist organisations undoubtedly gave state reconstruction peculiar and bloody characteristics, but has also served to obscure the broader and more complex aspects of the process.[11] Second and relatedly, this book considers the libertarian movement's collaboration with the Republican state to have been a lengthy process involving periods of reversal and consolidation, the study of which cannot be limited to the moments of anarchist representation in government but must incorporate attention to ideological and cultural questions, as well as to the activity of the anarchist organisations when not formally participating in government. Third, the book builds on studies of the socialisation campaign undertaken by the CNT in the first third of 1937.[12] Its attention to the upturn in revolutionary activity and the important alliances generated in this period suggests that the widespread conception that the revolution was a relatively brief affair, confined to the "short summer of anarchy," requires modification.

In addition to drawing from existing secondary works that serve to correct these persistent tendencies, the book offers several historiographical advances based on the close study of primary sources, chiefly the minutes of assemblies and meetings, the testimony of activists, and the anarchist press. Following François Godicheau and Ealham, and inspired by Anglophone

9   Stanley G. Payne, "A Critical Overview of the Second Spanish Republic," in *The Spanish Second Republic Revisited: From Democratic Hopes to Civil War (1931–1936)*, ed. by Manuel Álvarez Tardío and Fernando Del Rey Reguillo (Eastbourne: Sussex Academic Press, 2013), 18.

10   Helen Graham, *The Spanish Republic at War* (Cambridge: Cambridge University Press, 2002), 158–64.

11   I do not share Graham's scepticism as to the complicity of Stalinists in some of the more infamous murders committed in the Republican rearguard, such as the role of Soviet agents and Spanish Communists in the murders of Andreu Nin and Camillo Berneri. On the former case, see Pelai Pagès i Blanch, "El asesinato de Andreu Nin, más datos para la polémica," *Ebre 38*, 4 (2010), 57–76. On the latter, see Francisco Madrid Santos, "Camillo Berneri, un anarquista italiano (1897–1937)" (Unpublished PhD thesis, Universidad de Barcelona, 1979), 501–13, and Chapter Four of the present work.

12   Anna Monjo and Carme Vega, *Els treballadors i la Guerra civil* (Barcelona: Editorial Empúries, 1986); Antoni Castells Duran, *El proceso estatizador en la experiencia colectivista catalana (1936–1939)* (Madrid: Nossa y Jara Editores, 1996).

research into the Russian revolution, the book considers the role of mid-level activists who, for the most part, remained on the margins of both official positions of state administration and also what were known in such circles as the *comités superiores* of the Spanish libertarian organisations, but who nevertheless retained influence among wider sectors of the movement as union and affinity group delegates and prolific contributors to the anarchist press.[13] This focus has led to the unearthing of important interventions by, among others, Lucía Sánchez Saornil, Amador Franco, Juan Santana Calero and Julián Merino, the latter of whom is here afforded the centrality that his highly significant activity and role in the revolutionary rearguard deserves.

Beyond its individual champions, this work provides a more general account of the libertarian movement's radical currents than has been offered hitherto, and explains the complex affinities that linked their different manifestations. By examining the radical currents of Spanish anarchism as they cut across these different formations, we can perceive how opposition to collaboration and state reconstruction coalesced around specific positions that for the most part remained consistent with pre-war anarchist traditions while generating new revolutionary solidarities.[14] These positions formed a programmatic alternative to state reconstruction and demarcated the boundaries of the revolutionary achievements that radical anarchists fought to defend. The book shows that the radical position was both more widespread and more serious in its potential ramifications than has generally been understood.

The chapters are arranged in broadly chronological order. The first covers the pre-war years of the Spanish Republic and the tendencies and tactics of the libertarian movement in this period. Chapter Two outlines the extent of the revolution that accompanied the outbreak of the civil war in the summer of 1936. I examine the meaning and impact of state collaboration and the emergence of an oppositional strain within the Barcelona defence committees, the Juventudes Libertarias (Libertarian Youth – JJLL) and the anarchist press. The purpose of Chapter Three is to show the persistence of the revolutionary anarchist project and the renewal of its programmatic and practical characteristics in the first third of 1937. The chapter focuses

---

13   On mid-level anarchist activists in Spain, see François Godicheau, "Periódicos clandestinos anarquistas en 1937–1938: ¿las voces de la base militante?," *Ayer*, 55 (2004), 175–205 (204); Ealham, *Anarchism and the City*, 96. Works on Russia with a focus on middle-ranking worker-activists include: Simon Pirani, *The Russian Revolution in Retreat, 1920–24: Soviet Workers and the New Communist Elite* (London: Routledge, 2008); S. A. Smith, *Red Petrograd: Revolution in the Factories 1917–1918* (Cambridge: Cambridge University Press, 1983); Rex A. Wade, *Red Guards and Workers' Militias in the Russian Revolution* (Stanford: Stanford University Press, 1984).

14   In highlighting the development and subsequent fracturing of revolutionary alliances in this period, I have been influenced by the analysis in David Roediger, *Seizing Freedom: Slave Emancipation and Liberty for All* (London: Verso, 2015).

on the CNT's socialisation campaign and the new revolutionary alliances this helped to engender in and around the libertarian movement. These first chapters show the revolutionary movement in a period of expansion, albeit not without contradictions. By the spring of 1937, a radical anarchist programme had emerged, which drew on pre-war anarchist practices and the ideal of libertarian communism, and also on the basis of the revolutionary experience and its concrete achievements. Chapter Four examines the showdown between this revolutionary programme and the forces of the reconstituted state during the May events in Barcelona. It offers a significant new interpretation of why and how both the mobilisation and demobilisation took place. After this period of expansion and eventual explosion came a period of splintering and defeat. The fifth chapter analyses the renewed critique of state collaboration that followed the May days and the attempt of the Barcelona FAI to advocate a withdrawal from official positions. The evolving methods adopted by the leading cadres of the libertarian movement in combatting radical anarchism are also examined. Chapter Five discusses the defeat of this current, and departs slightly from the chronological order by covering three manifestations of this defeat in the period after the May days to the end of the civil war. It analyses the fracturing of revolutionary solidarities provoked by defeat and the hollow victory that this represented for the vitiated statist wing of Spanish anarchism. The attempts of the increasingly isolated radicals to bear witness to and draw lessons from their defeat are also discussed. The Conclusion discusses the historical import and contemporary relevance of the radical anarchists, evaluates their strengths and weaknesses, and posits the reasons for their ultimate failure.

Prior to the civil war, the libertarian movement in Spain had witnessed a boom in publications dedicated to outlining the post-revolutionary society. By imagining the world remade in the absence of a state, the anarchists advocated an end to private property, gender inequality and formal politics, proposing the socialisation of land and industry and the arming of the people. During the war, this imaginary provided the parameters of a mass revolutionary experiment. However, in a parallel process, the state re-established itself through a physical, ideological and economic assault on the manifestations of this libertarian programme that had emerged in the Republican rearguard. By examining the flashpoints where state reconstitution met libertarian recalcitrance, we find a broad and theoretically developed current of anarchism that attempted to retain its fidelity to pre-war traditions while analysing and drawing lessons from the revolutionary experience as it took place. This current requires a wide-ranging and synthetic history so that its historical and intellectual significance might be fully appreciated. This book is a contribution to that history.

CHAPTER ONE

Spanish Anarchists and the Republican State, 1931–1936

The Spanish Second Republic was declared, to mass jubilation, on 14 April 1931. It brought to an end a period of dictatorship during which anarchists had been driven underground or into exile, the CNT declared illegal and hundreds of its activists jailed. However, while the rebirth of democracy brought new opportunities for the CNT to propagate its ideas and build its organisational capacity, the Republic could not satisfy either the immediate economic demands of the organisation's working-class members or the long-term goals of its anarchist activists. Tensions were inevitable and not long in spilling over into violence and state repression. Activists found that constitutional guarantees could quickly be suspended, and within a short period anarchists considered that their insistence on the totalitarian essence of even democratic states had been vindicated. One episode that both encapsulated and accelerated this dynamic was the uprising of Alt Llobregat in 1932.

At the outset of the Republic, the population of the mining valley of Alt Llobregat in northern Cataluña lived in extreme poverty in labour colonies. The mining company, the greater part of which was owned by the Liverpool-born José Enrique de Olano, First Count of Figols, prohibited union organisation and paid its workforce in tokens redeemable only in the company stores.[1] Children of fourteen cried on the way to their first day of work, while men over twenty-five were considered surplus to requirements.[2] The first eight months of the Republic saw no changes to these conditions, and when the beginning of the new year brought word that workers in the nearby town of Berga had gone on strike, miners in the village of Figols decided that the moment had come to revolt. On 18 January 1932 a revolutionary committee was formed and, a few hours before work was to begin, its members called the villagers on to the streets to disarm the security forces.

---

1   Nicholas Rider, "Anarchism, Urbanisation and Social Conflict in Barcelona, 1930–1932" (Unpublished PhD thesis, University of Lancaster, 1987), 1064.

2   Cristina Borderias and Mercedes Vilanova, "Memories of Hope and Defeat: Catalan miners and fishermen under the Second Spanish Republic, 1931–9," in *Our Common History: The Transformation of Europe*, ed. by Paul Thompson and Natasha Burchardt (London: Pluto Press, 1982), 38–53: 43.

The success of the insurrection was confirmed by the hoisting of the red and black flag of the CNT over the town hall. The revolutionary general strike, characterised by the peaceful takeover of towns and villages and the declaration of "libertarian communism," spread like wildfire through the mining district before it was crushed, within a week, by the army.

The response of the CNT's committees was widely perceived to be too little, too late.[3] By the time the organisation declared a general strike in solidarity with the movement, Alt Llobregat was under military occupation. The fate of the insurrection provided a foretaste of how the episodic revolts that broke out in the following years would unfold: a workers' uprising established temporary dominance of an isolated region within Spain, the residents immediately attempted to put into practice a new social system based on the abolition of money and the sharing of resources, the workers' organisations throughout the rest of the country were unprepared, unwilling or unable to unite with the insurrection, the authorities crushed the rising and initiated a period of repression against the labour movement. After the rising in Alt Llobregat, more than a hundred anarchists, most of whom had only had a tangential relationship to it, were summarily deported to Spanish Guinea. Although the insurrections that followed, in January and December 1933 and October 1934, grew progressively in scale and levels of violence, the importance of the rising in Alt Llobregat for the anarchist movement is difficult to overstate. This is because it marked a definitive, worker-led break with the Republican state and pushed libertarian communism to the forefront of the movement's political imaginary, not as a vaguely agreed upon aim but as an immediately realisable practice.

Libertarian communism, a concept that drew heavily on the ideas of Peter Kropotkin and Errico Malatesta, and which conceived of the future society as a moneyless, free association of producers organised in federal communes, had been the stated goal of the CNT since 1919. For many influential figures in the organisation, however, this vision was a distant dream with little relevance to the more urgent organisational priorities of the day. At the outset of the Republic, the organisation's National Committee was dominated by gradualists, who tended to emphasise the importance of building and strengthening an organisation capable of remoulding society rather than embarking on an immediate attempt to overturn capitalism. Alt Llobregat showed, however, that many workers could not afford to wait.

What had the declaration of libertarian communism meant to the miners of Alt Llobregat? The oral history investigation of Cristina Borderias concluded that

---

3   Ealham, *Anarchism and the City*, 130–1.

Communism was a familiar word, although difficult to define, but to all it implied arms, justice and freedom. And because of this, most people agreed with the insurrection: "Yes, there everybody agreed, everybody wanted it... Communism – this had to be done... and everybody did it!"[4]

Inspired by anarchist propaganda, the workers in the district threw caution to the wind. In contrast to the gradualists, the revolt energised both the purist and voluntarist currents of the libertarian movement, who were convinced that it confirmed their prognoses as to the practicability of the anarchist ideal and the appetite of the masses for revolutionary action.[5] In its aftermath, the Peninsular Committee of the Iberian Anarchist Federation, the FAI, declared that "libertarian communism, labelled utopian by retrograde mentalities that have sold out to capitalism, has become a living and incontrovertible reality."[6] The purist review *La Revista Blanca*, which had welcomed the coming of the Republic as a progressive step and which tended to glorify industrial and technological advances in its pages, published an editorial on the front page of its edition of 15 February 1932 which declared: "It has been our custom to use the word future. Perhaps it would have been better to say near future and that is the term we will use from now on... The downfall of bourgeois society is at hand."[7] The reproductions of oil paintings and photos of bridges in its pages were replaced by scenes of striking workers and defeated insurrectionaries under armed guard. From this point on, few anarchists in Spain were prepared to dispute that the country was on the verge of revolution, and that libertarian communism would be its outcome. The question of how it could be brought about, and what its precise characteristics would be, was more vexed, however.

The upswing in insurrectionary activity in Spain ultimately served to reinforce the three-way division of the anarchist movement into gradualist, voluntarist and purist currents. In opposition to gradualists, voluntarists emphasised the revolutionary possibilities that could be brought about by insurrectionary activity, and purists prioritised propagandistic and cultural work in favour of the anarchist ideal. With the exception of "voluntarist," the labels of gradualist, voluntarist and purist were not ordinarily self-applied by libertarian activists, but they provide a descriptively accurate complement to the analogous contemporary terms which were deployed in the

4   Borderias and Vilanova, "Memories of Hope and Defeat," 44.
5   See Abel Paz, *Durruti in the Spanish Revolution*, 263–4.
6   *Tierra y Libertad*, 6 February 1932.
7   *La Revista Blanca*, 15 February 1932.

polemical context of faction fights, such as "reformist," "anarcho-Bolshevik" and "red-skin," respectively.

As we will see in this chapter, representative figures of each of these currents were capable of justifying a conciliatory attitude to the Republican state at various times. The gradualists, who tended to be more united in this regard, welcomed an end to the disruption to organisation that had been occasioned by state repression, while some voluntarists had participated alongside future state actors in insurrectionary essays against the dictatorship, and certain purists were mindful that the propagandistic and educational work they prioritised was easier to undertake under a democracy than a dictatorship. The birth of the Second Republic in 1931 had provided one example of when elements of the three strategic tendencies of Spanish anarchism contributed to a broadly conciliatory attitude towards the state and the democrats at its helm. Subsequently, an upsurge of working-class self-activity brought about a tactical convergence among purists and voluntarists from the middle ranks of the Spanish libertarian movement, who determined to reanimate their organisations with an anti-state purpose. This chapter provides an analysis of the background and outcomes of these divisions and alliances. The question of how to attain arms, justice and freedom was not a new one for anarchists during the Second Republic, but the radicalism and restlessness of the working class, and the severity of the measures adopted or considered by the authorities in response, gave it an ever-increasing urgency.

The libertarian movement in Spain

Although anarchism as both an ideology and a branch of the workers' movement is impossible to define narrowly, hostility to the state has been taken to be a common principle.[8] Anarchists have historically conceived of the state as the manifestation of authority and the negation of individual liberty.[9] When the Spanish section of the First International, the Federación Regional Española (Spanish Regional Federation – FRE) was founded in 1869, this anarchist interpretation of the state gained formal recognition within the country's labour movement, albeit not without debate.[10] The FRE thus assumed the thesis of Mikhail Bakunin, that the state could not be a tool of socialist transformation, either via parliamentary politics or the

---

8   See George Woodcock, *Anarchism* (Plymouth: Broadview Press, 2004), 28.

9   See José Álvarez Junco, *La ideología política del anarquismo español (1868–1910)* (Madrid: Siglo XXI, 1991), 222–4.

10   See Josep Termes, *Anarquismo y sindicalismo en España. La Primera Internacional (1864–1881)* (Barcelona: Ariel, 1972), 84–108.

Marxist concept of a dictatorship of the proletariat. The latter would represent nothing more than the "disguised resurrection of the state," which "could never produce any effect but the paralysis and death of the popular revolution's vitality and power."[11]

In the period covered by this book, the tendencies of Spanish anarchism were able to coexist, with varying degrees of harmony, within the framework provided by what came to be known as anarcho-syndicalism, but which was initially referred to as revolutionary syndicalism. The development of revolutionary syndicalism in France was embodied by the Confédération générale du travail (General Confederation of Labour – CGT) and had been formalised in the famous Charter of Amiens, which that union had adopted in 1906.[12] Inspired by the successes of the CGT, the belief had grown among Spanish anarchists that, as the Charter stated, an "apolitical" trade union – that is, a union unaffiliated to any political party – would be able to combine struggles of an economic nature with a wider project of revolutionary transformation.[13] In 1907, Solidaridad Obrera (Workers' Solidarity – SO), a union federation which produced a newspaper of the same name and which did not, at first, extend beyond Barcelona, was founded. SO was an amalgamation of ideologically varied unions that expanded rapidly and whose early success in bringing together Cataluña's unionised workforce led to a Congress in 1910 to decide whether it should be constituted on a national basis.[14] This was agreed to and the CNT was formed, with *Solidaridad Obrera* becoming the official newspaper of its Catalan region.[15]

The founding Congress of the CNT reflected the plurality of priorities and tactics favoured by its affiliates. It affirmed the need to overturn existing society and that, echoing the First International, the emancipation of the working class was to be the task of the working class itself.[16] It proclaimed

11   1872 letter from Mikhail Bakunin to one of the earliest and best-known of Spanish anarchists, Anselmo Lorenzo. Cited in Frank Mintz, "Las influencias de Bakunin y Kropotkin sobre el movimiento libertario español," *Historia Actual Online*, no. 21 (2010), http://www.historia-actual.org/Publicaciones/index.php/haol/article/viewArticle/415 [accessed 11 December 2017].

12   On the ideology and practice of the CGT, see F. F. Ridley, *Revolutionary Syndicalism in France: The Direct Action of its Time* (London: Cambridge University Press, 1970), 83–187.

13   Angel Smith, *Anarchism, Revolution and Reaction: Catalan Labour and the Crisis of the Spanish State, 1898–1923* (New York: Berghahn Books, 2007), 129.

14   On this Congress and the question of forming a national organisation, see Xavier Cuadrat, *Socialismo y anarquismo en Cataluña (1899–1911). Los orígenes de la CNT* (Madrid: Ediciones de la Revista de Trabajo, 1976), 462–77.

15   Ibid. 477. See also Carles Sanz, *La CNT en pie. Fundación y consolidación anarcosindicalista 1910–1931* (Barcelona: Anomia, 2010), 17–23; Manuel Buenacasa, *El movimiento obrero español 1886–1926. Historia y crítica* (Madrid: Ediciones Júcar, 1977), 37–40.

16   Cuadrat, *Socialismo y anarquismo*, 481.

its commitment to tactics of direct action, by which was meant the absence of third-party mediation in industrial disputes, but it also allowed for members of political parties to join the organisation, urged caution with regard to the general strike and committed itself to the short-term goal of establishing the eight-hour day.[17] The commitment to direct action was related to a further question under debate at the Congress: the advisability of constituting a new syndicalist organisation on a national level that would be separate from the pre-existing national trade union, the Unión General de Trabajadores (General Union of Workers – UGT), which had been founded in 1888. The UGT was the trade-union wing of electoral socialism, represented in Spain by the Partido Socialista Obrero Español (Spanish Socialist Workers' Party – PSOE). Contrary to revolutionary syndicalism's commitment to direct action, the UGT considered the mediation of its political allies to be potentially advantageous to its members. Despite assurances to the contrary from prominent figures within the CNT, the probability that the new organisation would provide a revolutionary alternative to the UGT was admitted by disappointed Socialists and hailed by enthusiastic anarchists in the weeks that followed the former's foundation.[18]

The CNT was organised federally into regional organisations. From 1918 these regions formalised their bottom-up structure. At the level of town or city, CNT members joined their local Sindicato Único (Single Union) according to the branch of industry they worked in. The representatives of each Single Union then elected delegates to a Local Federation. The elected delegates of these Federations then formed the Regional Committee. The CNT's National Committee was the temporary responsibility of one Regional Committee, to be chosen at the organisation's National Congress, its highest decision-making body.[19] In between National Congresses, the activity of the CNT was determined by decisions taken at Plenums. A Local Plenum was composed of delegates chosen at assemblies of the Single Unions, which would in turn decide the mandates and delegates to represent the locality at Regional Plenums. The Regional Plenums would likewise send mandated delegates to National Plenums. The structure was designed to prevent the accumulation of executive powers, with matters deliberated at assemblies at every level before being finally decided upon.

17   See Juan Gómez Casas, *Historia del anarcosindicalismo español* (Madrid: Zero, 1973), 83–5.

18   Cuadrat, *Socialismo y anarquismo*, 482–3.

19   In 1936 the National Committee would become a permanent body made up of delegates from all the regions. See the following chapter. For a comprehensive historical exposition and analysis of the functioning of the CNT's internal structure, see Anna Monjo, *Militants. Participació i democràcia a la CNT als anys trenta* (Barcelona: Laertes, 2003), 113–312.

Government repression was to provide the biggest logistical stumbling block to this patiently democratic and deliberative organisational form. The CNT was an illegal entity between 1911 and 1914, and at the beginning of this period the list of subscribers to *Solidaridad Obrera* was confiscated by the authorities, leading to hundreds of arrests across the country.[20] Its re-emergence, which owed a great deal to the economic conditions engendered by Spanish neutrality during the First World War, led to a membership spike which peaked in 1919 at over 700,000.[21] Spanish neutrality also meant that the CNT did not have to face the existential crisis of whether to continue oppositional activity against the government in wartime, the question that had split the socialist movement throughout the continent in 1914. In France, the CGT abandoned revolutionary syndicalism for the infamous "Union sacrée." In Spain, both notable purists such as Federico Urales and pragmatic union organisers such as Eleuterio Quintanilla voiced their approval of the position advanced by Kropotkin, among others, of support for the progressive, republican values supposedly embodied by France and threatened by Germany.[22] Although the abandonment of internationalism and anti-militarism generated a great deal of bitterness in Spain, the dispute did not lead to a lasting split in the CNT, where the questions it raised were set aside rather than resolved. When the Russian revolution led to the formation of Communist parties across Europe, in Spain, by contrast to the belligerent countries, it found no natural constituency of anti-war workers who felt betrayed by the labour movement.

Organised anarchism in Spain thus emerged strengthened after the war years, and was able to insist on its autonomy relative to the monopolising intentions of Moscow-directed international Communism, leading to a definitive fall-out in 1922. Meanwhile the growth of the CNT led to increased repression and violence. The peak of activity and membership in 1919 was followed by the years of *pistolerismo* in Barcelona, when local employers hired gunmen to target prominent organisers of the CNT, and the organisation's action-oriented voluntarists hit back. This period was brought to an end by the dictatorship of Primo de Rivera in 1923, but only after the death, in the spring of that year, of Salvador Seguí, the most prominent figure of Catalan anarchism, who was gunned down by *pistoleros* in the suburb of El Raval. The dictatorship brought a new period of illegality to the CNT, while the UGT initially cooperated with the regime. During this time, the questions that the war had brought to the surface, of whether anarchists should support a more

---

20   James Michael Yeoman, "Print Culture and the Formation of the Anarchist Movement in Spain" (Unpublished PhD thesis, University of Sheffield, 2016), 205.

21   Ealham, *Anarchism and the City*, 40.

22   On the debates in Spain, see Yeoman, "Print Culture," 225–31.

progressive, republican state over other, authoritarian forms, re-emerged. In exile, pragmatists in the CNT leadership and young gunslingers brought to prominence by the years of *pistolerismo* established contacts with republicans intent on forcing a change of regime in Spain.[23]

Concerns that the CNT might follow the UGT (as well as the erstwhile revolutionary syndicalists of the CGT) along the path of state collaboration would be reflected in the founding agreements of a specifically anarchist organisation, the FAI, which was formed in 1927, on a peninsular rather than national basis, affirming that: "The labour organization should turn to anarchism as it did in the past… and the anarchist organization of groups should be established alongside it, with the two organizations working together for the anarchist movement."[24] The organisational unit of the FAI was the affinity group, a collection of comrades united by ties of friendship and ideological kinship that did not normally number more than a dozen components. These were organised into town and city-wide Local Federations, and coordinated by Regional Committees and a Peninsular Committee, which were not intended to have any executive decision-making role. From its inception the FAI considered a semi-formal connection, a *trabazón*, to exist between itself and the CNT, which found an organisational expression in the *comités pro presos* (prisoner support committees), composed of equal parts FAI and CNT delegates.[25]

At the outset of the Second Republic, therefore, Spanish anarchism had two organisational reference points, the CNT and the FAI. While the former did not require that its members be anarchists, its most prominent activists considered themselves to be such, and its statutes contained the anarchist goal of libertarian communism. Yet Spanish anarchism could not be reduced to its organisational expressions, nor could these organisations be considered only in terms of their ultimate objectives. During the Second Republic, Spanish anarchism formed part of an oppositional cultural and moral universe, an "anti-state" that for many people influenced every aspect of their life and behaviour. Strongholds in working-class suburbs meant that anarchism was rooted in communities as well as workplaces, and even outside of such concentrations anarchist ideology and practice was sufficiently widespread to be a state-wide concern.[26] In spite of the challenges of the period, this universe would renew itself, giving rise to new organisations and

---

23   Throughout this book, "republican" will be used for those parties and individuals whose political priority was the establishment or defence of a republican state.

24   Quoted in Juan Gómez Casas, *Anarchist Organisation: The History of The FAI*, trans. by Abe Bluestein (Montréal: Black Rose Books, 1986), 110.

25   Gómez Casas, *Anarchist Organisation*, 110.

26   See Ealham, *Anarchism and the City*, 34–53.

sustaining the revolutionary vanguards that would prove crucial to the social upheavals of summer 1936.

Republic or revolution

Immediately prior to the declaration of the Second Republic, the CNT had been in contact with the animators of the Pact of San Sebastián, a broad-based alliance committed to establishing a democratic republic. The National Committee of the CNT, which included the veteran activists Joan Peiró and Ángel Pestaña, had agreed to support any insurrectionary action to that end while protecting the independence of the Confederation.[27] Public platforms were shared between anarcho-syndicalists and republicans throughout Spain. In the CNT stronghold of Gijón, another syndicalist of the old guard, Eleuterio Quintanilla, had proposed the initial republican alliance in that city, promising that Gijonese syndicalists would favour republicans with their vote and urging the CNT's state-wide "circumstantial solidarity" with the republican movement.[28] In Barcelona on 14 April, CNT activists, including some of those associated with voluntarist insurrectionism, ensured that the new authorities were able to occupy their posts.[29] In spite of the apolitical commitment in the statutes of the CNT, therefore, at the dawn of the Second Republic, "circumstantial solidarity" with the young Republican state was widespread, albeit not universal. Writing in *Tierra y Libertad*, the mouthpiece of the FAI, the rationalist schoolteacher José Alberola voiced his misgivings:

> To my mind there can be absolutely no convergence between what the bourgeoisie finds convenient and the aspirations of revolutionary syndicalism, else the latter renounce the goals for which it was founded... it is necessary that the Spanish anarchists break the self-imposed silence that, in the interests of proletarian harmony, we have submitted to, and confront that political and bourgeoisified current that has penetrated the depths of [the CNT].[30]

27   See John Brademas, *Anarcosindicalismo y revolución en España (1930–1937)* (Barcelona: Ariel, 1974), 30.

28   Pamela Beth Radcliff, *From Mobilization to Civil War: The Politics of Polarization in the Spanish City of Gijón, 1900–1937* (Cambridge: Cambridge University Press, 1996), 140.

29   See the memoirs of Ricardo Sanz, *El sindicalismo y la política. Los "Solidarios" y "Nosotros"* (Barcelona: Copa y Difon, 2013), 186.

30   *Tierra y Libertad*, 28 March 1931. José Alberola, from Aragón, was a prominent member of the FAI who frequently contributed radical articles to *Tierra y Libertad* in this period. His opposition to state collaboration would persist during the civil war. See below.

Engraving by Gustavo Cochet, photographed by Mario Gómez Casas, reproduced by permission of the Museo Gustavo Cochet and the Ministerio de Innovación y Cultura de Santa Fe. The caption reads: 'A FAI group holds a clandestine meeting prior to 19 July.'

This confrontation began within months and provided the backdrop to libertarian activity throughout the Republic's existence.

During this time, it was *Tierra y Libertad* that provided a platform to those who were most committed to combatting conciliatory attitudes towards the state within the CNT. Prior to the revolt in Alt Llobregat, the perspectives expressed in this organ were in contrast to those of the traditional mouthpiece of purist anarchism in Spain, *La Revista Blanca*, a review of international standing under the editorship of Joan Montseny and Teresa Mañé (better known as Federico Urales and Soledad Gustavo, respectively), and their daughter, Federica Montseny. *La Revista Blanca* defended a "progressive" acceptance of the Republic and an acknowledgement that the goal of anarchy remained some way off, a position that was close to that of the gradualist syndicalists in the CNT who, nevertheless, were dimly regarded within the pages of the review.[31] As such, "circumstantial solidarity" with the new regime cut across the gradualist, purist and voluntarist dividing lines of Spanish anarchism. What was to provide new impetus to the criticism of those inclined to conciliation was the rapid disillusionment of workers with the new order, which chimed with the desire of the voluntarists to force events in a more revolutionary direction.[32] The early and apposite scepticism expressed in *Tierra y Libertad* made this the ideal forum for the voluntarists to advance their agenda alongside the concerns of the anti-republican purists, and made the FAI the organisation that would appear to embody this confluence of voluntarist and purist perspectives in the years that followed.

This confluence found practical as well as journalistic expression in the early 1930s, embodied by new organisations connected to both the CNT and the FAI. The first of these emerged as a result of the Barcelona rent strike, which had begun in October 1930, and which would last in some neighbourhoods until after the end of the civil war.[33] Although not initiated by the CNT, this strike allowed the organisation to strengthen its links to community networks in its strongholds in the working-class quarters of Barcelona. The Barcelona branch of the CNT's Construction Workers' Union, strongly associated with the organisation's voluntarist wing, formed the Comisión de Defensa Económica (Commission for Economic Defence) to focus on working-class concerns outside of the workplace such as rent, food prices and unemployment.[34] In Gijón, the CNT formed a similar

31   See, for example, Federica Montseny's article, "España bajo la República," *La Revista Blanca*, 1 May 1931.

32   See Paz, *Durruti*, 216–7.

33   Nick Rider, "The practice of direct action: The Barcelona rent strike of 1931," in *For Anarchism: History, Theory and Practice*, ed. by David Goodway (London: Routledge, 1989), 79–105; Ealham, *Anarchism and the City*, 106–7.

34   Manel Aisa Pàmpols, *La huelga de alquileres y el Comité de Defensa Económica. Barcelona,*

organisation, the Sindicato de Defensa de los Intereses Públicos (Union for the Defence of Public Interests) that also organised beyond the workplace and made explicit calls to women, encouraging them to mobilise.[35]

Another such organisation was the defence committees. The formation of the defence committees was agreed to at a National Plenum of the CNT in April 1931, and responded to the prescient concern that the Confederation would be called upon to defend the Republic in the event of coup attempts from the right.[36] At a FAI Peninsular Congress in June, it was agreed that the specifically anarchist organisation would supply activists to this new body, which suggests that the defence committees were a further organisational expression of the *trabazón* between the CNT and the FAI.[37] However, in many regions and towns of Spain, defence committees were either not set up or existed on paper only, at least until a further organisational drive took place during the *bienio negro*, the two years of right-wing government that lasted from November 1933 to February 1936. Even in Barcelona, where their significance was trumpeted by local voluntarists, the formation of the defence committees does not initially appear to have implied anything more than the grafting of a command structure onto a loose network of "action groups" of the kind formed during the years of *pistolerismo*. The lack of effective organisation of the defence committees in the first years of the Second Republic would be demonstrated by the disastrous uprising of January 1933 and decried shortly afterward in a confidential report composed by Alexander Schapiro, then secretary of the International Working Men's Association (IWMA), the international revolutionary-syndicalist organisation to which the CNT was affiliated.[38]

The first National Congress of the CNT to be held since 1919 took place in Madrid in June 1931. There, the "confrontation" that Alberola had advocated in *Tierra y Libertad* took place, with the presence of FAI members at the Congress causing consternation among more moderate delegates.[39] The three principal issues of debate were the activity of the National Committee with regard to the republican conspiracies in the latter days of the monarchy, the articulation of a minimum programme that would

abril–diciembre de 1931. Sindicato de la Construcción de CNT (Barcelona: El Lokal, 2014), 55–90.

35   Radcliff, *Mobilization*, 287–8.
36   See the articles in *Solidaridad Obrera* urging the unions to take a lead in organising the armed self-defence of the people, *Solidaridad Obrera*, 17 and 19 April 1931. On the Plenum at which the decision was taken, see *Solidaridad Obrera*, 25 April 1931.
37   See the report from the Andalusian section of the FAI in *Tierra y Libertad*, 11 July 1931.
38   See Guillamón, *Los Comités de Defensa*, 8–9.
39   *Los Congresos del anarcosindicalismo. Tomo 1. Memoria del III Congreso extraordinario de la CNT. Madrid 1931* (Barcelona: Projecció Editorial, n.d.), 25.

be addressed to the government, and an alteration of the Confederation's internal organisation that would introduce national Federations of Industry, which incorporated the representatives of individual trades and professions into a broader structure. This latter proposal was passed in spite of the opposition mounted by radicals who saw in it the danger of bureaucratisation.[40] Attempts to censure the National Committee for its perceived collaboration with "political" elements were likewise unsuccessful, while the motion to address the Spanish parliament directly with a statement of perspectives was passed, albeit that the protests of several delegates were registered in the minutes.[41] At various points during these debates, the defenders of the majority positions took the opportunity to warn against inopportune revolutionary ventures, given the lack of preparation on the part of the CNT and the masses.[42] An apparent openness to "politics" and bureaucratisation thus became associated with antipathy to voluntarist insurrectionism.[43]

At the same time as radical anarchists were running aground against the seemingly entrenched positions of the gradualist majority in the CNT, the former current was more successful in setting its own house in order. The Peninsular Congress of the FAI also took place in Madrid in June, and there its Peninsular Committee was condemned for having participated in the republican conspiracy and temporarily barred from positions of responsibility in the Federation. The FAI thus emerged from its Congress shed of any lingering affinity with the Republic.[44] The articles carried by *Tierra y Libertad* in the weeks that followed combined criticisms of the new regime with declarations of revolutionary optimism that directly contradicted the warnings that Peiró, among others, had made at the CNT Congress in Madrid. Activists were therefore given the impression that the confluence of purist and voluntarist interests that had made itself felt at the CNT Congress through a minority fraction opposing perceived moderation, collaboration and bureaucratisation would be sustained by the positions and strategy of the FAI.

One non-FAI member who had made an impression at the CNT Congress was Juan García Oliver, who seemed to see the problem of revolution as a question of audacious leadership. He publicly blamed Pestaña and the deceased former General Secretary of the Catalan CNT Salvador

40   Ibid. 68–73.
41   Ibid. 105.
42   See the interventions of Joan Peiró and José Villaverde, ibid. 36 and 100, respectively.
43   "Politics" and the "political" were generally understood in Spanish anarchist literature to have to do with party politics and the machinations of state actors.
44   An account, from the point of view of one who was censured by this Congress, is given in Manuel Sirvent Romero, *Un militante del anarquismo español (Memorias, 1889–1948)* (Madrid: Fundación de Estudios Libertarios Anselmo Lorenzo, 2011), 226–8.

Seguí for having passed up the revolutionary opportunity of the post-war years, and compared them unfavourably to Lenin and Trotsky.[45] García Oliver had gained respect in anarchist circles for his activities as a leading member of the action group Los Solidarios during the years of *pistolerismo*. As impatient with theoretically inclined purist anarchists as he was with cautious gradualists, García Oliver's voluntarist conception of revolution would see him labelled an "anarcho-Bolshevik" by his purist opponents in the FAI.[46] Nevertheless, although Los Solidarios, which was renamed Nosotros in the summer of 1931, initially remained outside of the FAI, the group's components, which included similarly seasoned "men of action" such as Buenaventura Durruti and Francisco Ascaso, publicly associated themselves with the organisation.

At a FAI rally in Barcelona on 27 June, García Oliver, Ascaso and Durruti affirmed the imminence of revolution, with Durruti in particular signalling the part that would be played by the "Cuadros de Defensa Revolucionaria" (Revolutionary Defence Cadres, more commonly referred to as defence committees).[47] For the voluntarists, this new branch of libertarian organisation clearly had offensive as well as defensive potential, and Dionisio Eroles, a man close to the Nosotros group who had recently been released after eleven years in prison, wrote in *Tierra y Libertad* of the necessity that "all the activists of the CNT and the FAI realise the exceptional importance of these [defence] cadres, which will be the nerve centre, in the very near future, of actions of the Spanish proletariat that will amaze the world."[48]

Relations between the Republic and the Confederation became embittered soon after the former was founded, and as governmental repression impeded the normal functioning of the CNT, gradualists in the organisation were attacked, both by those who wished to defend the anarchist tenets of the organisation and by the voluntarists, whose chief concern was not to pass up an opportunity for a CNT-led revolution.[49] In response, the gradualists published a position paper at the end of August 1931, which came to be known as the Manifesto of the Thirty, due to the number of its signatories (who would henceforth be known as *treintistas*). While affirming that

45   *Los Congresos del anarcosindicalismo. Tomo 1*, 74.
46   See Guillamón, *Los Comités de Defensa*, 40–1.
47   *Tierra y Libertad*, 4 July 1931.
48   *Tierra y Libertad*, 27 June 1931. This article was signed "J. Eroles' as opposed to "D. Eroles." It is my assumption that they are one and the same person, as Dionisio Eroles contributed articles to *Tierra y Libertad* regularly at this time and I am unaware of other contemporary anarchists with this surname.
49   See Eulàlia Vega, *El trentisme a Catalunya. Divergències ideològiques en la CNT (1930–1933)* (Barcelona: Curial, 1980), 118–22.

Spain found itself in a revolutionary situation, the manifesto rejected the voluntarist conception of the revolution as an act of will, and did nothing to dispel the growing suspicion of the purists that the gradualist strain of anarcho-syndicalism was acting as a Trojan horse of Marxism and reformism within the CNT.[50] Alienated from the other principal currents of Spanish anarchism, the *treintistas* were both isolated and disinclined to fight for their positions within the CNT. Over the next two years, at Regional Plenums and meetings where gradualists could not, as at the Madrid Congress, rely on the majorities granted them by the bloc votes of larger unions and more moderately inclined Regional Committees, anarchists of proven "purism" were urged into positions of responsibility in the CNT. Throughout 1932 and into the beginning of the following year, the split was formalised, and the most prominent *treintistas* founded the syndicalist Opposition Unions in mid-1933, which would remain outside of the CNT until May 1936.

The position of the gradualists had been weakened by their slow and ineffectual response to the insurrection of February 1932, in Alt Llobregat. The instability of the alliance between voluntarists and purists was then revealed by the uprising of January 1933, launched on the initiative of the Catalan Regional Defence Committee (effectively the *Nosotros* group), which coordinated the region's defence committees. Conceived according to García Oliver's theory of "revolutionary gymnastics," it was a shambolic operation, the most significant consequence of which was a rising at the village of Casas Viejas in the province of Cádiz. There the revolt, which was undertaken in the mistaken belief that a nationwide insurrection was underway, was suppressed by the regional authorities and brought to a definitive end by the massacre of twenty-two villagers by members of the Civil Guard and the Republican police force, the Guardia de Asalto (Assault Guards).[51] According to the theory of "revolutionary gymnastics," groups of revolutionaries should be mobilised for insurrectionary activity, the repression of which would lead to an escalating spiral of revolutionary action in which the masses would lose their fear of the state.[52] In the absence of mass participation, the tactic had merely led to a handful of hugely uneven set-piece battles in which there could only be one outcome. The propagation of methods notable for their vanguardism and disregard for democratic organisational procedure earned the *Nosotros* group the pejorative description of

50   See, for example, the counterblast presented in the Manifesto of the *Agrupación Anarquista de Valencia, Tierra y Libertad*, 26 September 1931.

51   See Jerome R. Mintz, *The Anarchists of Casas Viejas* (Bloomington: Indiana University Press, 2004), 213–25.

52   See Juan García Oliver, *El eco de los pasos. El anarcosindicalismo…en la calle…en el Comité de Milicias…en el gobierno…en el exilio* (Paris: Ruedo Ibérico, 1978), 115.

"anarcho-Bolshevik." Much to the chagrin of anarchist purists, however, this was less commonly employed than "*faísta*," which, although intended to mean the same thing, had the effect of associating the FAI with events the organisation had little or nothing to do with.

The CNT would be involved in two further revolts prior to the outbreak of the civil war. Unlike the revolts of February 1932 and January 1933, however, which were products of the frustrated hopes that the Republic had aroused, those that followed were informed by the rise of fascism in Europe, and the conviction that only a revolution could prevent Spain from succumbing to a similar fate. The first of these anti-fascist revolts took place in December 1933 in the immediate aftermath of general elections, which had been preceded by an extensive abstention campaign carried out by the CNT and the FAI. This campaign repeatedly stressed the importance of fighting fascism on the street rather than through the ballot box, and urged Spain's working class to avoid the shameful fate of the German labour movement.[53] Notwithstanding such preparation, at least one regional section of the CNT warned in advance that the insurrection had no hope of success.[54] There was a jailbreak in Barcelona, and the adjacent town of L'Hospitalet, an anarchist stronghold, came under the control of the revolutionaries for four days. Libertarian communism was declared in several Aragonese villages, and workers' suburbs in Zaragoza were likewise held by the insurrectionaries for days, while there was heavy fighting in La Rioja.[55] The rising nevertheless posed little problem for the authorities, who crushed it within a week. Of greater scale was the insurrection in Asturias of the following year, which was of a similarly anti-fascist character. Socialists in Asturias had taken the repression of anarchists following the December revolt to be "proof of the fascist nature of the new government."[56] In Asturias, the insurrection was preceded by an accord of revolutionary unity, signed by the regional sections of the UGT and CNT, the latter acting against the policy of the national organisation. When the rising was crushed, the repressive violence of the state, directed by the Generals Manuel Goded and Francisco Franco, outstripped all previous experience under the Republic, while organisational

53   See Danny Evans, "'Ultra-Left' Anarchists and Anti-Fascism in the Second Republic," *International Journal of Iberian Studies*, 29, 3 (2016), 241–56.

54   See Horacio M. Prieto, *Secretario General de la CNT de España en 1936. Ex-ministro de la República en el exilio. Recuerdos. Tomo II, Utopistas (semblanzas de militantes libertarios)* (Unpublished memoir, BPA: n.d.), 103.

55   See Peirats, *The CNT, Vol. 1*, 57.

56   Adrian Shubert, "The epic failure: The Asturian revolution of October 1934," in *Revolution and War in Spain*, ed. by Paul Preston (London: Methuen, 1984), 123. See also Paul Preston, *The Coming of the Spanish Civil War: Reform, Reaction and Revolution in the Second Republic* (London and New York: Routledge, 1994), 120–30.

life was made impossible on a state-wide level as union buildings were closed and newspapers shut down.[57]

Although the splits and repression subsequent to these risings complicated the organisational life of the CNT, it is possible to overstate their impact.[58] The widely remarked upon decline in the union's fortunes in the period 1932–1935 must be balanced by an awareness of the continuing importance of the CNT as a reference point in the lives of both its members and wider support base, particularly through the libertarian cultural and educational centres, the *ateneos*.[59] The Libertarian Educational Youth Groups emerged from *ateneos* in Granada and Madrid, and combined with groups from Barcelona and Valencia to form the Federación Ibérica de Juventudes Libertarias (Iberian Federation of Libertarian Youth – FIJL) in Madrid in August 1932.[60] This organisation soon came to be seen as the third branch of the libertarian movement in Spain, although its Catalan section broke away at the end of the year to join the newly formed Culture and Propaganda group within the regional FAI, from which it was reluctant to disassociate.[61] Although it would re-join the FIJL at the outset of the civil war, the Catalan section was commonly known and is referred to in the literature as the Juventudes Libertarias (JJLL) rather than the FIJL.

It was through teaching at a CNT-affiliated workers' educational centre in Madrid that Mercedes Comaposada and Lucía Sánchez Saornil came to know one another and, in 1935, began soliciting support for an anarchist women's journal, *Mujeres Libres* (Free Women), the first issue of which

---

57   See Preston, *The Coming of the Spanish Civil War*, 177–8; Gabriel Jackson, *The Spanish Republic and the Civil War 1931–1939* (New Jersey: Princeton University Press, 1965), 159–64.

58   See, for example, Casanova's exaggerated contention that "the CNT had been destroyed by a combination of the 'intrusion of the FAI' and the formation of syndicates of opposition": Julián Casanova, *Anarchism, the Republic and Civil War in Spain: 1931–1939*, trans. by Andrew Dowling and Graham Pollok (London: Routledge, 2005), 63.

59   See Javier Navarro, *A la revolución por la cultura. Prácticas culturales y sociabilidad libertarias en el País Valenciano (1931–1939)* (Valencia: Universitat de València, 2004), 117–21; "Mundo obrero, cultura y asociacionismo: algunas reflexiones sobre modelos y pervivencias formales," *Hispania*, 63, 2 (2003), 467–84: 476–7; Dolors Marín Silvestre, "Anarquistas y Sindicalistas en L'Hospitalet. La creación de un proyecto de autodidactismo obrero," in *El cinturón rojinegro: radicalismo cenetista y obrerismo en la periferia de Barcelona 1918–1939*, ed. by José Luís Oyón and Juan José Gallardo (Barcelona: Ediciones Carena, 2003), 125–46.

60   See Antonia Fontanillas, "Nacimiento de la FIJL," in Felipe Alaíz, Víctor García and Antonia Fontanillas, *Vidas cortas pero llenas. 80 aniversario de la fundación de la FIJL* (Badalona: Centre d'Estudis Llibertaris Federica Montseny, 2012), 7–8.

61   See Juan Manuel Fernández Soria, *Cultura y libertad. La educación en las Juventudes Libertarias (1936–1939)* (Valencia: Universitat de Valencia, 1996), 32–3; Sònia Garangou, *Les Joventuts Llibertàries de Catalunya (1932–1939)* (Maçanet de la Selva: Editorial Gregal, 2017), 42–9.

was published in May 1936. During the war, the group around the journal would join forces with the Agrupación Cultural Femenina (Women's Cultural Grouping) in Barcelona, itself an outgrowth of women's activity in neighbourhood *ateneos* and unions, which had been formed in 1935.[62] Although the need for such groups highlights the fact that women members of the CNT tended to be marginal to organisational life, their emergence also testifies to the self-renewing capacities of Spanish anarchism, in which autonomous organisational practices facilitated the identification and rectification of deficiencies by the people they affected. Whereas, for the other branches of the workers' movement, a successful revolution was expected to bring about a period of transition during which questions of gender equality could be attended to in due course, libertarian communism held open the possibility of freedom and equality as immediate practice. Because worker mobilisations during the Republic had put libertarian communism at the centre of the anarchist agenda, it therefore made sense for anarchist women to take practical steps towards their full participation in the new society.

On the eve

It has been suggested that the impetus for the reunification of the libertarian movement at the Zaragoza Congress of May 1936 came from the relative organisational paralysis brought about by repression and disunity.[63] However, a contemporary ideological shift in the FAI, embodied by Diego Abad de Santillán's Nervio affinity group, also helped to make this rapprochement possible. Santillán, the pseudonym of Sinesio Baudilio García Fernández, had spent most of his life in Argentina, where his polemics in favour of a specifically anarchist workers' organisation had won him the favour of many purists in Spain.[64] This may help to explain the immediate impact he had on the FAI on his return to the country in 1934, by which time he had become a convert to "the idea of toleration among all revolutionary parties."[65] In Barcelona, Nervio joined in the effort to sideline the Nosotros group.[66] As much had previously been attempted by the purist José Peirats,

62   Vega, *Pioneras y revolucionarias*, 123–8.
63   Eulàlia Vega, *Entre revolució i reforma. La CNT a Catalunya (1930–1936)* (Lleida: Pagès, 2004), 396–8.
64   Ealham, *Living Anarchism*, 61.
65   Quoted in James A. Baer, *Anarchist Immigrants in Spain and Argentina* (Chicago: University of Illinois Press, 2015), 215.
66   See Stuart Christie, *We, the Anarchists: A Study of the Iberian Anarchist Federation (FAI) 1927–1937* (Oakland: AK Press, 2008), 158–9; García Oliver, *El eco de los pasos*, 132.

of the affinity group *Afinidad*, appalled by the "anarcho-Bolshevik" methods of Nosotros. Peirats, however, soon tired of Santillán's "disciplinary anarchism" when the latter endeavoured to undermine the autonomy of the affinity groups by subjecting them to organisational control.[67] Under the editorship of Santillán, *Tierra y Libertad* turned sharply away from insurrectionism, provoking angry criticism from a former contributor, Alfonso Nieves Núñez, while his industry-centred vision of the future society was not far removed from that advocated by Joan Peiró, the most prominent *treintista*.[68]

While the *bienio negro* saw the groundwork laid for the reunification of the CNT, therefore, the three-way split in the movement as a whole, between voluntarists, purists and gradualists, appears to have been reinforced during this time. As much was suggested by the campaign to reorganise the defence committees. Initiatives in this regard were undertaken in Barcelona, where they were spearheaded by the Nosotros group, and also Madrid and Andalucía.[69] However, in the FAI stronghold of La Felguera in Asturias, no defence committees were ever set up, their objectives instead entrusted to affinity groups, while in Galicia it was not until July 1935 that the FAI agreed to supply delegates to the defence committees.[70] In Barcelona, where the most coordinated and well-equipped network of defence committees had been established, the plans of the Nosotros group to convert it into a "revolutionary army" met with the concerted and near unanimous opposition of both the purist and gradualist currents. Even within the network of the defence committees, discipline was not guaranteed. García Oliver's "authoritarian" posture caused him to lose support at its youthful periphery, while on the eve of the civil war the Nosotros group could not even rely on the obedience of its lieutenants in Barcelona.[71]

67   See Ealham, *Living Anarchism*, 69–70 and 77.

68   See Mintz, *Anarchism and Workers' Self-Management*, 204–5. Alfonso Nieves Núñez, an Argentinian who had spent most of his life in Spain, would maintain an oppositional position over the years that followed. His letter, which complains of the "reformist" nature of the "so-called anarchist press," can be found in the Centro Documental de la Memoria Histórica (CDMH), PS Barcelona, 1335/11.

69   See, respectively, Guillamón, *Los Comités de Defensa*, 9–25; Julián Vadillo, "Desarollo y debates en los grupos anarquistas de la FAI en el Madrid Republicano," *Germinal*, 4 (2007), 27–65 (56); José Luís Gutiérrez Molina, *Crisis burguesa y unidad obrera. El sindicalismo en Cádiz durante la Segunda República* (Madrid: Madre Tierra, 1994), 329.

70   See, respectively, the Eladio Fanjul Roces file, Col·lecció Ronald Fraser, AHCB, 20; and Eliseo Fernández, "The FAI in Galicia," in *Anarchism in Galicia: Organisation, Resistance and Women in the Underground*, ed. and trans. by Paul Sharkey (London: Kate Sharpley Library, 2011): 7–8.

71   See the following chapter. On García Oliver's loss of support among young activists at this time, see the recollections of Diego Camacho: Abel Paz, *Chumberas y alacranes (1921–1936)* (Barcelona: Medusa, 1994), 195.

In the build-up to the general elections of February 1936, the CNT and the FAI did not mount the kind of concerted abstention campaign that had preceded the elections and attempted insurrection at the end of 1933. Whether this was due primarily to the exhaustion of activists and resources occasioned by the repression of the *bienio negro*, or thanks to what Santillán would revealingly describe as a "happy coincidence of opinion" among the "activists whose views counted for a great deal in our ranks," remains a subject of debate.[72] The CNT and the FAI concentrated much of their propaganda at this time on the need for an amnesty for political prisoners, which formed part of the platform of the Popular Front, a broad electoral alliance which had been animated chiefly by Manuel Azaña, leader of the centrist Acción Republicana (Republican Action) and Prime Minister of the Second Republic during the first *bienio*, and Indalecio Prieto, a leader of the moderate wing of the PSOE.[73] As several of the most prominent figures from across the spectrum of Spanish anarchism, from Peiró to Federico Urales, called, explicitly or otherwise, for a vote for the Popular Front, a resurrection of the "progressive" alliance that had ushered in the Republic with the support of gradualist, purist and voluntarist anarchists could be perceived.[74]

On an official level, however, neither the CNT nor the FAI considered parliament to be a potential terrain in the fight against fascism. Following a Plenum of FAI Regional Federations at the end of January, *Tierra y Libertad* affirmed: "The anarchists consider it deplorable that workers are called to the ballot boxes in the name of socialism, and propose as a true dike against fascism the united revolutionary action of the proletariat."[75] Two days before the elections and a full five months before the civil war began, the National Committee of the CNT issued a communiqué calling for workers to be "on a war footing," identifying Morocco as the "epicentre" of the conspiracy, and urging that every attempt be made to "ensure that the defensive contribution of the masses may lead to the real social revolution and libertarian communism... pursued to its utmost consequences without

72   Diego Abad de Santillán, *Por qué perdimos la guerra. Una contribución a la historia de la tragedia española* (Madrid: Toro, 1975), 53. For a discussion of the abstention campaign of 1936, see Roberto Villa García, "'Obreros, no votéis.' La CNT y el Frente Popular en las elecciones de 1936," *Pasado y Memoria. Revista de Historia Contemporánea*, 13 (2014), 173–96.

73   See Paul Preston, "The Creation of the Popular Front in Spain," in *The Popular Front in Europe*, ed. by Helen Graham and Paul Preston (New York: St. Martin's Press, 1987), 84. The signatories of the Popular Front included all of the moderate and leftist organisations other than the CNT, including the newly formed dissident communist organisation, the Partido Obrero de Unificación Marxista (Party of Marxist Unification – POUM).

74   See Ealham, *Anarchism and the City*, 167.

75   *Tierra y Libertad*, 12 February 1936.

tolerating attempts by the liberal bourgeoisie and its Marxist allies to hold back the course of events."[76] In spite of tactical differences with regard to voting in February, the dominant feeling in the CNT was that bourgeois democracy was unlikely to survive any existential conflict with fascism. At the beginning of the year, Durruti had declared at a meeting of his union: "Our slogan must be: dictatorship of the bourgeoisie or libertarian communism. Bourgeois democracy is dead in Spain and it is the republicans who have killed it."[77]

The victory of the Popular Front slate allowed the CNT to call a National Congress, which began in Zaragoza on 1 May. Assemblies were held to debate the agenda for the Congress on successive Sundays throughout the country and hundreds of CNT members made their way to Zaragoza, where 649 delegates representing 550,595 members celebrated the first Confederal Congress since 1931. However, this apparently thriving democratic culture disguised the fact that the Congress did not discuss in any detail what was apparently the chief preoccupation of the organisation, namely, the imminent threat of a coup d'état, and how best to respond to it. It appears that the national coordinating body of the defence committees discussed its plans at a private session.[78] The principal outcomes of the Zaragoza Congress were the agreements to ratify the readmission of the Opposition Unions, the approval of a document outlining the content of libertarian communism, and the sending of a unity proposal to the UGT.

In the preparatory assemblies leading up to the Congress, it was the debate around the definition of libertarian communism that had produced the most enthusiasm. Unions and affinity groups submitted 150 different proposals for the consideration of the Congress, which it was the unenviable task of a working group to synthesise. The vision of libertarian communism that emerged was a compromise between the purist and gradualist currents, and was criticised from the floor by the former for considering the union organisation to have a role in a post-revolutionary society and by the latter for not granting it a more prominent position.[79] Historians have since wondered at the document's attention to such details at the expense of questions of armed conflict and wartime production. Yet the vision of libertarian communism that was produced by the Congress, and above all

76   Peirats, *The CNT, Vol. 1*, 90.
77   See Abel Paz, *Durruti en la Revolucion Española* (Madrid: Fundación de Estudios Libertarios Anselmo Lorenzo, 1996), 443. The English translation of this volume cited above provides a slightly different rendering. Subsequent citations of Paz, *Durruti*, are taken from the English translation.
78   Abel Paz, *The Story of the Iron Column: Militant Anarchism in the Spanish Civil War*, trans. by Paul Sharkey (Oakland: Kate Sharpley Library and AK Press, 2011), 6.
79   C.N.T., *El Congreso Confederal de Zaragoza* (Bilbao: Zero, 1978), 200–7.

the multiple and varied discussions that it was the product of, demonstrate that a desire for libertarian communism and a collective effort to imagine its parameters were not the preserve of ideologues or deluded and isolated villagers, but were at the very heart of this mass, working-class organisation. In spite of the fact that the document did not claim to provide a rigid formula for a post-revolutionary society and failed to win unreserved approval, it is worth noting that the principles that were affirmed here as integral to the revolutionary project would soon re-emerge as priorities for radical anarchists during the revolution. These included the arming of the populace, economic equality, assembly-based decision-making procedures, federalism, and the equality of the sexes.[80]

The unity proposal sent to the UGT was arrived at after a similarly heated debate. It urged the Socialists to abandon their political illusions and commit to the social revolution. In another example of compromise, however, an additional article recognised the right of the UGT to elaborate further conditions for an alliance, which were to be negotiated by appointed liaison committees from both organisations, that would then return to their members with the results for ratification.[81] This proposal was opposed on purist grounds by the delegate from L'Hospitalet, José Peirats: "There can be no entente between liberty and authority," he declared. "The criterion of class… is Marxist, and therefore artificial. Men are polarised principally according to their ideas, their passions and their mentality."[82] Speaking in favour of the proposal, the delegate from the fishing industry of Barcelona affirmed that ideas could not be sufficient to make a revolution when they were not shared by the majority of even the CNT's own members, and that the impetus for an alliance came from below.[83] The dangers of a unity negotiated via liaison committees and which made no stipulations as to the elaboration of workers' power during and after the revolution were not highlighted.[84] In the brief period that followed the Congress of Zaragoza before the outbreak of the civil war, the UGT displayed no desire to respond to the CNT proposal.[85] The trumpeting of the alliance in the CNT press was not, as the National Committee admitted, "because we believe that [the

80   Ibid. 226–42.
81   Ibid. 224–6.
82   Ibid. 182–3.
83   Ibid. 185–6.
84   In this respect, the proposal differed from the influential 1934 appeal for an alliance written by the CNT activist Valeriano Orobón Fernández, who by the time of the Zaragoza Congress was terminally ill. See José Luis Gutiérrez Molina, *Valeriano Orobón Fernández. Anarcosindicalismo y revolución en Europa* (Valladolid: Libre Pensamiento, 2002), 268–77.
85   See Horacio M. Prieto, *Secretario General de la CNT de España en 1936. Ex-ministro de la República en el exilio. Recuerdos* (Unpublished memoir, BPA: n.d.), 54.

UGT] will agree to it, since they have no honesty within them," but rather because of the advantageous light in which this presented the Confederation in the eyes of pro-alliance workers.[86] However, the question of an "entente between liberty and authority" could not be sidelined, and would soon be posed of the organisation again amidst the rubble and gunpowder smoke of July 1936.

Conclusions

The fact that anarchists shared ideas relating to rational education and human progress with liberal republicans and socialists, and attended talks and debates at the larger *ateneos* frequented by republicans, has led historians to include anarchists within a broad definition of Spanish republicanism.[87] In Spain as elsewhere, a common belief in "progress, education, science, and the need to overcome a tradition that stood in the way of both personal and collective liberation" gave rise to alliances of convenience between revolutionary, socialist, working-class movements and liberal, bourgeois republicans.[88] Since the foundation of the CNT, the libertarian movement had been divided by such temporary and informal alliances on three occasions in particular: during the First World War, prior to and at the outset of the Second Republic, and during the election campaign of 1936. The question would be posed again, with brutal clarity and urgency, during the civil war. On each of the occasions noted above, the alliance with "progressive" and statist elements cut across the three-way division of the libertarian movement into gradualist, voluntarist and purist currents.

The ease with which examples from each tendency can be found urging support for the more "progressive" form of state is suggestive of a related

86   See Thomas Corkett, "Interactions between the Confederación Nacional del Trabajo and the Unión General de Trabajadores in Spain and Catalonia, 1931–1936" (Unpublished PhD thesis: University of Glasgow, 2011), 185.

87   See José Álvarez Junco, "Los 'amantes de la libertad': la cultura republicana española a principios del siglo xx," in *El republicanismo en España (1830–1977)*, ed. by Nigel Townson (Madrid: Alianza, 1994), 265–92 (270); and the discussion in Álvaro Girón Sierra, "Una historia contada de otra manera: librepensamiento y 'darwinismos' anarquistas en Barcelona, 1869–1910," in *Cultura y política del anarquismo en España e Iberoamérica*, coord. by Clara E. Lida and Pablo Yankelevich (Mexico City: El Colegio de México, 2012), 95–133. The question is also discussed by a contemporary French anarchist: Gaston Leval, *Collectives in the Spanish Revolution* (London: Freedom Press, 1975), 327–8.

88   E. J. Hobsbawm, "Religion and the Rise of Socialism," in E. J. Hobsbawm, *Worlds of Labour: Further Studies in the History of Labour* (London: Weidenfeld and Nicolson, 1984): 43.

contradiction within the CNT: that a massive, democratic organisation whose functioning derived largely from the anonymous labour of its thousands of activists and supporters nevertheless gave rise to famous spokespeople with privileged access to public platforms.[89] The scrupulously bottom-up organisational forms adopted by Spanish anarchists had not prevented the rise of *notables*, "big names" whose influence gave them a leading role in the movement. During periods of repression, when the organisational functioning of the CNT became necessarily less transparent, such *notables* could have a decisive influence on strategy, as in the period immediately preceding the Republic. When organisational normality returned, the pronouncements of *notables* had the potential to outweigh the agreements of regularly constituted Plenums and assemblies, as arguably occurred during the election campaign of February 1936. We have seen, however, how important developments within the libertarian movement took place that bypassed such prominent figures. As the lifelong activist Germinal Gracia would later reflect:

> It would be a crass error to imagine that the CNT can be reduced to a few dozen men at the top. Its true strength resided in a wellspring of anonymous activists, who wrote infrequently and expressed themselves crudely. Situated between the great mass of the membership and the famous higher-ups, these were the ones who carried the weight of the organisation at its base, in direct contact with the factories… These mid-level activists constituted, in successive generations, a great reserve of energies for the organisation. When the unions were closed by the authorities, activity persisted underground thanks to this ant's nest of militants, which the police could never penetrate.[90]

This chapter began with a discussion of the rising in Alt Llobregat because it marked a crucial moment in the CNT's relationship with the young Second Republic. It revealed a dynamic by which the desire of workers to live in a new kind of society animated the anarchist movement and drew a line in the sand that confirmed the difficulty of a progressive alliance with the Republic. The rising did not provide a strategic model for accelerating the revolutionary process but it did bring the question of strategy into dialogue with the desire for libertarian communism, so much so that by the eve of the civil war, activists at all levels of the movement were preoccupied with the question of what the revolutionary society would look

---

89   This point is also made in Richards, *Lessons of the Spanish Revolution*, 199.

90   Cited in Carlos Díaz, *Víctor García, "el Marco Polo del anarquismo"* (Madrid: Madre Tierra, 1993), 19.

like – pragmatists like Peiró and Santillán no less so than their maximal-ist counterparts.[91] Meanwhile, the movement had produced new organisa-tional forms, the defence committees, the libertarian youth and the women's groups, which were shortly to play a key role in defining the parameters of one of the most extraordinary events of the twentieth century: the Spanish revolution.

91   See the discussion in Alejandro R. Díez Torre, *Trabajan para la eternidad. Colectividades de trabajo y ayuda mutua durante la Guerra Civil en Aragón* (Madrid and Zaragoza: La Malatesta Editorial and Prensas Universitarias de Zaragoza, 2009), 32–5; and Mintz, *Anarchism and Workers' Self-Management*, 204–5.

CHAPTER TWO

Revolution and the State, July–December 1936

As libertarian activists had long promised would happen, the alliance of the working class against fascism was not hammered out in the headquarters of unions and political parties but in fact occurred "on the street" in July 1936.[1] The attempted coup d'état, initially headed by José Sanjurjo and prominent generals such as Emilio Mola, Queipo de Llano and Francisco Franco, was the catalyst for the declaration of a general strike and the creation of ad hoc anti-fascist alliances between trade unions and workers' parties. In some areas, sympathetic members of the army and the police added crucial weight. The coup was routed in many of Spain's major cities, but important regional capitals such as Sevilla, Oviedo and the anarchist stronghold of Zaragoza were lost. Where the revolt was defeated, the initial collaboration of the CNT with other organisations was established as an emergency defensive alliance against an external threat. The committees created to coordinate the anti-fascist forces, however, were by force of circumstances obliged to challenge existing power relations in their cities and towns, controlling movement through barricades and checkpoints and taking charge of supplies in order to keep local populations fed. In most areas, these committees also rapidly concerned themselves with questions that went beyond the defence of the Republic to address long-standing demands of the workers' movement. As the defeat of the revolt was everywhere accompanied by the dislocation of state power, the nature and durability of these anti-fascist alliances would consequently be tested by an emerging revolutionary situation in Republican Spain.

Barcelona, the traditional bastion of the CNT and the first major city in which the military revolt was comprehensively defeated, would provide the test case for the organisation's attitude to the state, revolution and anti-fascist alliances in this new context. There, the rising had met with the determined response of the CNT defence committees, which had mobilised around 2,000 members according to the plans of the Catalan Regional Defence Committee, which was chiefly composed of members of the Nosotros

---

1   On the frequency with which this appeal to a unity of "the street" was made, see Gutiérrez Molina, *Crisis burguesa*, 36.

group.[2] They had been able to count on the support of a significant proportion of the city's security forces, the intervention of activists from the dissident communist party, the Partido Obrero de Unificación Marxista
(Workers' Party of Marxist Unification – POUM) and a mobilised working-class population that thronged the plazas clamouring for arms and that
filled the streets in festive spirit as the rising was defeated. What remained
of the Republican state in Cataluña was discredited, through its pusillanim-
ity in the face of the rising and initial refusals to arm the people, while its
functioning had been thrown into chaos.[3]

The fall of the Atarazanas barracks on 20 July, following an anarchist-led
assault during which Francisco Ascaso was killed, marked the definitive end
of the military revolt in Barcelona. The veteran union organiser Andrés
Capdevila recalled: "We went into the street to defend ourselves and once
we had triumphed, once the barracks were under our control, we said 'The
time has come for the revolution.'"[4] The transformation of the city, familiar
from the abundant literature, photography and cinema that have sought to
capture it, was underway.[5] A labyrinthine network of barricades established
proletarian hegemony on the streets. Churches, with notable exceptions
such as the cathedral and the Sagrada Familia, were set alight. Men and
women in workers' overalls held rifles aloft and exclaimed "*vivas!*" to the
revolutionary organisations, while requisitioned cars and trucks sped back
and forth, their horns beeping out the rhythm of the omnipresent chant:
"CNT-FAI!" Buildings belonging to the wealthy, large private compa-
nies or religious orders were taken over. The well-dressed, if not all of the
better-off, disappeared from the streets, as the working-class periphery of
the city took over the centre.[6] As one eyewitness declared:

2   The figure of 2,000 is given by the anarchist teacher Félix Carrasquer in Ronald Fraser,
     Blood of Spain: The Experience of Civil War, 1936–1939 (London: Penguin, 1979), 107.
     The importance of the Regional Defence Committee to the success of the street fight-
     ing in Barcelona is demonstrated in a highly detailed account of its activities on 19 and
     20 July in Guillamón, *Los Comités de Defensa*, 53–90.

3   See Ángel Ossorio y Gallardo, *Vida y Sacrificio de Companys* (Barcelona: Nova Terra,
     1976), 186; Pelai Pagès i Blanch, *La Guerra Civil espanyola a Catalunya (1936–1939)*
     (Barcelona: Els llibres de la Frontera, 1997), 43; Fraser, *Blood of Spain*, p.141; Ignacio
     Iglesias, *Experiencias de la Revolución. El POUM, Trotski y la intervención soviética* (Barce-
     lona: Laertes, 2003), 101.

4   Andrés Capdevila file, Col·lecció Ronald Fraser, AHCB, 13.

5   For an evocative, nuanced and comprehensive account of the transformation that Bar-
     celona underwent in the summer of 1936, see Chris Ealham, "The myth of the mad-
     dened crowd: class, culture and space in the revolutionary urbanist project in Barcelona,
     1936–1937," in *The Splintering of Spain: Cultural History and the Spanish Civil War, 1936–
     1939*, ed. by Chris Ealham and Michael Richards (Cambridge: Cambridge University
     Press, 2005), 111–32.

6   Ibid. 119.

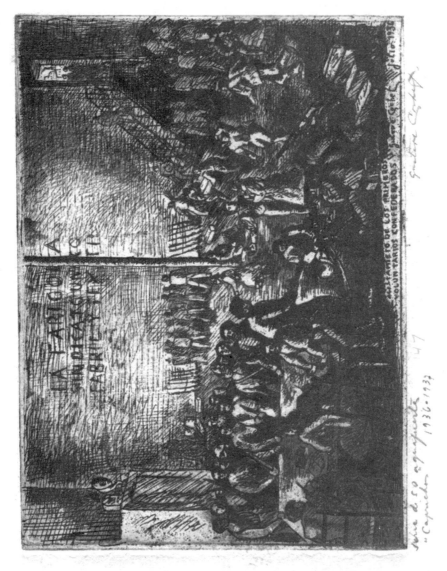

Engraving by Gustavo Cochet depicting CNT members volunteering for the front at the rational school "Natura", better known as "La Farigola", in the neighbourhood of Clot. Photographed by Mario Gómez Casas, reproduced by permission of the Museo Gustavo Cochet and the Ministerio de Innovación y Cultura de Santa Fe.

Today there is not a hat, a collar, or a tie to be seen among them; the sartorial symbols of the bourgeoisie are gone, a proletarian freedom has swarmed in along the Calle Hospital and the Calle del Carmen from the Parallelo.[7]

Even taking into account the forbidding national and international context, it is clear that, in its twenty-six-year history, the CNT had never before found itself at the heart of a mobilisation with so much revolutionary potential.

Proletarian freedom and its limits

By 20 July, the defence committees in Barcelona had constituted themselves as "neighbourhood revolutionary committees" and their members had taken to calling themselves *"milicianos."*[8] Movement around the city was controlled by barricades overseen chiefly by such *milicianos*. They still dominated the streets when Franz Borkenau, a refugee from Hitler's Germany, arrived on the night of 5 August:

They sat on the benches or walked the pavement of the Ramblas, their rifles over the right shoulder, and often their girls on the left arm. They started off, in groups, to patrol out-lying districts. They stood, as guards, before the entrances of hotels, administrative buildings, and the larger stores. They crouched behind the few still standing barricades, which were competently constructed out of stones and sand-bags... The fact that all these armed men walked about, marched, and drove in their ordinary clothes made the thing only more impressive as a display of the power of the factory workers. The anarchists, recognizable by badges and insignia in red and black, were obviously in overwhelming numbers.[9]

It was such *milicianos* who formed supply committees to ensure that the families of those undertaking revolutionary work were fed, and set up

7   John Langdon-Davies, *Behind the Spanish Barricades: Reports from the Spanish Civil War* (London: Reportage Press, 2007), 99.

8   Guillamón, *Los Comités de Defensa*, 91. In the literature on the anarchist movement in the civil war, these committees are frequently referred to as both revolutionary committees and defence committees. To avoid confusion, I refer to them as defence committees throughout this book.

9   Franz Borkenau, *The Spanish Cockpit: An Eye-Witness Account of the Political and Social Conflicts of the Spanish Civil War* (Ann Arbor: University of Michigan Press, 1974), 70.

huge public canteens, most famously at the Ritz hotel, renamed Hotel Gastronómico No. 1. They also organised the first militia divisions that left in the direction of Zaragoza on 24 July, with Durruti and Antonio Ortiz, both Nosotros members, leading anarchist columns.

One of the most striking indications of the rupture that had taken place in the life of Barcelona was the visible protagonism of women, and the emergence of the militia woman, the *miliciana*, dressed in the uniform of blue overalls and carrying a rifle, as an emblem of the revolutionary moment. For women, wearing workers' overalls had "an even deeper significance, as women had never before adopted such masculine attire... [it] not only meant an exterior identification with the process of social change but also a challenge to traditional female attire and appearance."[10] Women had participated in the street fighting to put down the coup and it was a 19-year-old anarchist woman, Concha Liaño, who headed up the expropriation of the enormous Casa Cambó building on 19 July, which, renamed the Casa CNT-FAI, would become the headquarters of the libertarian movement in Cataluña until the fall of Barcelona.[11] The women's prison was stormed and the inmates set free.[12] Remembering the behaviour of women at this time, Antonia Fontanillas would later assert that "one breathed in a different kind of atmosphere, more natural, more human. The barriers of convention were being broken down."[13]

By 20 July it was clear to anarchists that the defensive measures they had undertaken to defeat the military coup in Barcelona had developed along revolutionary lines, in accordance with the predictions of the National Committee's February communiqué. That document, drafted by Horacio M. Prieto, had enjoined activists to pursue any revolutionary development to its "utmost consequences," without "tolerating attempts by the liberal bourgeoisie and its Marxist allies to hold back the course of events." That day, the Liaison Committee the regional CNT had delegated to maintain communication with the seat of Catalan government, the Generalitat, was called to a meeting with the Catalan President, Lluís Companys. The Liaison Committee was composed of three members of the Regional Defence Committee, García Oliver, Durruti and Francisco Ascaso, who was replaced after his death by Aurelio Fernández Sánchez, a further long-standing member of the Nosotros group, along with another,

10   Mary Nash, *Defying Male Civilization: Women in the Spanish Civil War* (Denver: Arden Press, 1995), 52.
11   Eulàlia Vega, *Pioneras y revolucionarias*, 134–6.
12   Partially demolished in the act, the complete destruction of the building would be carried out by the CNT Construction Workers' Union mandated by an assembly of anarchist women. See Ealham, "The myth of the maddened crowd," 126.
13   Antonia Fontanillas, "De lo aprendido y vivido," unpublished memoir (Dreux, 1996), 8.

Josep Asens, in representation of the Regional Committee of the CNT, and Santillán, an opponent of the tactics employed by the Nosotros group, in representation of the FAI.

They arrived at the Palace of the Generalitat bleary-eyed and covered in the dust and gunpowder of battle. There, these representatives of triumphant proletarian freedom met those of the "liberal bourgeoisie and its Marxist allies," who were busily discussing the creation of a new body, the Comité Central de Milicias Antifascistas (Central Committee of Anti-Fascist Militia – CCMA), which would unite the anti-fascist organisations in Cataluña in order to coordinate the war effort and maintain order.[14] The viability of the project depended on the participation of the anarchists. The Regional Committee of the CNT, in communication with the Liaison Committee via telephone, agreed to the proposal, subject to its ratification at a Regional Plenum to be held the following day. By that time, however, the CCMA was already operational, a fact declared by decree of the Generalitat on 21 July. For the Regional Committee of the CNT to agree to participation in a body incorporating the representatives of a democratic system in crisis, subject to the regional government, represents an apparent paradox. It appears still more paradoxical when we consider that the Liaison Committee mediating the discussion was dominated by those members who had been most associated with the voluntarist wing of the organisation during the Second Republic.

It seems at first glance that it would have been feasible for the voluntarist wing to have asserted its authority at this stage, in the name of the Regional Defence Committee. The prestige and power of the Barcelona defence committees, long considered the potential shock troops of the revolution, had never been greater, and with the revolutionary developments in Barcelona led primarily by *milicianos*, it is unlikely that any remaining governmental body would have been able to countermand any initiative carried out in their name. The recollections of Ricardo Sanz, a member of the Nosotros group, suggest that such an initiative would have provoked a crisis within the CNT: "We knew that the organisation was opposed to dictatorship. And that's what it would have been if our position [of pursuing the revolution to its utmost consequences] had been accepted."[15] By this reading, the Regional Defence Committee, unwilling to provoke such a schism, surrendered the initiative it held after the defeat of the military rising to the gradualists and purists opposed to authoritarian measures.

14   See the recollections in García Oliver, *El eco de los pasos*, 176–8; and the discussion in Agustin Guillamón, *La Revolución de los Comités. Hambre y Violencia en la Barcelona Revolucionaria. De junio a diciembre de 1936* (Barcelona: Aldarull Edicions, 2012), 56–9.

15   Quoted in Fraser, *Blood of Spain*, 112.

Nevertheless, it should also be borne in mind that the defence committees, in spite of the efforts undertaken to reorganise them along more disciplined and militaristic lines, were a heterogeneous and unpredictable entity, even in the eyes of García Oliver.[16] Beyond a core of militants that the Regional Defence Committee could depend on to obey orders, the bulk of the defence committees represented a broader network, animated chiefly by affinity groups.[17] There is evidence to suggest that between this wider network and the core were "mid-level" shop stewards and FAI activists who had helped combat *treintismo* in the previous years but who could not be relied upon to simply follow the orders of the Regional Defence Committee. As much had been demonstrated on 17 July when activists from the Maritime Transport Workers' Union, without waiting for the directions of the Regional Defence Committee, stormed the boats anchored in the port of Barcelona and carried off their stores of weaponry. The initiative for the raid has been attributed to Juan Yagüe and Julián Merino, activists in the CNT-affiliated Maritime Transport Workers' Union and mid-level delegates in the defence committees.[18] The event caused consternation among the Nosotros group, who hastened to intervene in order to avoid a state of emergency being declared.[19] Such apparent mutual mistrust may help to explain why, for men in negotiations with the Generalitat both before and after the July days, the unpredictable and broadly autonomous wider network of the defence committees may not have appeared to be a reliable basis for extending the power and influence of the CNT in the direction they intended.

The Regional Plenum called by the Barcelona CNT to debate participation in the CCMA took place on 21 July. It set a precedent for the way in which the CNT's democratic procedures would be undermined by the war. The urgency of the circumstances meant that assemblies were called hastily, with little time for delegates to be elected and their positions debated by the wider membership. The key debates to be discussed were proposed by the *comités superiores* (the name given to the Regional, National and Peninsular Committees of the different branches of the libertarian movement), and the function of the assembly was reduced to merely ratifying or rejecting

16   On the attempts to reorient the defence committees, see Guillamón, *Los Comités de Defensa*, 9–25.

17   This is the impression given by the recollections of former members of defence committees. See Paz, *Chumberas*, 203–4, and "Entrevista amb Joan 'Remi' per Joan Casanovas Codina, Barcelona, 13/3/1986," AHCB, Fonts Orals, 33–8.

18   Juan Yagüe's relationship to the defence committees can be surmised from his leadership role in the Roja y Negra Column. He would die at the front in September. Julián Merino was the delegate of the Barcelona FAI to the Catalan Regional Defence Committee during the Second Republic. See José Manuel Márquez Rodríguez and Juan José Gallardo Romero, *Ortiz, general sin Dios ni amo* (Barcelona: ed. Hacer, 1999), 80.

19   See Santillán, *Por qué perdimos la guerra*, 61; García Oliver, *El eco de los pasos*, 420–1.

them. While the *comités superiores* had formerly taken on an executive role in circumstances of heightened repression or emergency, the permanent emergency situation brought about by the war led, in the months that followed the rupture of July, to such decision-making procedures gradually assuming a routine quality, which would become increasingly formalised over the course of the war. According to Fidel Miró, the 21 July assembly was made up of "committees and *notables*" and was not a regularly constituted Plenum.[20]

Three positions emerged: one favouring collaboration, one opposing it on revolutionary grounds, and one which considered collaboration to be of potential short-term use to the CNT, which could strengthen its position before proceeding to a more complete revolutionary transformation.[21] Montseny and Santillán spoke in favour of the first position, the former considering the revolutionary option tantamount to an "anarchist dictatorship," the latter warning against the probability of international intervention against any such revolutionary endeavour.[22] Whether persuaded of these arguments or content to bide their time and await developments, the delegates present approved collaboration with the CCMA, with only the vote of José Xena, delegate for Baix Llobregat, opposed, whose position had been supported by García Oliver.[23] The CCMA met that same night, with the components of the CNT's Liaison Committee attending as the delegates of the CNT and the FAI.

It is far from clear that the controversy implied by the decision to join the CCMA, identified subsequently by activists and historians, was understood to be so significant by CNT activists in Barcelona at the time. Diego Camacho, then a member of the JJLL, recalled:

> Only a handful of activists were aware of the founding [of the CCMA], the immense majority were either ignorant of it altogether, or else it sounded to them like one more revolutionary committee among the many others that were operating all over the place.[24]

Certainly, the constitution of the CCMA did not prevent the revolution from maintaining its upward curve. By the end of the month, the return

---

20   Fidel Miró, *Vida intensa y revolucionaria* (Mexico City: Editores Mexicanos Unidos, 1989), 180. Miró was a leading figure in the JJLL and a close associate of Santillán.

21   See the recollections of García Oliver, *El eco de los pasos*, 184–8; and the discussion in Guillamón, *La Revolución de los Comités*, 59–61.

22   García Oliver, *El eco de los pasos*, 185–6.

23   Ibid. 185–8.

24   Abel Paz, *Viaje al Pasado* (Madrid: Fundación de Estudios Libertarios Anselmo Lorenzo, 2002), 59.

to work had seen a wave of expropriations, as factories and whole industries were taken over by union activists.[25] Mary Low, a Trotskyist poet from England who arrived in August to aid the POUM in Barcelona, provides an account of her first walk round the city centre:

> We began to walk about the narrow streets which wind in and out between the main thoroughfares. Every now and then a big sheet of white paper pasted over the name-plate of a shop or business made us stop and look. It said: "Taken over by..." and then followed the name of one of the workers' parties. The houses were hastily scrawled with big initials in red, the names of parties to which they now belonged. It was extraordinarily exciting. I looked about me. A feeling of new strength and activity seemed to radiate from the crowds of people in the streets.[26]

However, while the CCMA was a product of the revolution, it was not a revolutionary organ, and it remained subordinate to the pre-existing institutions of state governance. Meanwhile, because the CCMA operated on the basis of delegates proposed by the different anti-fascist organisations, there was no opportunity for a directly democratic process to influence it. For anti-fascist politicians such as Companys, who did not wish to see state power abolished, the CCMA provided a seemingly revolutionary legitimacy and a base from which to reorganise and marshal their strength.[27]

The defacto collaboration of the libertarian movement with the state in Cataluña had thus begun. This was a complex process that not only included the presence of CNT representatives in the CCMA but also found expression in libertarian involvement, indeed frequent predominance, in the bodies set up by Generalitat decree in the days and weeks that followed. These included the Consejo de la Escuela Nueva Unificada (Council of the New Unified School – CENU), responsible for education, established on 27 July; the Comisión de Indústrias de Guerra (War Industries' Commission) created on 7 August; the Workers' and Soldiers' Councils, charged with ensuring the continued loyalty of officers who had served in the army prior to July; the Comité Central de Abastos (Central Committee of Supplies); the Consejo de Economía de Cataluña (Council of the Economy of Cataluña), established on 11 August; and the *Patrullas de Control* (Control Patrols) founded on the

---

25   Peirats, *The CNT, Vol. 1*, 139–45.

26   Mary Low and Juan Breá, *Red Spanish Notebook: The First Six Months of the Revolution and the Civil War* (San Francisco: City Lights Books, 1979), 19–20.

27   See Pozo González, *Poder legal*, 62–3; Antoni Castells Duran, "Revolution and Collectivizations in Civil War Barcelona, 1936–9" in *Red Barcelona: Social Protest and Labour Mobilization in the Twentieth Century*, ed. by Angel Smith (London and New York: Routledge, 2002): 137.

same day, which was a police force directed by the Investigation Committee of the CCMA, led by Aurelio Fernández and Salvador González (this latter a member of the Partit Socialista Unificat de Catalunya [Unified Socialist Party of Cataluña – PSUC]).[28] While the revolutionary situation lasted in Cataluña, in which the balance of power remained conditioned by the presence of armed workers on the street, it was far from clear that this process of collaboration would be definitive or irreversible, and in the case of some of the bodies enumerated above, it did not prove to be.[29] Nevertheless, in a pattern that was to accelerate over the autumn, the process ensured that the CNT's most prominent activists were absorbed into what were called "official posts" in administrative organs, while the restructuring of education, public order, the economy and the war industry represented a further layer of state collaboration that involved thousands of CNT members. The scale of state collaboration was such that when oppositionists later attempted to advocate a withdrawal from official positions, they would be confronted not only by ideological arguments in favour of anti-fascism but also by the daunting logistical and economic implications of their proposal.[30]

Throughout much of what remained of Republican Spain, a comparable process to that which had taken place in Cataluña was underway, in which committees of anti-fascist unity with a variety of different names were formed in cities and towns with the participation of the CNT. The organisation dominated the Comité de Guerra (War Committee) in Gijón, where industry was run by the unions and the Committee also took over the city's branch of the Bank of Spain.[31] A Comité Ejecutivo Popular (Popular Executive Committee) was established in Valencia on 20 July, which immediately came into conflict with the central government in Madrid.[32] In Almería, a Comité Central Antifascista (Anti-fascist Central Committee) was constituted by 23 July, although the CNT, outnumbered by the UGT in the region, did not join until the beginning of August, which may be suggestive of disquiet regarding the question among the Confederal affiliates.[33]

28   The PSUC had formed in July through the amalgamation of the Catalan branches of the PSOE and PCE with the Unió Socialista de Catalunya (Socialist Union of Cataluña) and the Partit Català Proletari (Proletarian Catalan Party).

29   The case of the *Patrullas de Control* would be instructive in this regard, and is discussed in more detail in the following chapter.

30   See the discussion in Chapter Four.

31   Fraser, *Blood of Spain*, 238–40.

32   See Richard Purkiss, *Democracy, Trade Unions and Political Violence in Spain: The Valencian Anarchist Movement, 1918–1936* (Brighton: Sussex Academic Press, 2015), 238–9.

33   On the formation and composition of the committee, but not the basis for the delayed entry of the CNT, see Rafael Quirosa-Cheyrouze y Muñoz, *Almería, 1936–37. Sublevación militar y alteraciones en la retaguardia republicana* (Almería: Universidad de Almería, 1996), 86–7.

In Málaga, a Liaison Committee was formed on 19 July, and on 26 July the Comité de Salud Pública (Committee of Public Safety) was formed to oversee public order, with Francisco Millán, of the FAI, as secretary.[34] In these areas, and many more, the anti-fascist Committee was the symbol and embodiment of the new state of affairs, providing an alternative structure of power to local and regional governments, which in most cases were reduced to a nominal role. The central governmental power of Madrid, after the chaotic first days of the rising, sought to re-establish its presence and authority on the streets through the mobilisation of the security forces and government-issued passes guaranteeing safe passage.[35] Nevertheless, these measures could not disguise the marginalisation of the government, and the consequent importance of the CNT in the organisation of resistance and public order in the capital, where its activists found their greatest rivals to be the rapidly growing PCE.[36]

The composition of the anti-fascist committees in each region was largely dependent on the balance of political forces prior to July 1936, albeit with the exclusion of the rightist parties. In certain cases, particularly outside of the larger cities, how the organisations had responded to the military rising was also a factor in deciding their participation in the new committees. In Lleida, the workers' organisations initially felt strong enough to exclude what were seen as the bourgeois parties – in this case the Esquerra Republicana de Catalunya (Republican Left of Cataluña – ERC).[37] In La Felguera in Asturias, the committee was initially entirely made up of CNT members.[38] The committees were often presented at mass assemblies in town centres where they were ratified, and in areas where only one organisation dominated or where the workers' organisations had little strength, the assembly might have a more open and active character.[39] Assemblies as a forum for debate and decision-making were features of several revolutionary phenomena – factories taken over by their workers, collectives

34   See Amorós, *Los Incontrolados*, 162–5; Julio Aróstegui, *Por qué el 18 de Julio… Y después* (Barcelona: Flor del Viento, 2006), 335. It is common to see this and other similarly named committees translated literally as Committee of Public Health. However, they were named after the Comité de Salut Public of the French Revolution, universally referred to as the Committee of Public Safety in English.

35   See Pierre Broué and Emile Témime, *The Revolution and the Civil War in Spain* (London: The MIT Press, 1972), 145.

36   See César M. Lorenzo, *Los anarquistas españoles y el poder* (Paris: Ruedo Ibérico, 1972), 171–4.

37   Lleida was a key base of support for the POUM, which agitated for the creation of a wholly proletarian government. See Pelai Pagès, *Andreu Nin: Su evolución política (1911–1937)* (Madrid: Zero, 1975), 212.

38   Eladio Fanjul Roces file, Col·lecció Ronald Fraser, AHCB, 25.

39   See Pozo González, *Poder legal*, 315–8.

established in rural areas, neighbourhood defence committees and militia columns at the front – but did not impinge upon the activity and direction of the quasi-governmental anti-fascist committees in the major cities, in which delegates were answerable to the organisations they belonged to. The democratic deficit evident in the collaborationist organs and the official structures of the CNT itself was therefore counterbalanced to an extent by the assembly-based procedures that characterised the broader revolutionary experience.

Assemblies of CNT activists provided the basis for the collectivisation of land in Aragón. As the militia columns marched on Zaragoza, the parts of the region that fell to their advance underwent revolutionary changes. The extent to which coercion was employed by the militias in ensuring that collectivisation of agricultural land in Aragón took place is a matter of dispute, although, as Graham Kelsey has pointed out, the collectives would subsequently respect the rights of the so-called individualists who did not wish to take part in them.[40] It must further be remembered that land was also collectivised in swathes of Castilla La Mancha and Andalucía; the collectivisations of Aragón were exceptional only insofar as they took place on land that had been liberated by, for the most part, anarchist militia. Assemblies were held throughout those parts of Aragón during August, at which CNT activists debated the restructuring of their economies, often with the participation of the UGT, which was the smaller union in the liberated zone. On 6 October, the Regional Defence Council of Aragón was formed at a Plenum of the CNT in Bujaraloz and was initially dominated by libertarians under the presidency of Joaquín Ascaso, cousin of Francisco.[41]

Meanwhile, the front line in the region had stabilised by the end of summer, in sight of the capital, Zaragoza. An assault on the city never materialised, as military personnel who had remained loyal to the Republic advised the anarchists to cover their flanks.[42] The situation in Aragón was not unique. The militia columns raised in Gijón were convinced to delay before advancing on Oviedo. Those marching on Granada from Alicante, including the anarchist Maroto Column, dug in at Baza, in the north of the Andalusian province. The strikes declared in the cities under rebel control

40   See Graham Kelsey, *Anarcho-syndicalism, Libertarian Communism and the State: The CNT in Zaragoza and Aragon, 1930–1937* (Amsterdam: International Institute of Social History, 1991), 161. For a contrary perspective, see Julián Casanova, *Anarquismo y Revolución en la Sociedad Rural Aragonesa, 1936–38* (Barcelona: Crítica, 2006), 120.

41   At the founding Plenum, the CNT had initially agreed to offer only two posts on the Council to the UGT and one to the republicans, as compared with the seven that would be taken up by the CNT. The minutes of this Plenum are reproduced in Juan Zafón Bayo, *El Consejo Revolucionario de Aragón* (Barcelona: Editorial Planeta, 1979), 123–33.

42   Paz, *Durruti*, 485.

were worn down by the systematic use of terror. The mutinous army did not have to face its enemy on two fronts, and the fighting developed along the lines of attrition warfare, characterised by sieges and trenches. In such a war, the military strengths of the anarchist movement – urban street fighting, mobility and impetuosity – were rendered increasingly superfluous, while the practice of direct democracy and autonomous organisation became a hindrance to effective military action.

From late July, the rebel commanders had received the active assistance of the German and Italian air forces, enabling the transfer of men and weaponry from Spanish Morocco to Andalucía.[43] Confronted by trained military reinforcements, civilian resistance to the rising in Cádiz was overwhelmed, and while systematic repression of workers' and democratic organisations took place there and in the cities of Sevilla and Granada, General Yagüe's army swept north through Extremadura. At Badajoz, which had offered serious resistance, the repression was of such a scale that it was to become one of the most infamous episodes of the civil war, as hundreds of its inhabitants were massacred in the bullring day after day for weeks after the city fell in mid-August.[44] The isolation of the Republic was confirmed by the Non-Intervention Agreement signed by the major European powers in August on the diplomatic initiative of Britain and France. An effective arms embargo was thereby placed on the Spanish Republic that brought the question of weaponry, and the desire to reassure foreign powers, to the forefront of the problems facing the workers' organisations. Such considerations undoubtedly impacted on the internal debates of the CNT taking place during these months as to the attitude it should adopt towards the question of government and military reorganisation.

On 4 August, the CNT held a National Plenum in Madrid. This event was illustrative of the extent to which the normal functioning of the Confederation had been compromised by the war, as only three regions, the Centre, Cataluña and Levante, were able to send delegations. The Plenum debated the question of CNT collaboration in a hypothetical National Anti-Fascist Committee, which had apparently been mentioned to the National Committee of the CNT by government ministers.[45] The Cataluña and Levante delegations spoke in favour, while the Central region's delegation expressed reservations, with no final decision being taken due to the lack

43   Graham, *The Spanish Republic*, 105.

44   See Julián Casanova, "Rebelión y revolución" in *Víctimas de la guerra civil*, coord. by Santos Juliá (Madrid: Temas de Hoy, 2004), 76–7; Paul Preston, *The Spanish Holocaust: Inquisition and Extermination in Twentieth-Century Spain* (London: Harper Press, 2012), 316–24.

45   See Pozo González, *Poder legal*, 196.

of representation of several regions. The reticence of the Central delegation towards the vague proposal of a National Anti-Fascist Committee may have been influenced by calls from the Madrid section of the CNT for the central government to be replaced by a Junta de Defensa (Defence Council) without moderate republican representation. This argument, in favour of government by an exclusively working-class committee, was the unifying characteristic of the left wing of Spanish anti-fascism at this time, both from within the ranks of the CNT, and also the POUM, for whom this was official policy.[46]

This argument was strengthened by the ominous military situation in which the Republic found itself. At this time, many activists in Barcelona considered that the revolutionary changes that had taken place in the city were laying the ground for a more complete transformation, which would follow the anarchist-led capture of Zaragoza. The city was considered to be of vital importance, perhaps more for its symbolic than strategic value.[47] The longer it remained in the hands of the reactionaries, the weaker became the hand of the maximalists. Such activists therefore found themselves in a double bind: they could not impel the revolution to its "utmost consequences" without the moral authority of a military victory, but they could not elaborate a revolutionary military strategy as long as the impasse of "temporary" collaboration persisted. Throughout Republican Spain there was a widespread perception that "bourgeois politicians" were incapable of prosecuting the war with sufficient vigour. By summer's end, in the words of Helen Graham, "Worker confidence in the republican leadership was reduced to virtually nil."[48]

On 13 September, San Sebastián, the only city in the Basque Country for which July had represented a revolutionary rupture comparable with the rest of Spain, was surrendered to the rebels without a shot being fired. As the city was evacuated, Basque nationalist police remained behind in order to disarm anarchist militia and prevent the retreating forces from burning the city.[49] While such losses added urgency to the arguments of the collaborationists, they also illustrated the extent to which collaboration prevented the militia from adopting the guerrilla tactics associated with revolutionary warfare. On the front line, audacious schemes based on the infiltration of rebel-held cities and simultaneous uprisings from within and assaults from without went untested.[50] This failure to elaborate a strategy appropriate to

46   See Andreu Nin, *La revolución española* (Madrid: Diario Público, 2011), 248.
47   See Borkenau, *The Spanish Cockpit*, 87–8.
48   Graham, *The Spanish Republic*, 127.
49   Fraser, *Blood of Spain*, 189.
50   For a detailed discussion of the failure of the CNT to mount a concerted offensive against

the organisational form of the militias was, in part, due to the revolutionary organisations' commitment to participation in the anti-fascist front.[51] This is not to say that a revolutionary strategy would have been victorious, and anarchist self-confidence in this regard was shaken at this time by the failure of the Mallorca expedition, in which many anarchist volunteers had participated, and where initial victories preceded the intervention of the Italian air force, and a hasty and bloody retreat.[52]

Nevertheless, the relationship of the war to the revolution hinged on the question of state collaboration. From very early on in the conflict, Horacio M. Prieto, National Secretary of the CNT from September to November 1936, had considered that the only course open to the organisation was "to be a solid force within anti-fascism, identified with it and protected by it."[53] Prieto was a veteran of the anarchist movement, whose purist scruples had prevented him from joining the CNT until 1932. Once a member, however, he had immediately been entrusted with influential posts, and he began to move away from purist positions. In 1932 he edited the national review *CNT*, where he was referred to as "Sergeant Prieto" by his colleagues, and from 1935 until May 1936 he served his first term as National Secretary.[54] As the democratic functioning of the CNT had been severely compromised by the war, the National Secretary of the organisation was well placed to define the terms and outcomes of the various debates underway in the Confederation during the first months of the conflict.[55] While Prieto was tenacious in his advocacy of collaboration, however, the momentum towards participation in government emanated primarily from developments in Barcelona that were driven by the regional rather than national organisation of the CNT.

There, the decision to participate in the government of the Generalitat was taken in unclear circumstances towards the end of August. According to César M. Lorenzo, Prieto's son, the decision was taken at a secret Regional

Zaragoza, see Eduardo Pons Prades, "Summer 1936: Why did we fail to take Zaragoza," trans. by Paul Sharkey, Christie Books website (2011), http://www.christiebooks .com/ChristieBooksWP/2011/07/summer-1936-why-did-we-fail-to-take-zaragoza-by -eduardo-pons-prades-translated-by-paul-sharkey.

51   A similar point is made in George Esenwein and Adrian Shubert, *Spain at War. The Spanish Civil War in Context, 1931–1939* (London: Longman, 1997), 147. See also Antony Beevor, *The Battle for Spain: The Spanish Civil War 1936–1939* (London: Phoenix, 2006), 142–3.

52   See Michael Alpert, *A New International History of the Spanish Civil War* (Basingstoke: Palgrave Macmillan, 2004), 68–9.

53   Prieto, *Secretario General de la CNT de España en 1936, Tomo II*, 99.

54   See ibid. 56; and Miguel Iñiguez, *Esbozo de una enciclopedia histórica del anarquismo español* (Madrid: Fundación de Estudios Libertarios Anselmo Lorenzo, 2001), 388.

55   The National Secretary at the outbreak of the war was David Antona, although this was an interim position due to Prieto falling ill. The National Plenum of 4 August referred to above confirmed Prieto's re-election, and he returned to the post in September.

Plenum in which the committees of the CNT, FAI and JJLL were represented and the Peninsular Committee of the FAI also had a vote.[56] A Regional Plenum of the Catalan CNT had already agreed to the dissolution of the CCMA on 17 August, a decision approved by a Plenum of Barcelona anarchist groups on 21 August.[57] The wider membership of the CNT was not made aware of the decisions of the Catalan *comités superiores* until the end of the following month, when the CNT's representation in the Generalitat was negotiated. Mary Low wrote of this time that "events, with their separate details which had seemed to have no importance when taken one by one, had been following each other all this time in a slow crescendo and now the wave broke."[58] The CCMA was officially dissolved on 1 October.

The reconstruction of the Republican state

On 4 September 1936, a new national government was formed with Largo Caballero as Prime Minister and in which the PCE also participated for the first time. The previous day a National Plenum of the CNT had agreed in principle to intervention in government but rejected immediate participation. The Catalan delegation proposed, as had the Madrid delegates a month before, the creation of a new central organ of power composed of representatives of the CNT and the UGT, which would be headed by Largo Caballero. In accordance with this restatement of the "left" option, *Solidaridad Obrera* declared its preference for a National Revolutionary Council (Junta) "of all the workers' and peasants' organisations," affirming that "the current moment is one hundred per cent proletarian."[59] However, at the same time as the Catalan Regional Committee was urging the creation of a Junta composed of the unions, it entered a process of bringing autonomous and localised initiative back under central control. In spite of the calls from some elements of the CNT and the POUM for proletarian government, the organisations' representatives in the CCMA did not oppose the decision taken by that body on 2 September, to oblige the antifascist committee in Lleida to accept the participation of the ERC.[60] The case of Lleida was a small example of a wider picture of state reconstruction on the basis of centralisation and class collaboration. This process would be

56   See Lorenzo, *Los anarquistas españoles*, 99.
57   See Pozo González, *Poder legal*, 199.
58   Low and Breá, *Red Spanish Notebook*, 120.
59   *Solidaridad Obrera*, 6 September 1936.
60   Joan Sagués, "'Lleida la Roja.' El poder obrer a la capital de la Terra Ferma," in *Breu Història de la Guerra Civil a Catalunya*, ed. by Josep M. Solé Sabaté and Joan Villarroya (Barcelona: Edicions 62, 2005), 181–2.

contradictory and take place in stages because its apparent logic, of creating a strong state with a mobilised population capable of waging a modern war, depended on the defeat of a revolution which had, in the absence of such a state, prevented the collapse of the Republic and sustained the war effort up to that point.

On 15–17 September, two days after the fall of San Sebastián, the CNT held another National Plenum in Madrid. The proposal to form a Junta de Defensa to coordinate the regionally organised anti-fascist committees was here officially adopted. By contrast to the original proposal of an exclusively proletarian council, however, this body was to be presided over by Largo Caballero and formed by five delegates from the CNT and five from the UGT, with four moderate republicans also represented and Azaña continuing in his post as President of the Republic.[61] The proposal was thereby stripped of its "left" content, and Prieto considered that the principle of governmental participation had now been conceded, as the reconceived Junta differed only superficially from the existing administration.[62] The momentum was now with those who favoured collaboration, and although the Catalan Regional Committee would continue to advocate the constitution of a Junta after it had been rejected by Largo Caballero, its case was severely undermined by the participation of the Catalan CNT in the Generalitat from 26 September. An equally important outcome of the Plenum was the decision, proposed by Prieto, to change the composition of the National Committee of the CNT, which would henceforth be a permanent body made up of delegates from the Regional Committees.[63] Previously, the formation of the National Committee had been the temporary responsibility of a Regional Committee chosen at the National Congress, its duties supposedly limited to coordination. Its refoundation as a representative, executive body therefore represented a significant shift away from the CNT's founding statutes.

Such a retreat from Confederal democracy was a necessary component of both the constraints imposed by the war and the contortions required by state collaboration, which was as much an ideological process as it was one of formal political participation. This was shown clearly in the recasting of the civil war as a war of national independence. On the one hand a reaction to the aid the rebels received from Italy and Germany, and the presence in Spain of the Army of Africa under the supreme command of General

61   Pozo González, *Poder legal*, 216–7.
62   See Horacio M. Prieto, *Secretario General de la CNT de España en 1936. Ex-ministro de la República en el exilio. Recuerdos. Tomo III, ¡Ananké! Mi curriculum vitae: ilusión, aventura, frustración* (Unpublished memoir, BPA, n.d.), 169.
63   Ibid.

Franco, this was also indicative of the Republican state's need for a common mobilising agent other than that of class. Prior to the war, the FAI had made its position clear: "The struggle against fascism, an international phenomenon, must be carried out internationally by the workers' and revolutionary organisations, to the exclusion of any nationalist idea or sentiment."[64] In April, French Communists had been ridiculed in the pages of *Solidaridad Obrera* for their "integralist nationalism" in the face of Hitler's Germany: "Today, socialists and Communists follow the same methods as in 1914," the paper noted.[65] At the end of August 1936, however, in a radio broadcast published in *Solidaridad Obrera*, Federica Montseny described the civil war as one of national independence against "fascist civilisation," characterised in racist terms as "not... a Christian civilisation but a Moorish civilisation."[66]

Illustrative of the nationalist component in the reconstitution of the Republican state was the mission of the Comité de Acción Marroquí (Moroccan Action Committee), which arrived in Spain in September, seeking a declaration of Moroccan autonomy from the government, in exchange for which they would attempt to organise an uprising in the rebels' African rearguard and to disrupt recruitment to the Army of Africa.[67] García Oliver had been in contact with this Committee since July, but although he was able to arrange for a pact to be signed with the CCMA, the meeting of the delegation with Largo Caballero proved fruitless. The Prime Minister was concerned that any such declaration of autonomy would provoke a hostile reaction from France.[68] The Spanish Republic thus maintained the colonial policies that had incubated the ultra-nationalist and authoritarian military caste that had rebelled against it, and "anti-fascist" nationalism became an ideological corollary of state reconstruction in the Republic. Tragically, although *Solidaridad Obrera* called for the complete independence of Morocco at this time, Montseny's speech was only one of many examples of Spanish anarchists promoting this increasingly dominant ideology.[69] One of the more egregious was provided by the openly colonialist speech of the geographer Gonzalo de Reparaz, published by the CNT-FAI's propaganda office, which lamented that "the Moroccan zone... well led, well administrated, could have been the cradle of a new Spanish empire."[70]

64   Quoted in *Tierra y Libertad*, 7 February 1936.

65   *Solidaridad Obrera*, 17 April 1936.

66   Guillamón, *La Revolución de los Comités*, 165.

67   See Paz, *Durruti*, 517–24.

68   Alpert, *A New International History*, 105.

69   *Solidaridad Obrera*, 28 August 1936. "

70   Gonzalo de Reparaz, *Lo que pudo hacer España en Marruecos y lo que ha hecho. Conferencia pronunciada en el cine Coliseum de Barcelona, el día 17 de enero de 1937* (Barcelona: Oficinas de propaganda CNT FAI, n.d. [1937?]), 13.

Voluble nationalism went hand in hand with a reassertion of patriarchal values that further undermined the achievements of the revolution. As noted above, women in workers' overalls brandishing rifles was one of the most striking images of July in the major cities. Every observer of Spanish affairs commented on the public transformation of the role of women. On 20 July, *Solidaridad Obrera* noted that women had fought alongside men at the barricades in Barcelona.[71] The involvement of women at the front was initially exalted by the workers' organisations and the image of the *miliciana* was used in recruitment posters and propaganda, which were aimed at women as well as men.[72] The process whereby this exaltation was turned into its opposite ran parallel to the reconstitution of the Spanish state.[73] For the authorities seeking to "normalise" the Republican rearguard, putting women back in their place was a first step. An early indication that this process would not be unanimously opposed by the revolutionary forces was a note carried in *Solidaridad Obrera* on 30 September stating that a new column formed in Poblet in Tarragona would only admit *milicianas* who were related to or a partner of male recruits.[74] This was followed days later by denunciations in the official newspaper of the Badalona anti-fascist committee of women deemed to be "showing off," criticising "photos of women armed with a gun who have never fired a shot in their lives."[75]

Learned patriarchal behaviours were not dispelled overnight, in spite of the profound challenge to traditional gender norms that the rupture of July had represented. However, determined women were able to persuade anarchist commanders to accept their presence in the columns, even when this was against their better judgement. Such was the case of Antonia Fontanillas, who along with two friends convinced Juan Yagüe to allow them to enlist in the column he was organising for the ill-fated Mallorca expedition.[76] Mary Low also recounts the story of her friend, Margaret Zimbal,

71   Amorós, *La Revolución traicionada*, 100.

72   Lisa Lines, *Milicianas: Women in Combat in the Spanish Civil War* (Lanham: Lexington Books, 2012), 55.

73   See Giovanni C. Cattini, "La Dona entre la Guerra i la Revolució. L'ocupació de l'espai públic i la superació de les restriccions de gènere tradicionals," in *Breu Historia de la Guerra Civil* ed. by Josep M. Solé Sabaté and Joan Villarroya (Barcelona: Edicions 62, 2005), 329. This process followed the chronological formulation proposed by Tabea Alexa Linhard: "Within discourses of domestication, three mechanisms that subdue and often erase women's political agency can be identified: the exaltation, the silencing, and the demonization of revolutionary women": Tabea Alexa Linhard, *Fearless Women in the Mexican Revolution and the Spanish Civil War* (Missouri: University of Missouri Press, 2005), 2.

74   Guillamón, *La Revolución de los Comités*, 266.

75   Quoted in Nash, *Defying Male Civilization*, 52.

76   Fontanillas, "De lo aprendido," 9. In the event, Fontanillas was persuaded by her father not to leave, although her two friends took part in the expedition, and one later fought on the Aragón front in the Roja y Negra column.

a nineteen-year-old German Jew who also participated in the Mallorca expedition as part of a POUM column. Initially persuaded to remain in the rearguard after her return, she ran to catch up with her company when it was departing for the front at Huesca. She would die shortly afterwards, caught by a sniper while tending to a wounded comrade.[77] Such individual cases were not uncommon, but the respect that the *milicianas* were able to gain from their fellow combatants was undermined by the campaign of "normalisation" that was gaining traction at state level, accompanied by the slogan "men to the front, women to the rearguard." That prominent anarchists propagated this slogan showed that sexist "common sense" could be made to serve, consciously or not, the process of state reconstruction. For the anarchist Conxa Pérez, who left the front, this was "what hurt me more... because it was our comrades, Ortiz, who was a friend of mine... and Durruti... they had always been comrades, fighting for equality, but on this point I don't think they got it."[78]

State reconstruction in the Republican zone must therefore be seen as a broader process than that implied by the reorganisation of administrative bodies. By the time the CNT officially entered the government of Largo Caballero, a fact announced at a rally in Valencia on 19 October, sectors of the organisation were already involved in this process, both in terms of formal relations with the state and in public support for its constitution as a patriarchal and racial/national entity. That the news implied simultaneously a moment in an ongoing process and a crossing of the Rubicon that would intensify the CNT's state collaboration, with all of its implications for the internal life of the organisation, was reflected in the varied response it generated from within the ranks of Spanish anarchism. For one sector, it was a "bombshell" greeted with disbelief, while for others it was accepted as a pragmatic response to the demands of the situation.[79] For Prieto, it was a logical continuation of collaboration with other anti-fascist forces, and he was particularly dismissive of the "metaphysics" of accepting positions in regional governments, the judiciary and the police while continuing to renounce representation at the level of central government.[80] According to some sympathisers, the CNT's acceptance of a secondary role in the central government, and the ideological concession this implied, was proof of the

---

77   Low and Breá, *Red Spanish Notebook*, 177–9.

78   Vega, *Pioneras y revolucionarias*, 166.

79   For the former response, see Josep Peirats Valls, *De mi paso por la vida* (Barcelona: Flor de Viento, 2009), 314; Abel Paz, *Viaje al pasado*, 66–7. For the latter, see the recollections of a Gijonese anarchist, Ramón Álvarez Palomo file, Col·lecció Ronald Fraser, AHCB, 50–2.

80   Prieto, *Secretario General de la CNT de España en 1936, Tomo III*, 162.

sincerity of the organisation's anti-fascism.[81] Meanwhile, *Solidaridad Obrera*, which was operating with a temporary, transitional editorial board at this time, because the Regional Committee of the CNT had removed the purist editor, Liberto Callejas, greeted the presence of anarchist ministers in the Republican government with ingenuous enthusiasm: "The entrance of the CNT into central Government," it declared, "is one of the most transcendental occurrences in the political history of our country. The State and Government will oppress the people still less with the intervention in them of elements of the CNT."[82]

Any possibility that the ministers and councillors representing the organisations that supported the revolution could change the oppressive nature of the state was compromised, however, by the fact that they were at all times outnumbered by an emerging bloc determined to, in its words, "normalise" the Republican rearguard, thereby enabling the reconstitution of the Republican state.[83] This bloc was composed, in Cataluña, of the ERC, the PSUC, the Unió de Rabassaires (an organisation of Catalan peasants that was traditionally sympathetic to the political left but hostile to collectivisation) and Acció Catalana Republicana (Republican Catalan Action). In the Generalitat, it was represented by seven councillors (three from the ERC, two from the PSUC and one each from the Unió de Rabassaires and Republican Catalan Action), as compared with three from the CNT and one POUM councillor. In the newly organised central government, the four CNT ministers were accompanied by fourteen other, Socialist, Communist and republican ministers.[84] While it should be borne in mind that many rank-and-file Socialists and UGT members were active participants in the revolution, their representatives in government, while belonging to different tendencies, were united in conceiving the revolution, if they supported it at all, as a secondary consideration to the war and the construction of a strong state.

The ministries given to the CNT were Health, Justice, Industry and Commerce, whose ministers would be, respectively, Montseny, García Oliver, Peiró and Juan López, the latter a convinced syndicalist who had joined the CNT aged eleven.[85] The relative impotence of the four anarchist

81   See the editorial of *Frente Libertario*, a Madrid-based newspaper which had recently been established by the Defence Committee of the Central Region of Spain for free distribution at the front, quoted in Dolors Marín, *Ministros Anarquistas. La CNT en el Gobierno de la II República (1936–1939)* (Barcelona: Random House, 2005), 142.

82   *Solidaridad Obrera*, 4 November 1936. On the dismissal of Callejas, see the following chapter.

83   Pozo González, *La Catalunya antifeixista*, 78.

84   See Marín, *Ministros Anarquistas*, 138–41.

85   Graham, *The Spanish Republic*, 129–35

ministers with respect to the anti-revolutionary bloc was immediately made clear. As soon as they entered the government they were called to an emergency meeting to debate the removal of the seat of the Republican government from Madrid to Valencia in the face of the fascist advance. This debate took two days to resolve because of the opposition to the move mounted by the anarchists.[86] Faced with the unanimous opposition of their ministerial colleagues and desirous of averting a crisis in the new government, however, they eventually acquiesced. The abandonment of the capital caused a scandal, and libertarian embarrassment was heightened when ministers leaving the city were detained at anarchist-controlled checkpoints.[87] The affair cost Prieto his post as National Secretary of the CNT, and he was replaced by the then Regional Secretary of Cataluña, Mariano Rodríguez Vázquez, who was, however, similarly committed to collaboration in government.

Libertarian ire in Madrid was to an extent channelled into the defiant fervour required for the defence of the city, encapsulated by the mobilising slogan "Long live Madrid without a government!"[88] It was further sated by the ad hoc organisation created by Largo Caballero, the Junta de Defensa de Madrid (Madrid Defence Council – JDM), charged with taking on governmental authority in the capital and mounting its defence in the absence of the Spanish parliament. Superficially resembling in composition and appearance the anti-fascist committees then being wound down under the terms of the municipal reorganisation ordered by the Largo Caballero government, the CNT in Madrid greeted the creation of the JDM as a vindication of the perspective it had maintained in the previous months, of regional anti-fascist committees being coordinated by a National Council of Defence.[89] Several anarchists would later recall in interviews with Ronald Fraser that Madrid at this time experienced a revolutionary atmosphere.[90]

Nevertheless, once the immediate danger of the city's fall had passed, the CNT's delegates to the new body found themselves pressurised by their colleagues with regard to an issue that was becoming familiar throughout

86   Juan García Oliver, *Mi gestión al frente del ministerio de justicia, conferencia pronunciada en el Teatro Apolo de Valencia el 30 de Mayo de 1937* (Valencia: Ediciones de la Comisión de Propaganda y Prensa del Comité Nacional de la CNT, 1937), 6–7.

87   Paul Preston, *The Spanish Civil War: Reaction, Revolution and Revenge* (New York: W. W. Norton & Company, 2007), 166.

88   *Frente Libertario*, 10 November 1936, quoted in Julio Aróstegui and Jesús A. Martínez, *La Junta de Defensa de Madrid, Noviembre 1936 – Abril 1937* (Madrid: Comunidad de Madrid, 1984), 82.

89   Aróstegui and Martínez, *La Junta de Defensa*, 127.

90   See the testimonies contained in the Eduardo De Guzmán, "Pedro" and Lorenzo Íñigo Granizo files, Col·lecció Ronald Fraser, AHCB. This contrasts with the references in the literature to Madrid as a non-revolutionary counterpoint to Barcelona. See, for example, Graham, *The Spanish Republic*, 215.

the Republican rearguard: the problem posed to public order by the continued presence of armed CNT members on the streets. Complaints about the
organisation from members of the Junta had to do with the apparent refusal
of the CNT's members to disarm, or abide by the agreements of the JDM.
Lorenzo Íñigo Granizo, the delegate of the FIJL, acknowledged that CNT
members did indeed refuse to accept the authority of the Junta with regard
to the question of arms, because the organisation dreaded the possibility
that the Communist-controlled public order authorities would be able to
draw up a register of the names and addresses of armed CNT activists. He
even challenged José Cazorla, delegate of public order, to disarm him outside a meeting of the JDM "if you have the balls," as the only licence he held
for his weapon was signed by the Local Federation of the CNT![91] An essential problem of the CNT's collaboration with the state was thereby revealed:
that the will to collaborate in an anti-fascist bloc did not easily translate into
an acceptance of governmental authority at ground level, particularly when,
as in the case of disarmament, this was both a life-and-death issue and an
affront to the libertarian conception of the revolution.

As shown by the example of Madrid, "normalisation" of the rearguard,
the most explosive aspect of which was the confrontation over public order
and internal security, where libertarian influence tended to be important,
was deemed necessary even in areas of Republican Spain where revolutionary transformation had been more limited than in Cataluña and Aragón.
So it was that in Almería the Civil Governor was moved to declare in an
order of early November that "all authority and competence with regard to
Government and public administration remains linked to accordance with
the laws of the Republic, to the town halls, mayors and their legitimately
designated agents."[92] Expropriations were to end while arrests and registers
would henceforth only be undertaken by governmental and military authorities. Likewise in Málaga, the foremost form taken by state reconstruction in
the autumn was the reorganisation of public order, whereby the functions of
the Committee of Public Safety were transferred to newly established bodies. The "*patrullas mixtas*," which had operated as a rearguard militia, were
dissolved, and the official police force, responsible to the Civil Governor,
was put in control of "everything pertaining to the tranquillity and vigilance
of the city."[93]

As partners in this process of state reconstruction, the CNT and the
FAI could do little to oppose the restoration of public order in an official
capacity. The same was true of the conversion of the militia into a regular

91   Lorenzo Íñigo Granizo file, Col·lecció Ronald Fraser, AHCB, 45.
92   Quirosa-Cheyrouze y Muñoz, *Almería, 1936–37*, 136–7.
93   See Antonio Nadal, *Guerra Civil en Málaga* (Málaga: Editorial Arguval, 1984), 170.

army, the process known as militarisation, promulgated by Largo Caballero in a raft of legislation and appointments over the autumn and winter of 1936.[94] Above all, the process sought to establish a *mando único* (unified command) of the armed forces. Among the organisations of the Republican rearguard, interpretations of what a *mando único* would imply varied from the increased cohesion and internal coordination of the militia system with its high proportion of voluntary, democratic units controlled by political or union organisations, to the creation of a new Republican army based on traditional military hierarchies and discipline. In Málaga, for example, the Regional Committee of the CNT called for a *mando único* to be established at a regional level on the basis of a Provincial Council of Unified Militia.[95] Nevertheless, the insistent propagation of the *mando único* as a campaigning slogan by Communist and republican parties was, as Juan Andrade, an activist of the POUM, noted in the party newspaper *La Batalla*, intended to suggest that "there are some on the left of 'anti-fascism' who oppose general mobilisation and unity of command... they [Communists and republicans] are making a mistake, unless it is a conscious manoeuvre on their part."[96] We might surmise that "*mando único*" was being used euphemistically by the proponents of militarisation to hasten the return of those aspects of soldiery that this "left of anti-fascism" did oppose: martial discipline, military rank and the loss of political and revolutionary characteristics.

The possibility that a voice as influential as that of Durruti could be added to those opposing militarisation had been extinguished by a bullet on the Madrid front in November 1936. Until that point, the Durruti Column had resisted militarisation.[97] Although Durruti had not openly used his influence to defy the CNT, and had reluctantly taken a squad of militia with him from the Aragón front to join the defence of Madrid at the behest of the organisation, a speech he had made before his departure, delivered on the radio and transmitted across loudspeakers in Barcelona, had indicated the widespread unease felt at the front with regard to the compromises made in the rear.[98] After his death, his legacy was to become a battleground, symbolised by the slogan "We renounce everything except victory," a phrase falsely attributed to him by anti-fascist allies that would

94 Michael Alpert, *The Republican Army in the Spanish Civil War, 1936–1939* (Cambridge: Cambridge University Press, 2013), 59–70.
95 This was in November 1936. See Nadal, *Guerra Civil en Málaga*, 282–3.
96 Juan Andrade, *La revolución española día a día* (Barcelona: Nueva Era, 1979), 138. Andrade had been a founder member of the PCE who was expelled in 1928, and had subsequently joined the international opposition to Stalin headed by Trotsky.
97 Guillamón, *Barricadas en Barcelona*, 128.
98 Paz, *Durruti*, 633–4.

soon be employed by the *comités superiores* of the libertarian organisations.[99] Former members of his column, meanwhile, recalled Durruti having stated that militarisation would be rejected regardless of decisions made in the rearguard.[100] Suspecting that their commander had been murdered, either by Communists or even by his eventual replacement, the former military officer José Manzana, the reluctance of the Durruti Column in Madrid to reincorporate into the front became a cause of severe embarrassment to the *comités superiores* of the CNT.[101]

Meanwhile, these committees entrusted the veteran activist Miguel González Inestal with a particular mission to convince their members at the front to accept the introduction of martial discipline and rank in the libertarian trenches.[102] In so doing, however, the CNT and the FAI were undermining the bases of their power, and removing the conditions that had made their collaboration a necessary precondition for the recovery of the Republican state's legitimacy. By the end of the year, as opponents of the revolution continued to regain ground lost in July, many anarchists began to take stock, and to advance alternative strategies to that of state collaboration. This would bring them into conflict with those engaged in the process of state reconstruction, including, inevitably, the *comités superiores* of the libertarian movement.

Revolutionary resistance

As we have seen, the presence of arms in the rearguard was integral to the question of who held power in revolutionary Spain – the state or the organised working class – and as such it became a test case for anarchists committed to defending and strengthening the revolutionary achievements

99   Guillamón, *Barricadas en Barcelona*, 139.
100 See the intervention of the delegate from Cardona, "Acta del pleno de locales y comarcales celebrado el día 4 de febrero de 1937," CDMH, PS Barcelona, 531/1.
101 Guillamón, *La Revolución de los Comités*, 432. Durruti had initially been replaced by Lucio Ruano, whose brutal methods caused consternation in the ranks (see Chapter Four). Reference to the rumours regarding Manzana is made in the correspondence of Diego Camacho, "Correspondencia entre Diego Camacho ('Abel Paz') y Juan García Oliver," *Balance. Cuaderno de historia*, 38 (2014), 29, and is also discussed extensively in Gimenólogos, *En busca de los Hijos de la Noche*, 398–413. The cause of Durruti's death remains a source of speculation. Contemporary rumours of foul play were angrily denounced by the National and Peninsular Committees of the CNT and the FAI, respectively, in *Solidaridad Obrera*, 24 November 1936.
102 Miguel González Inestal file, Col·lecció Ronald Fraser, AHCB, 72. González Inestal was nominated for this task by Prieto, who later claimed to have committed the CNT to militarisation "on the sly." See Prieto, *Secretario General de la CNT de España en 1936*, Tomo II, 182–3.

of the summer. In Cataluña, the creation of the *Patrullas de Control* as the legitimate guarantors of the revolutionary order in the region, in addition to the scarcity of arms at the front, had led the *comités superiores* to back a campaign for the remainder of the rearguard to be disarmed. Diego Abad de Santillán put the case for such disarmament to a Plenum of anarchist affinity groups in Barcelona on 21 August, which agreed to his proposal. At a meeting of the Barcelona *comités superiores* held the following day, however, a representative of the city's defence committees was present, who stated that "in various assemblies held in the neighbourhoods of Barcelona it has been agreed that, prior to handing over weapons for the front, the armed bodies responsible to the government should be disarmed first."[103] Diego Camacho would later recall a manifesto of Barcelona defence committees that declared: "The defence groups will not lay down their arms while the problem of political power is unresolved and there is an armed force that obeys the Madrid government and isn't under workers' control."[104]

This assertion of the right of revolutionaries to bear arms was an appeal to revolutionary legitimacy as opposed to Republican legality that had as its basis the ongoing revolutionary situation in Spain.[105] Even at this early stage, however, the adoption by anarchists of positions that were outside and against the state would be treated by the *comités superiores* as a breach of internal discipline. At a further meeting of the *comités superiores* on 5 September, in response to the continued autonomy of action of the defence committees, the then Regional Secretary of the Catalan CNT, Mariano Rodríguez Vázquez, and Marcos Alcón Selma, a member of the Nosotros group, insisted that the committees were responsible to the CNT and the FAI and that members should raise any concerns with their respective unions.[106] Union democracy had been severely curtailed by the conditions of war, however, and the political culture of workplaces had been diluted by the obligatory unionisation of the Catalan workforce and the departure of seasoned activists for the front or for official positions. In such circumstances, it was inevitable that the defence committees would continue to provide both a meeting point for disaffected voluntarists and purists in Barcelona, and a network through which the armed defence of the revolution could be effected. The fact that the defence committees were, a month after 19 July, represented by delegates in conflict with the collaborative policies of the *comités superiores* further reinforces the interpretation offered above as

103   Guillamón, *La Revolución de los Comités*, 150.
104   Paz, *Durruti*, 517.
105   The distinction between revolutionary legitimacy and Republican legality is made in Pozo González, *La Catalunya antifeixista*, 54–60.
106   Guillamón, *La Revolución de los Comités*, 191–2.

to the existence of a core and a wider network of defence committees that was mediated by radicals whose obedience could not be relied upon. Once the pre-war Regional Defence Committee had dissolved in order to take up positions either at the front or in the CCMA, new defence committee representatives were chosen from among these radicals who swiftly came into conflict with their predecessors.

In September, an affinity group was formed among JJLL members in the Barcelona suburb of Gràcia who also belonged to their local defence committees. Named Los Quijotes del Ideal, the group was set up to reaffirm the essential principles of anarchism in opposition to what was seen as the degeneration of the CNT and the FAI, to which latter organisation it did not affiliate.[107] It can therefore be perceived that the combative approach adopted by the activist delegates at the heart of the defence committees was echoed at their youthful, purist periphery. That veteran purists were also among the dissenters became clear in December, when the municipal reorganisation begun in autumn made its delayed appearance in Aragón. The reorganised Regional Defence Council, the make-up of which was announced on 21 December with the blessing of the central government, contained seven CNT delegates, and two members each of the Left Republicans, the UGT and the Communist Party. A fifteenth member, Benito Pavón, was a member of the Partido Sindicalista and had been a long-standing member of the CNT.[108] This reorganisation prompted the resignation of José Alberola, a veteran of the struggle against the republican alliance of 1931. In a speech in Lleida in March 1937, he gave an indication of his reasoning:

> [I]f the vanguard retreat, those who are less advanced will justify their own retreat with that of the most advanced and no one will remain at their post. The anarchist will accept "politics" to share this sphere with the bourgeoisie and authoritarians; the socialist will become a republican and the republican will turn still further to the reaction, which is exactly what is happening... A half completed revolution represents a set-back.[109]

Anarchist women also organised to bring the revolution to completion. The fusion of the group around the review *Mujeres Libres* in Madrid with the Women's Cultural Grouping in Barcelona, led to Mujeres Libres (MMLL)

---

107   Paz, *Viaje al pasado*, 58–62.
108   The Partido Sindicalista (Syndicalist Party) had been formed by Pestaña on his withdrawal from the CNT in 1932.
109   José Alberola, *Interpretación anarquista de la revolución* (Lérida: Ediciónes Juventudes Libertarias, 1937), 13–5.

groups springing up throughout the Republican zone, and the review reappeared in the autumn as the mouthpiece of what was fast becoming a nationwide organisation. The MMLL formed a self-organised presence in the rearguard via which the patriarchal implications of state reconstruction would be combatted. Its vision and practices, as Martha Ackelsberg puts it, "differentiated it both from other left-wing women's organizations and, to some extent, from other organizations of the anarcho-syndicalist movement":

> While the founders of the journal saw their programs and policies as consistent with the theory and goals of the larger anarchist movement, they believed that, left to its own devices, the movement was incapable of mobilizing women effectively for the social revolution and the recon-struction of society.[110]

That the grouping was, by contrast to such grandees of the move-ment as Federica Montseny, able to perceive the danger to the revolution posed by the intertwined re-emergence of gendered and racial discourse is demonstrated by an article in its review at the end of the year. It was written in response to a recruitment poster in Madrid which played on racist and sexist fears of the Army of Africa (near identical versions had appeared in Barcelona addressed to Catalan men), under the slogan "*Madrileños*, do not allow your women to be despoiled by the Moors!":

> *Madrileño*, comrade, brother: do not join the struggle out of fear of the Moorish "razzias," the bane of Christian women... There is no reason to revive the instinctive, primitive motives that years of spiritual cultiva-tion have calmed, you do not need the spurs of opportunists who, to win a victory – almost always for their party – resort to the lowest of incite-ments... You are struggling for yourself; out of your deepest conviction and not because of the ridiculous threats, of greater or lesser accuracy and terror, of humiliation to your wife who, what is more, shares your ideal and knows how to defend it and herself.[111]

Opposition to state collaboration would grow in coherence over the first months of 1937, and the continued contacts between radical women, anar-chist purists in the JJLL and the defence committees would be crucial to the revolutionary mobilisation in May of that year. As had occurred during the first years of the Second Republic, the revolutionary press played a signifi-cant role in establishing a shared platform for these sectors to express their

110   Ackelsberg, *Free Women*, 136.
111   *Mujeres Libres*, December 1936.

misgivings about state collaboration. This became clear above all following the acceptance of ministries in the government of Largo Caballero. The old guard of the *Solidaridad Obrera* editorial board had been cleared out before this news was announced, but the revolution had allowed new publications to be established, or old ones to be revived, and several voiced their scepticism at this turn of events.

The newspaper of the FAI in Valencia, *Nosotros*, in an article entitled "The anarchists and the 'circumstances'," declared that, if anarchist principles were not maintained, "we will end up not knowing who is an anarchist and who is a republican."[112] *Línea de Fuego*, the mouthpiece of the Iron Column, an anarchist division on the front at Teruel, went further: "What was always attacked is now to be embraced and the very foundations of our beliefs torn up. From now on there is to be no more talk of freedom, but of obedience to 'our' government instead."[113] *Acracia*, the publication of the CNT-FAI in Lleida, which had, under the stewardship of José Peirats, also made clear its opposition to state collaboration, considered the sudden jump from the social to the political terrain to be a "senseless contradiction" even from a collaborationist perspective, requiring that activists in the libertarian movement "split up in order to form a separate body in organisations unsuited to a revolutionary movement." The workers of the CNT, it went on, did not require the distractions of the "political" sphere to carry forward the revolution.[114]

By December 1936, several of those sacked from *Solidaridad Obrera* were collaborating in *Ideas*, the newly established weekly mouthpiece of the libertarian movement in Baix Llobregat, an area known for its revolutionism and the only Catalan locality whose representative (José Xena) had voted against the CNT participating in the CCMA.[115] The editors of *Ideas* made it clear that they thought the CNT was making a strategic error in subjugating its principles to the war against fascism, considering the situation to be uniquely propitious for the organisation to put forward its perspective. Nor were punches pulled in regard to the CNT's anti-fascist allies:

> the politicians, all the Spanish politicians of the so-called left, are as responsible as the fascists for the battle that bloodies the Iberian soil, because they allowed the fascist movement to organise itself from the

112   *Nosotros*, 7 November 1936. The paper continued to hold a line critical of collaboration and of official politics until it was taken over by the Peninsular Committee of the FAI in the summer of 1937.
113   Quoted in Mintz, *Anarchism and Workers' Self-Management*, 212.
114   *Acracia*, 28 October 1936.
115   Xena was on the editorial board of *Ideas*, along with Jaime Balius, Liberto Callejas and Vicente Galindo Cortés, who wrote under the pen-name "Fontaura." The latter three had all been on the editorial board of *Solidaridad Obrera* at the beginning of the war.

ministries, barracks and colonies of Spain... To those, today as yesterday, we must say: ... The time of Governments has passed; the time of
politics has passed... the social hour has sounded. You are victims of
your own errors; you think of nothing other than Power and Money.[116]

Leaving little doubt as to its position, the front page headline of this first
edition read: "Neither Law nor Official Army. Socialisation and the People
Armed!"[117] The issues this headline raised – obedience to the law, militarisation, socialisation and the disarmament of the rearguard – demonstrate
that the contributors to *Ideas* had identified the dividing lines that were to
prove fundamental to the coalescence of a revolutionary alliance opposed to
state reconstruction. On the other side of the divide stood not only the anti-
revolutionary bloc but the *comités superiores* of the CNT.

Conclusions

At the first meeting of the CCMA on the night of 21 July 1936, the question was raised as to who had been responsible for the defeat of the army in
Barcelona. To this, Aurelio Fernández, a veteran activist of the CNT and
member of the Nosotros group, replied: "the usual suspects: the *piojosos*
(lowlife)." Agustín Guillamón has expanded on who was understood to fall
into this category:

> the unemployed, the recent migrants and the marginalised and im-
> poverished population of the *"casas baratas"* (cheap houses)... and the
> mistreated industrial proletariat who, in extremely tough conditions,
> assailed by mass unemployment, long working days, hunger wages and
> precarious piecework, lived in the working-class neighbourhoods... in
> rented or sublet hovels, rooms or bare flats which they had to share due
> to unaffordable rent.[118]

These were the conquerors of July, who had "swarmed" into the centre
from the workers' districts, described by Francisco Lacruz, who despised
them, as "terrifying-looking whores," "former men," "subhuman beings full
of psychopathic defects... This mad and maddening humanity, which ordinarily lives hidden from and extraneous to the city."[119]

116   *Ideas*, 29 December 1936.
117   Ibid.
118   Guillamón, *Barricadas en Barcelona*, 58. *"Piojoso"* literally means "lice-ridden."
119   The words of Francisco Lacruz, cited in Ealham, "The myth of the maddened crowd," 111.

The unlikely coincidence of Fernández and Lacruz in their naming of the revolutionary protagonists reveals July as the triumph of those who had been excluded from bourgeois society, a fact recognised by their champions as well as their enemies. The victory of the workers was also a victory for women, "terrifying-looking" in their "masculine" attire, brandishing rifles, occupying buildings and demolishing the women's prison. It was moreover an internationalist victory, and as anarchist patrols began to dominate the French–Catalan frontier, revolutionary Barcelona acted as a magnet to radicals and refugees from fascist states. This was the cosmopolitan working-class alliance, which, understood in pathological, gendered and racist terms, was what the international phenomenon of fascism had set out to destroy. But its triumph was also incompatible with the continued existence of the democratic, bourgeois nation-state. The profundity and scale of the revolutionary moment and the expansiveness of its horizons meant that briefly this state appeared to have evaporated, leaving anarchy and fascism to behold each other as irreconcilable opposites. Yet the Spanish revolution was also to reveal the reservoirs of power that the modern state could draw upon even after its administrative mechanisms and monopoly of violence had disappeared.

Working-class men who had been frequently dehumanised due to their association with radical politics were now appealed to in gendered terms to control the "frivolous" displays of power and pleasure of their rifle-wielding sisters and daughters. Anarchist men were encouraged to repudiate the presence of women at the front due to the dangers of venereal disease but not to eschew brothels while on leave. Men whose status as "true" Catalans or Spaniards had never been recognised when they were militant organisers were now encouraged to enlist in order to protect "their women" from the "Moorish hordes." In this way, unpredictable and expansive revolutionary energies could be channelled back into the service of a system whose iniquities had nurtured those sectors of society that now sought to cast all democracy and progress aside.

Democracy and progress were further resources of the stricken state. It has been argued that the division of the Spanish anarchists into gradualists, voluntarists and purists was rendered meaningless by the onset of the civil war.[120] Although porous, these categories in fact retained their validity. The libertarian activists that backed state collaboration in 1936 formed an alliance that was reminiscent of the movement at the moment of the

120   See Pere Gabriel, "Un sindicalismo de Guerra: sindicatos y colectivizaciones industrials y agrarias en Cataluña, 1936–1939," *Actes II Seminari sobre la guerra civil i el franquisme a Catalunya, Barberà del Vallès 14 i 15 de març de 1997* (Barberà del Vallès: Ajuntament de Barberà del Vallès, 1997), 59; Pozo González, *Poder Legal y Poder Real*, 271.

Republic's declaration in April 1931, and it was justified in such terms in a speech by the prominent Asturian anarchist and future mayor of Gijón, Avelino Mallada, on 11 September 1936: "During the democracy, dictatorship, and whenever it was necessary, the anarchists struggled against tyranny. In the years of Primo de Rivera… we anarchists stood at the side of the democrats to put an end to that shameful episode."[121] The organisational priorities consistently maintained by gradualists such as Mallada and Joan Peiró were reinforced during the first months of the civil war by the National Secretary of the CNT, Horacio M. Prieto, while the purist Montseny's "progressive" defence of a national, democratic civilisation in August 1936 likewise echoed the sentiments she had expressed at the birth of the Republic. Although the most prominent voluntarists – in particular García Oliver and Durruti – had been more enigmatic, in some respects their role in July recalled their activity in Barcelona on 14 April 1931, when CNT activists ensured that Lluís Companys was able to occupy the office of the Civil Governor, or in exile prior to the Second Republic, when they maintained close relations with Catalan separatists in opposition to the dictatorship.[122] Having castigated his forebears for missing the opportunity to take on the mantle of "Lenin and Trotsky" in Spain, García Oliver, at the helm of the Barcelona defence committees, acquiesced in the decision of an unconstitutionally assembled Regional Plenum to participate in the CCMA and, rather than attempt to gain support for his revolutionary position among the wider membership, would go on to become one of the most notable figures of state collaboration.

As in the case of Russia twenty years earlier, the advances of the revolution in Spain in the summer of 1936 were predicated on the decomposition of the state and the creation of alternative sources of legitimacy and power by armed workers. When those alternatives began to be closed down by the reconstituted state, this process could be understood as a counterrevolution, even though in both instances the revolutionary organisations were involved in this "disguised resurrection of the state" prophesied by Bakunin.[123] What would complicate matters further in the Spanish case was that the CNT's apparent allies in the project of state collaboration were ambivalent in their relations with the *comités superiores*, and wholly hostile to the organisation's grassroots activists. As a result, the latter were pushed into a twofold defence

121   Ramón Álvarez, *Avelino G. Mallada. Alcalde Anarquista* (Barcelona: Historia Libertaria de Asturias, 1987), 276.

122   See Prieto, *Secretario General de la CNT de España en 1936, Tomo II*, 88–9, on García Oliver's positive attitude to anti-dictatorial alliances at that time; and García Oliver, *El eco de los pasos*, 82–9.

123   Mintz, "Las influencias de Bakunin y Kropotkin."

of anarchism, on the one hand attempting to maintain fidelity to their anti-state traditions, and on the other resisting the attempts of rival organisations to sideline the libertarian movement.

In spite of these setbacks, the forces that the rupture of July had set in motion could not easily be contained. After a period of disorientation and regroupment, radical anarchists began to push back against the reconstruction of the state, defending the conquests of July, and moving forward with structural challenges to the capitalist economy. Over the course of this process, alliances began to emerge that reaffirmed the initial, expansive parameters of the Spanish revolution. This process, and the new organisational expressions it gave rise to, is the subject of the following chapter.

CHAPTER THREE

Radical Anarchism:
Programme and Alliance, January–April 1937

By the end of 1936, a division within the CNT on the basis of attitudes to the state could be perceived. On the one hand, many members advocated a defence of the revolution in the rear through a socialised economy and armed populace, and at the front through a war waged by a voluntary, popular militia. This was summed up in the slogan advanced by the publication *Ideas*: "Socialisation and the people armed!"[1] On the other hand, the organisation's *comités superiores* were now committed to participation in national and regional governments of anti-fascist unity, the principal objective of which was to re-establish the Republican state in order to wage a conventional war. Either side of this divide, the decision-making processes employed by the partisans of each tendency were at variance. The radical tendency was characterised by assemblies of activists in the neighbourhoods, workers in the factories, and combatants at the front. The *comités superiores*, by contrast, made decisions at closed meetings, often in haste and in response to urgent situations. Over the winter and early spring of 1937, the parameters of this division would become more clearly defined.

One factor that initially served to obscure the tensions within the libertarian movement was an awareness of the threat to the CNT's influence posed by the increasing coherence and confidence of those organisations that made the fight against fascism conditional upon the suppression of the social revolution, in particular the PCE and its Catalan sister party, the PSUC. The PSUC is unlikely to have numbered more than a few thousand members at its foundation, but it grew rapidly during the first year of the war, appealing to anti-fascists among the middling classes with a programme committed to the defence of parliamentary democracy and private property.[2] The line of the Comintern, to which the PSUC and PCE belonged, was of presenting Spain to Britain and France as a fellow democratic state under siege from fascism and requiring their aid. In order to do this, it was imperative to downplay, deny or curtail the revolutionary

1   See preceding chapter.
2   See Pagès i Blanch, *La Guerra Civil espanyola a Catalunya*, 45

aspect of the Spanish civil war, while attempting to maintain anti-fascist unity.[3] In practice, however, these aims proved to be mutually exclusive. Early observations from Comintern agents such as André Marty stressed the desirability of splitting the CNT between those of its components who favoured unity and those who threatened it by pressing ahead with the revolution.[4]

The libertarian camp had generally been slow to react to the position the PCE and the PSUC had taken on in the summer of 1936. Attempts had been made to ostracise the latter party from revolutionary phenomena in certain parts of Cataluña because it was regarded as an arriviste organisation without established credentials, not because of its political positioning.[5] Consequently, the offensive carried out by the PCE and the PSUC against the dissident communist POUM was characterised in *Solidaridad Obrera* as relating to "personal or party political questions, questions of pride" rather than representing an attack on the revolution's most vulnerable adherents.[6] Even the POUM, however, did not initially consider the Communists to be external to its conception of "proletarian" anti-fascism. For this reason Andreu Nin, the de facto leader of the party in this period, considered there to be a working-class majority in the Generalitat.[7]

Nevertheless, by the end of 1936, a "counterrevolutionary" threat had become apparent to all sectors of the CNT and not only those already sceptical about anti-fascist collaboration.[8] This counterrevolution was defined in the official press of the Catalan CNT in terms of political intrigue, primarily with regard to the "provocations" and "rumour mongering" of the Communists in their attempts to sideline the Confederation.[9] The radicals had a broader, and more realistic, understanding of the process as one of

3   See the telegrams exchanged between the PCE and the Comintern and Soviet authorities in the first days of the conflict, reproduced in *Spain Betrayed: The Soviet Union in the Spanish Civil War*, ed. by Ronald Radosh, Mary R. Habeck, and Grigory Sevostianov (London: Yale University Press, 2001), 7–15.

4   Antonio Elorza and Marta Bizcarrondo, *Queridos Camaradas. La Internacional Comunista en España, 1919–1939* (Barcelona: Planeta, 1999), 327. Marty was a member of the French Communist Party and the Secretariat of the Comintern who had arrived in Spain soon after the outbreak of the civil war. He would later become Political Commissar of the International Brigades.

5   See Juan José Gallordo Romero and José Manuel Márquez Rodríguez, *Revolución y guerra en Gramenet del Besòs (1936–1939)* (Barcelona: Grupo de Estudios Históricos Gramenet del Besòs, 1997), 81.

6   *Solidaridad Obrera*, 13 December 1936.

7   See Nin, *La revolución española*, 262. It was not until a speech in April that Nin publicly declared that the PSUC was "not a workers' party": ibid. 313.

8   See, for example, the front page of *Solidaridad Obrera*, 29 December 1936, and the editorial in *Ruta*, the mouthpiece of the Catalan JJLL, 1 January 1937.

9   See *Solidaridad Obrera*, 29, 30, 31 December 1936.

reconstructing the Republican state at the expense of revolutionary projects. Such an analysis had cost the veteran purist Liberto Callejas his job as editor of *Solidaridad Obrera*, following the publication of an editorial that opposed the Decree of Militarisation in terms that struck at the heart of the problem: "There is a mentality that... of a piece with the position it held before 19 July, tends almost involuntarily towards the reconstruction of that which existed then but which has since been destroyed by... the revolutionary process."[10] The article, which insisted that militarisation must not be allowed to undermine the revolutionary character of the war or resurrect a pre-revolutionary militarist spirit, prompted the PSUC and the Catalan branch of the UGT to send a letter of complaint to both the Regional Committees of the CNT and the FAI, precipitating the dismissal of Callejas.[11]

Callejas's understanding of the counterrevolution as a phenomenon of state reconstruction rather than organisational rivalry reflected the division of the CNT into street-level and high political perspectives. This divergence would be exposed most clearly during the May events in Barcelona, when the *comités superiores* considered the revolutionary mobilisation of the libertarian movement to have as its end the mere rectification of yet another Communist-inspired "provocation."[12] If the widespread identification of an external enemy, the "counterrevolution," in the months prior to these events served to obscure the differences within the libertarian movement, this chapter will demonstrate that it did not prevent the emergence and crystallisation of a radical programme defined in opposition to the reimposition of state power per se. As much was made clear at the start of the year by the rationalist teacher Floreal Ocaña in the pages of *Ideas*, the new journalistic home of Liberto Callejas:

> The "fifth column," formed by all the political parties, has begun its attack on the people's revolution. With typical guile it has increased the size of the old organs of state repression in the hope that, as before, they will follow the state's orders... If the political world, which bears the blame for the rise of fascism, succeeds in making the people obey laws intended to put the brakes on social and economic progress, and swallow the double pill of an official army and armed institutions recognised as the only forces and organisational forms permitted to struggle at the front and... "conserve revolutionary order in the rear," then soon, very soon, we will see a campaign for those who aren't enlisted in one or other mercenary body to immediately hand over weapons

10   *Solidaridad Obrera*, 31 October 1936.
11   See Pozo González, *La Catalunya antifeixista*, 71.
12   The May events are discussed in the following chapter.

and munitions. And after this campaign will come…registers of homes intended to complete the disarmament of the proletariat.[13]

This bleak perspective, which would prove to be remarkably prescient, was shared by other revolutionaries in Spain. Mary Low described the ebb of the revolution and the linked reassertion of militarism, nationalism and traditional gender roles:

> It was in the air… The regiments going down the streets marched in perfect formation, one two, one two, the arms swinging chest high and the hundreds of feet striking down on the pavement with a single, thunderous blow. The Catalan flag was carried automatically with the red banners and the black, there were less women mingled among the men going to the front, there were no longer dogs and cats following on the end of a string, or perched on kit-bags. It was all as it should be, and we stood more chance of winning the war perhaps, but meanwhile the chance of winning the revolution was growing gradually fainter.[14]

In spite of this relative decline, however, the revolution retained a great deal of resources and potential. Across Republican Spain, over one and a half million workers and peasants began the year participating in the revolutionary experiment of collectivisation.[15] It was, after all, as late as December 1936 that George Orwell arrived in Barcelona and described it as a place where "the working class was in the saddle."[16] Furthermore, following the heroic defence of Madrid, sufficient optimism remained as to the course of the war for the branches of the libertarian movement to advance policies that went beyond the merely defensive or reactive.

Detectable in this period was an increasing restlessness among radicals who did not accept the "circumstantial" arguments of the *comités superiores* and were unprepared to be swept along by the tide of events. In an overview of the movement published at the outset of 1937, the editorial board of *Acracia* predicted a change of course:

> Anarchism, in spite of ministerial collaboration, has not betrayed itself, which is not to say that the ministers and councillors are behaving

---

13   *Ideas*, 21 January 1937.
14   Low and Breá, *Red Spanish Notebook*, 214.
15   See the convincing estimates and periodisation in Mintz, *Anarchism and Workers' Self-Management*, 139.
16   George Orwell, *Orwell in Spain: The Full Text of* Homage to Catalonia *with Associated Articles, Reviews and Letters from* The Complete Works of George Orwell (London: Penguin, 2001), 32.

like anarchists, but rather that not all anarchism is ministerial and nor does it make a dogma out of the facts as they stand. There are many of us who have remained faithful to the most rigorous anti-statism... We anticipate, therefore, a brilliant Confederal and anarchist resurgence... that will return to the resolutions adopted and rectify abuses... The revolution will not be strangled with the complicity of its most enthusiastic champions. Let us react for the good of everyone. For a humanity without classes and a society of free producers.[17]

The stage was set for an alliance among radical revolutionaries that would seek to alter the collaborationist course of the libertarian organisations, as had occurred at the outset of the Second Republic, while simultaneously attempting to deepen and extend the revolutionary process. The result was a surprising upturn in revolutionary initiatives and the coalescence of new revolutionary solidarities in the first third of 1937. As we will see in this chapter, however, this resurgence was complicated by the disastrous loss of Málaga, the increasing violence of state reconstruction, and the widening gap between the grassroots activists and the *comités superiores*, leading radicals to consider a return to the barricades the only remaining option for the salvation of the Spanish revolution.

The people armed?

As intimated in the above citation from Ocaña, the successful reconstitution of the Republican state depended on the governing authorities establishing a monopoly of violence at the front and at the rear. Opposed to this, the slogan of "the people armed" lost ground to campaigns urging the sending of weapons to the front and the establishment of a *mando único* to oversee the war effort. The position of those resisting militarisation was much weakened by the fall of Málaga in February. *Hombres Libres*, the newspaper connected to the Maroto Column in the province of Granada, had continued to affirm in January that the revolution and the war were inseparable.[18] However, once Málaga had fallen, its defenders starved of ammunition and support by the central government, the Maroto Column agreed to militarisation at a general assembly.[19] Miguel García, a Catalan militia volunteer and CNT member who had joined the front at Madrid, recalled that anarchists "let

17   *Acracia*, 23 January 1937.
18   Amorós, *Maroto*, 102.
19   Ibid. 114. On the fall of Málaga, see Nadal, *Guerra Civil en Málaga*, 359–79, and Beevor, *The Battle for Spain*, 223–5.

themselves be persuaded into accepting the inevitable for the sake of the promised arms."[20] González Inestal, the man who had been charged with imposing militarisation on anarchist columns by Prieto, told more recalcitrant militia that they would be unable to count on organisational support in requesting arms and ammunition if the decision of the CNT to accept militarisation was not respected.[21]

On 5 February, a Plenum of anarchist and Confederal columns took place in Valencia.[22] It had been called by the Iron Column, in operation on the front at Teruel, in consultation with the Maroto Column, which was unable to send delegates because of the advance of the mutinous army on Málaga. The reasons given for the calling of the Plenum were, first, that the "enormous quantity" of decisions made in the rearguard had taken place without consulting the militia columns, and, second, that those in the rear had seemingly forgotten "the revolutionary meaning of the moment."[23] As if to confirm the timeliness of this assembly, at a Regional Plenum of the Catalan CNT the previous day, delegates from Baix Llobregat and Cardona had affirmed that militarisation "annuls the revolutionary organisation," while the delegate from Badalona suggested that representatives from the militia columns be granted representation at National Plenums of the CNT, a proposal rejected by the Regional Committee.[24]

While several attendees at the Plenum of militia stressed the "historic" or "transcendental" nature of the gathering, the representative of the National Committee of the CNT made plain his irritation at the manner in which the Plenum had been called and denied its authority. He reported, furthermore, that Largo Caballero had personally informed him that "the arms of the state will be given to the forces of the state… if [the militia] do not want to enter into [the state] then their organisations can supply them with arms."[25] It was clear, therefore, that the price paid for military supplies would be an acceptance of state authority. The alternative, as was swiftly becoming clear, was abandonment by both the General Command and the libertarian organisations.

The continued viability of columns operating in accordance with

20   See Miguel García, *Miguel García's Story* (London: Miguel García Memorial Committee, 1982), 46–7.

21   Miguel González Inestal file, Col·lecció Ronald Fraser, AHCB, Fonts Orals, Casa de l'Ardiaca, 74.

22   "CNT-FAI Acta del Pleno de Columnas Confederales y Anarquistas celebrado en Valencia el día 5 de febrero de 1937," http://www.fondation-besnard.org/spip.php?article428 [accessed 1 December 2017].

23   Ibid.

24   "Acta del pleno de locales y comarcales celebrado el día 4 de febrero."

25   "CNT-FAI Acta del Pleno de Columnas Confederales y Anarquistas."

anarchist principles at the front depended on the persistence of the revolutionary interregnum in the rear. In the case of the Iron Column, its attempt to rely on the resources of this revolution came under sustained attack from the forces of the state in the first months of 1937. A small socialised factory in Burriana that supplied the column with munitions was subject to an attempted occupation by members of the Republican police force, the Assault Guards, which was only averted on the intervention of armed militia and the negotiation of the CNT's National Committee.[26] Then, on 8 March, the occupation of a workers' centre in Vinalesa by Assault Guards prompted clashes that led to the occupation of the district by government forces and the arrest and imprisonment of two hundred libertarians, including ninety-two members of the Iron Column.[27] Appeals for the release of the prisoners were persistent in *Nosotros* in the following weeks and echoed in the pages of *Acracia*. The Italian anarchist Camillo Berneri, a refugee from Mussolini's Italy, who had fought at the front before ill-health forced him to return to Barcelona, described the events as "reminiscent of Casas Viejas."[28]

On 21 March, the Iron Column finally agreed to militarisation at an assembly.[29] The previous month, the similarly recalcitrant components of the del Rosal Column had been loaded on to trucks and taken from the front line to Cuenca, where a representative of the National Committee informed them that they would be expelled from the organisation if they failed to militarise.[30] Following militarisation, the significance of "the people armed" shifted to the rearguard, where many activists, male and female, continued to bear arms. In the first half of 1937, these activists would be joined by a steady stream of combatants leaving the front. By far the most significant group to abandon the lines en masse was that from the Gelsa section of the Durruti Column, of which eight hundred components returned to Barcelona with arms in hand in February, although desertion in opposition to militarisation appears to have been a more widespread phenomenon than has hitherto been claimed, and requires further study. While militarisation had settled the question of the monopoly of violence at the front in favour of the state, in the rear, and particularly in Cataluña, it remained open to contestation. There the police forces jostled for hegemony with the defence committees and with the *Patrullas de Control*.

26   See Paz, *The Story of the Iron Column*, 171.
27   Ibid. 221–2.
28   Camillo Berneri, *Entre la Revolución y las trincheras* ([Paris?]: Ediciones Tierra y Libertad, 1946), 24.
29   *Nosotros*, 22 March 1937.
30   Fraser, *Blood of Spain*, 338.

Although initially intended to comprise affiliates from all of the anti-fascist organisations, the *Patrullas* were in effect controlled by the CNT, and in some cases were answerable to the local defence committee.[31] Those same committees pressured anarchists to overcome their reluctance to enlist in a body which had the appearance of a police force, challenging militants who complained of abuses to join in order to safeguard the "revolutionary morality" according to which the *Patrullas* were to operate.[32] Early in 1937, however, the *Patrullas* would become a target of the propaganda and law-making of the republican and Communist parties, particularly in the wake of the much-publicised events in La Fatarella in January. La Fatarella was an agricultural town in Cataluña, where an attempt to form a collective by a minority of its inhabitants, affiliated to the CNT, led to the crystallisation of an anti-collectivisation bloc composed of the PSUC, the ERC, the UGT and the *Unió de Rabassaires*. Growing tension in the town led to a bloody showdown between some of its anti-revolutionary inhabitants and the *Patrullas de Control* sent from Barcelona, resulting in tens of deaths, mostly of townspeople.[33] The uprising of La Fatarella was represented by the libertarian organisations as the work of the "fifth column" but was defended by the anti-revolutionary bloc as an expression of legitimate grievances.[34] The UGT subsequently withdrew its members from the *Patrullas de Control* and in February the PSUC organised a protest, in which the official police bodies participated, calling for their dissolution.[35] In spite of decrees issued in March and April, the Generalitat did not succeed in dissolving the *Patrullas de Control*, many of whose members in this period appear to have responded directly to the orders of their local defence committee.[36]

Jaime Balius wrote in *La Noche* of the necessity of maintaining the *Patrullas de Control* as a guarantee of the revolution that would not be subject to or incorporated into the traditional forces of public order:

31   According to one former member, this was the case in the Barcelona suburb of Sants: Joan Casanovas, "La Guerra Civil a Barcelona: les patrulles de control de Sants vistes per un del seus membres," *Historia y Fuente Oral*, 11 (1994): 59. The *Patrullas* in the Catalan town of Gramenet del Besòs were also subject to the control of the local, Confederal, defence committee. See Gallordo Romero and Márquez Rodríguez, *Revolución y guerra en Gramenet del Besòs*, 72.

32   Casanovas, "La Guerra Civil a Barcelona," 56–7.

33   See Pelai Pagès i Blanch, "La Fatarella: Una insurrecció pagesa a la reraguarda catalana durant la guerra civil," *Estudis D'Historia Agrària*, 17 (2004), 659–74.

34   The CNT's version of events was given in *Solidaridad Obrera*, 26 January 1937. Two days later *Acracia* also described the events as a "fascist" uprising, and stated that the presence of fascists in "left" organisations was due to the "unscrupulous" way in which certain organisations had attempted to increase their memberships: *Acracia*, 28 January 1937.

35   Chris Ealham, "Una revolución a medias: los orígenes de los *hechos de mayo* y la crisis del anarquismo," *Viento Sur*, 93 (2007): 97.

36   See Casanovas, "La Guerra Civil a Barcelona," 64–5.

It must not be the *Patrullas de Control* that are incorporated into the uniformed bodies, but rather the members of the institutions of the old regime who, after a rigorous selection process, should then form part of the *Patrullas de Control*, and it must be our comrades of the workers' organisations that control absolutely everything pertaining to public order.[37]

At issue was one of the questions considered fundamental to a classical understanding of the state as "a relation of men dominating men, a relation supported by means of legitimate (i.e. considered to be legitimate) violence."[38] In the Catalan rearguard in this period, as Balius's article makes clear, a power struggle was underway between those who claimed their legitimacy from legality and those whose claim to violence was based on the revolution of July 1936. Who dominated whom had yet to be decided, but Balius was not alone in linking this question to his concern that the revolution had not gone far enough. In this respect, the economic question was as significant as that of public order, and the relevance of one to the other would be made explicit in this period.

The socialisation campaign

A recognition that the CNT had allowed the direction of the economy to escape its control following the first burst of revolutionary activity in the summer had, by the end of 1936, become general within the libertarian movement. This resulted in the socialisation campaign that, in the first half of 1937, became crucial to the question of whether the revolution, or the project of state reconstruction, would triumph. The campaign would also reveal fault lines within the libertarian movement, with the *comités superiores* understanding socialisation to imply union control of the economy, while radical sectors defined it as a complete transformation in the relations of production leading to "a community of free producers."[39]

On 30 December 1936, an editorial in *Solidaridad Obrera* declared the intention of the CNT to "prepare the intervention of the unions in the highest direction of production and of the economy in general," retrospectively suggesting that its initial acceptance of a system of partial

37   *La Noche*, 26 February 1937.
38   Max Weber, "Politics as a Vocation," in *From Max Weber: Essays in Sociology*, ed. by H. H. Gerth and C. Wright Mills (London: Routledge, 1995), 78.
39   See, for example, the declaration of the National Committee of Spanish Transport Workers' Unions cited in Castells Duran, *El proceso estatizador*, 29–30.

collectivisations, in which union control was not, in the main, assured, had been intended as a "transitional solution."[40] Dissatisfaction regarding the collectivisations as they had functioned hitherto stemmed from several factors. The existence of variables in prices within the same industry suggested that collectives in both the town and country were operating in competition with each other and not according to the needs of society at large.[41] Furthermore, in some cases activists felt that the effect of the committees set up to administer collectivised factories was that one boss had been replaced with five.[42] On 6 December 1936, at the first Regional Plenum of the FAI to be held in Cataluña since July, the delegate from the affinity group *Viejos Acratas*, based in the radical stronghold of L'Hospitalet, declared that "the [factory] control committees do the same as the bourgeoisie."[43]

For radical anarchists, the collectivisations fell short of their revolutionary aspirations. The veteran activist Severino Campos, known as "the little Jacobin," lamented in the first issue of *Ideas* that:

> While the revolution has begun its rapid march, its constructive phase has not yielded the kind of results on the economic terrain that could satisfy the broad conceptions of anarchism… nevertheless we must not hold ourselves back nor take… collectivism as a model of the social future… the collectivisations cannot continue in the manner in which they have been interpreted and practised until now. It is necessary to think of something that will guarantee bread and work for all, while at the same time suppress the exorbitant wages of those who contribute the least work.[44]

The December Plenum of the Catalan FAI called for the socialisation of production and distribution, "avoiding the partial collectivisation of enterprises, which represents a complete negation of the spirit of socialisation."[45] In early January, a Plenum of Catalan peasants affiliated to the CNT was held, at which the continued malign influence of the middleman was denounced by delegates, that of Pi de Llobregat declaring that "until such a

40   *Solidaridad Obrera*, 30 December 1936.
41   See Leval, *Collectives in the Spanish Revolution*, 291; and Mintz, *Anarchism and Workers' Self-Management*, 146–7.
42   Jacinto Borras file, Col·lecció Ronald Fraser, AHCB, 9.
43   "Acta del Pleno Regional de grupos anarquistas de Cataluña, celebrado el día 6 de diciembre de 1936," CDMH, PS Barcelona, 531/1.
44   *Ideas*, 29 December 1936.
45   "Acta del Pleno Regional de grupos anarquistas de Cataluña, celebrado el día 6 de diciembre."

time as there may be an across-the-board socialisation of wealth it will necessarily be very difficult to attain the end in view."[46]

For the *comités superiores*, there were further potential advantages to the campaign. Its initiation enabled a return to the question of Federations of Industry, a reorganisation of the CNT's structure that had been debated at the Madrid Congress of 1931.[47] Using the argument that the CNT as it stood would be unable to implement socialisation, long-time advocates of the Federations of Industry, such as Joan Peiró, attempted to persuade those sectors of the CNT that had obstructed their implementation for five years that the unions should be reorganised, with the concomitant increase in bureaucracy and centralisation this implied.[48] *Tierra y Libertad*, the weekly publication of the FAI, dedicated double-page spreads of consecutive issues to explaining the need for both socialisation and Federations of Industry and how they would function.[49] On 7 January, Fidel Miró, Secretary of the JJLL in Cataluña, published an article in *Ruta*, the mouthpiece of that organisation, which also stressed the revolutionary import of socialisation and the need for it to be preceded by the organisation of Federations of Industry.[50]

Socialisation also appealed to the more radical sectors of the CNT, and, in this sense, the campaign had the potential to unify the organisation. From the perspective of the *comités superiores*, an increase in union control over the economy might have mitigated the CNT's decreasing influence at the level of state administration, while socialisation may also have been viewed as an opportunity to bring the union's membership into line. Problematic in this regard was that the radical sectors of the libertarian organisations did not consider the socialisation campaign as a question of internal discipline. Nor did they view it in the staid and unromantic terms of Peiró, who declared that:

> Socialisation and nationalisation is, in essence, the same thing. Socialisation loses part of its virtues if it is the state that carries it out. It conserves all of them… when its enactor is the anti-state, specifically, the union. For this reason it is necessary that the required reaction is produced among Confederal affiliates, and the superstructure of the

46   Quoted in José Peirats, *The CNT in the Spanish Revolution, Volume 2*, trans. by Paul Sharkey and Chris Ealham (Hastings: Christie Books, 2005), 28.

47   See Chapter One.

48   See, for example, an article from the end of January, in which Peiró argued that "creating the organs and capacity for directing and administrating the new economy without the need for any tutelage from the state should take precedence": *La Vanguardia*, 31 January 1937. See also Monjo and Vega, *Els treballadors i la Guerra civil*, 130.

49   See *Tierra y Libertad*, 26 December 1936 and 9 January 1937.

50   *Ruta*, 7 January 1937.

industrial unions and the creation of the National Federations is proceeded to rapidly...[51]

By tapping into the mood of the movement's radical sectors, the campaign
risked measures being taken before the new union structures could be im-
plemented, and an initiative which had been expected to shore up the internal cohesion of the CNT threatened to produce a quite different outcome.

Radicals in L'Hospitalet had already undertaken, under the auspices of
the socialised supplies industry, the expropriation of two cooperatives on
Christmas Day 1936, which had resulted in the resignation of the ERC
and the UGT representatives from the municipal council.[52] In January, the
local CNT took steps to socialise the entire economy of the town. This
was agreed to by the CNT union of L'Hospitalet and announced in *Ideas*,
21 January 1937. Collectivisation of individual enterprises had been widespread in L'Hospitalet, and their coordination was to be enacted "within
days." This example of socialisation was to be controlled not by national
federations but by a Regional General Council of the Economy composed
of elected delegates from each branch of industry, in line with proposals
sketched out by José Xena.[53] The radicals read this development in a maximalist light:

> We give this idea to the comrades of other localities so that, if they are
> not afraid of being labelled extremists, they can put it into practice and
> facilitate the creation of the Regional General Council of the Economy,
> the basis for bringing to a happy conclusion the free commune within a
> Federation of the Free Peoples of Iberia.[54]

Furthermore, radicals expanded on their conception of socialisation to incorporate calls for the strict observance of "union federalism" and a critique
of governmental collaboration.[55] For the CNT in Lleida, socialisation likewise implied that "everything pertaining to the life of the town should be
controlled and administered by the collective as a whole."[56] An open assembly was held at which the townspeople proclaimed the socialisation of hous-
ing as the first stage in a process intended to lead to complete socialisation.[57]

51   *Solidaridad Obrera*, 17 January 1937.
52   See *La Vanguardia*, 27 December 1936.
53   *Ideas*, 14 January 1937.
54   *Ideas*, 21 January 1937.
55   *Ideas*, 14 January 1937.
56   *Acracia*, 26 January 1937.
57   José Peirats, *Figuras del movimiento libertario español* (Barcelona: Ediciones Picazo,
      1977), 279–80.

In Aragón, a Congress took place in Caspe in February, where 456 delegates representing 275 collectives agreed to the creation of a Regional Federation of Agrarian Collectives in order to improve coordination among themselves.[58] While this rationalisation of the gains of the revolution was unanimously agreed to, the Congress also revealed tensions between the delegates in attendance and the *comités superiores*. When the delegate of the Regional Committee of the CNT suggested that Adolfo Arnal Gracia, a CNT member and Councillor of Agriculture in the Regional Defence Council of Aragón, act as an advisor in the drawing up of the functions of the new Federation, the delegate of Alcorisa declared that "there can be no place whatsoever for political meddling at this Congress," while that of Binéfar alleged that the Council of Agriculture behaved in a counterrevolutionary manner.[59] The assembled delegates were subsequently lectured to by a representative from the National Committee:

[W]hen it was only ourselves who were making the revolution we were able to mount an immovable defence of the ideas that we carry in the deepest recesses of our hearts; if the current revolution was ours alone, that of the CNT, the one we want, then we would consider refusing to compromise on any issue... Remember that not everywhere is like Aragón. Here, fortunately, you form an undeniable majority, but in the provinces of Cuenca, Murcia, Albacete and some others the Confederal organisation has barely any representatives; that is why it is necessary that in those places where we are the greater force... we compromise somewhat in our aspirations. All I am trying to remind you of is that it was you yourselves, in your unions, who conferred on your Regional Committees the mandate and the agreement to constitute municipal councils and, without realising it, you are wrecking your own agreements.[60]

Nevertheless, the uncompromising mood of the delegates to the Congress was reflected in the election of José Mavilla, the man Arnal had replaced as Councillor of Agriculture in the Regional Defence Council, as Secretary of the newly established Regional Federation of Collectives. Mavilla was

58   See the minutes of the Congress reproduced as an appendix in Díez Torre, *Trabajan para la eternidad*, 344–78.

59   Ibid. 358. Although in his mid-twenties at this point, Arnal Gracia was already something of a veteran in the CNT and had served on the National Committee during the Second Republic. He left his position in the Regional Defence Council later in the year and joined the front, where he died at Alfambra in early 1938. See Iñiguez, *Esbozo de una enciclopedia*, 53.

60   Díez Torre, *Trabajan para la eternidad*, 359–60.

a radical who had once claimed to "prefer the sweet sound produced by the crash against the pavement of a saint's head fallen from a church to Beethoven's most harmonious sonata."[61]

It has been suggested that the *comités superiores* did not, in fact, envisage the wartime implantation of socialisation but were desirous of preparing the union for a leading role in post–civil war economic reconstruction while, in the meantime, conceding ultimate control of industry to the state.[62] If this was the case, the campaign for socialisation must be understood to have ultimately undermined as much as promoted libertarian unity, as radical sectors, mobilised by this objective, would come into conflict, not only with reluctant colleagues and open opponents of the revolutionary process, but also the leadership of their own organisations. According to one CNT veteran, attempts to socialise the glass industry in the Catalan city of Mataró were obstructed by the "selfishness" of workers organised in cooperatives, and "Peiró was one of those who took their side."[63] The *comités superiores* of the CNT saw socialisation as fundamentally concerned with internal union discipline, while radicals saw the campaign as emanating from the base of the workers' organisations, resulting in a marginalisation of the political sphere. *Ideas* trumpeted the fact that calls for socialisation had emerged from Congresses and not "individuals, committees, councils and governments that do not respond to the general interest of anti-fascist Spain."[64]

Viewed from either perspective, the possibility that the trade unions could recover a protagonism denied them by the reconstituted state depended, on a national level at least, on the collaboration of the UGT. Working-class unity on the basis of fidelity to the revolution thus became a priority for many radical anarchists in this period. However, there were serious stumbling blocks to revolutionary unity as conceived by radical anarchists, not least that posed by the Socialist trade union, the UGT. Unity between the two Spanish labour unions was promoted on the pages of *Ideas* in spite of the fact that the opposition of the UGT was an obstacle to socialisation in Cataluña. For the editorial board, it was an article of faith that the unions were the guarantee of the proletarian character of the revolution.[65] The time of "politics" having passed, the question of how social life was to be organised had become a function of the economy, where the primacy of the unions would be assured through socialisation and the unity

61   Quoted in José Luis Ledesma, *Los días de llamas de la revolución. Violencia y política en la retaguardia republicana de Zaragoza durante la Guerra Civil* (Zaragoza: Institución "Fernando el Católico," 2003), 61.

62   See Monjo and Vega, *Els treballadors*, 129–31.

63   Joan Saña i Magriña file, Col·lecció Ronald Fraser, AHCB, 48.

64   *Ideas*, 11 March 1937.

65   *Ideas*, 14 January 1937.

of the CNT and the UGT. Some CNT propagandists evidently believed that the UGT base was more radical than its leadership, and complaints in *Solidaridad Obrera* about the lack of democratic procedure at the Congress of Catalan Land Workers reflected unease that those in charge of the UGT would be able to sway its affiliates from their revolutionary aspirations.[66] The paper returned to the theme in April: "The workers must prevent, for the good of the revolution and the triumph of the people in arms over the invading armies, anyone from interfering [in their affairs]... in the manner of the comrades who currently lead, in the autonomous region, the union organisation of the UGT."[67]

This interpretation implicitly, and somewhat ingenuously, denied that the growth of the UGT in Cataluña since the beginning of the war had anything to do with its opposition to revolutionary measures. Yet, since the introduction of compulsory union membership in Cataluña in August 1936, the UGT had established a foothold in industries where the union had, prior to July, no serious implantation. Obligatory unionisation was considered a "barbarity" and a "crime" by Jacinto Borras, who had been on the editorial board of *Solidaridad Obrera* at the outset of the war, a sentiment that was widely shared in the Catalan libertarian movement.[68] By forcing non-revolutionary workers to join a union, the policy not only served to increase the membership of the UGT, but also provided those sectors of the workforce most opposed to revolutionary experiments with an organisational base from which to obstruct them. Far from heralding the proletarian moment, therefore, the rise of the UGT in Cataluña was based on a reassertion of "petit-bourgeois" privileges against the levelling aspirations of the local CNT unions. Baix Llobregat, a traditional stronghold of radical Spanish anarchism, even hosted a PSUC mayor by November 1936, in the town of Molins de Llobregat, where conflicts had centred on the forced collectivisation of small businesses and the union takeover of cellars and woods.[69] In the Catalan countryside, the UGT operated according to a similar logic, displaying a banner at the aforementioned Congress of Catalan Land Workers which read: "Less experiments in collectivisation, more produce," the insincerity and intended effect of which were denounced in

66   *Solidaridad Obrera*, 26 January 1937.
67   *Solidaridad Obrera*, 6 April 1937.
68   Jacinto Borras file, Col·lecció Ronald Fraser, AHCB, 47. At the Congress of Catalan Land Workers referred to above, the "vast majority of the peasants spoke up against the decree on compulsory unionisation": Peirats, *The CNT, Vol. 2*, 27. See also "Entrevista amb Joan 'Remi,'" 81.
69   See Remi Cases et al., "La col·lectivització a Molins de Llobregat," in J. Lluís Adín et al., *Col·lectivitzacions al Baix Llobregat (1936–1939)* (Barcelona: Publicacions de l'Abadia de Montserrat, 1989), 193–4 and 215–9.

Solidaridad Obrera.[70] Catalan peasants affiliated to the CNT complained that former landlords had joined the UGT, while the outright opposition of the latter to further collectivisation in the countryside had the effect of driving a wedge between the CNT and the *Unió de Rabassaires.*[71] The UGT also opposed collectivisation in parts of Aragón, where the regions in which the UGT had outnumbered the anarcho-syndicalist organisation prior to the civil war had fallen to the rebels.[72]

The aggressively anti-revolutionary policy of the UGT in Cataluña is not to be wondered at, given that it was in line with the tactics of the PSUC, which controlled the Catalan branch of the union to such an extent that it had become estranged from the national leadership.[73] Even in areas where PCE and PSUC influence within the UGT was not so marked, however, the prospects for joint union initiatives in this area were not great. On 12 February, after the fall of Málaga, the UGT National Executive issued a manifesto stating that "everything done in the rearguard to establish social methods and administration regarding the future of our economy must today be completely suspended."[74] In Asturias, where the experience of October 1934 had made cooperation between Socialists and anarchists easier to achieve, conflict arose over the reintroduction of small businesses in Gijón, the freedom of which both Socialists and Communists wished to protect.[75] Opposition to the restoration of elements of capitalism led to the jailing of some two dozen members of the CNT supplies union. The CNT members of the Council of Asturias had them released almost immediately after visiting the home of the Civil Governor, where the anarchist baker and union activist Ramón Álvarez Palomo alleged that:

> You want to return to the enemy, whether he is fascist or not... what you call his interests, but we do not want to give the working class the

70   *Solidaridad Obrera*, 26 January 1937.

71   See Peirats, *The CNT, Vol. 2*, 27.

72   See Julián Casanova, "Socialismo y Colectividades en Aragón," in *Socialismo y Guerra Civil*, coord. by Santos Juliá (Madrid: Editorial Pablo Iglesias, 1987), 283–93. The reasons for this opposition are suggested to be the influence of the PCE in the Aragonese UGT, the persistence of pre-war rivalry and resentment of CNT activity in the collectives.

73   Walter Schevenels, General Secretary of the International Federation of Trade Unions (IFTU), to which the UGT belonged, remarked in a report to the IFTU that the Catalan section of the UGT is "practically identical with" the PSUC: "Summarised report on the mission to Spain of the 21 to 29 January 1937," Archives of the Trade Union Congress, University of Warwick, 292/946/15b/7. See also Helen Graham, *Socialism and War. The Spanish Socialist Party in Power and Crisis, 1936–1939* (Cambridge University Press: Cambridge, 1991), 210–1; Pere Gabriel, *Historia de la UGT, Vol. 4. Un sindicalismo de guerra, 1936–1939* (Madrid: Siglo XXI, 2011), 196–7.

74   Quoted in Gabriel, *Historia de la UGT*, 63.

75   Gabriel, *Historia de la UGT*, 165.

idea that they are fighting for the bourgeoisie... for now all aspirations have to be kept intact.[76]

The contention that the wartime sacrifices demanded of the working class could only be guaranteed by acknowledging the validity of revolutionary aspirations was made frequently at this time. In an editorial linking the war to the question of socialisation, *Tierra y Libertad* declared that: "A popular army can only be victorious if it fights for a revolutionary ideal, which is the expression of the hopes of the proletarian masses to be free from capitalist exploitation."[77] Attempts to unify the workers' organisations on this basis were fraught with difficulty, however.

Reactions to the activity of the UGT among many Spanish anarchists were notable for their confusion and naivety. In a speech of March 1937, José Alberola, the radical former member of the Regional Defence Council of Aragón, wondered why the UGT should oppose collectivisation, when this form of organisation corresponded to the "gradualism" of the Socialists, in contrast to the conceptions of the anarchists, for whom the collectives were a compromise.[78] In an article regarding the affiliation to the UGT in Lleida of the Gremis i Entitats de Petits Comerciants i Industrials (Associations and Bodies of Small Traders and Industrialists – GEPCI), *Acracia* declared: "The workers of the UGT must demand the immediate expulsion of that organisation which... wants to hold back the movement initiated on 19 July."[79] *Solidaridad Obrera* likewise commented on its front page that "it would be timely if these 'representatives of the proletariat' that speak so much of the interests of the petite-bourgeoisie would think a little more about the interests of the workers."[80]

Some radicals were not so sanguine, however. As an article in the review of *Mujeres Libres* put it, such a "timely" change of course was improbable given that, "the petite-bourgeoisie, forced to join a union... chose the lesser evil" between the revolutionary CNT and "reformist" UGT.[81] An indication that as much was understood by the mid-level union delegates of the CNT is given by the minutes of a Plenum of Barcelona unions held on 23 January 1937. There it was widely accepted that an ideological gulf existed between the CNT and the UGT and that only radical measures could bring about an understanding between the organisations. The existing liaison

76   Ramón Álvarez Palomo file, Col·lecció Ronald Fraser, AHCB, 41.
77   *Tierra y Libertad*, 27 February 1937.
78   Alberola, *Interpretación anarquista*, 10–1.
79   *Acracia*, 5 April 1937. The GEPCI was a pressure group formed primarily by small businesspeople.
80   *Solidaridad Obrera*, 8 April 1937.
81   *Mujeres Libres*, February 1937.

committee between the CNT and the UGT was strongly criticised, and the health workers' delegate even contemplated the possibility of an armed showdown between the unions on the streets. Less dramatic were the proposals urging mass assemblies of workers of both unions.[82] Such tactics, which were also promoted in the press of the POUM, had the advantage of allowing decision-making procedures to bypass the bureaucracies of both unions and the revolutionary majority to prevail in those industries where one existed.[83] Contrary to the wishes of the *comités superiores* of the CNT, the socialisation campaign had revealed a willingness among radical anarchists to revive direct democracy and mass assemblies in the interests of consolidating revolutionary achievements and forging new revolutionary solidarities. As the following subsection will show, the momentum this generated spilled over the boundaries of the workplace and laid the basis for the revolutionary alliance that would mobilise against the state during the Barcelona May days of 1937.

Revolutionary alliances

By the end of 1936, any lip service that the CNT's anti-fascist allies in the Socialist, Communist and republican parties had previously made to the revolution had largely been replaced by appeals to "anti-fascist unity." It was far from clear whether such unity necessarily contained any revolutionary component at all. As an article in *Mujeres Libres* put it in the autumn:

> To be an antifascist is too little; one is an antifascist because one is already something else. We have an affirmation to set up against this negation… [that] can be condensed into three letters: CNT, which means the rational organisation of life on the basis of work, equality, and social justice. If it weren't for this, antifascism would be, for us, a meaningless word.[84]

For radicals, therefore, the question of unity was meaningful only insofar as it was linked to fidelity to the revolutionary process. The Italian Camillo Berneri wrote in November 1936: "Taken as a whole, the Spanish government is just as opposed to social revolution as it is to monarchic and clerical fascism."[85] An editorial in *Acracia* admitted: "The sacred commonplace

---

82   See Guillamón, *La Guerra del pan*, 202–6.

83   For examples from the press of the POUM, see *Emancipación*, 29 May 1937.

84   *Mujeres Libres*, October 1936. Taken from the translated citation in Ackelsberg, *Free Women*, 135.

85   Berneri, *Entre la Revolución y las trincheras*, 10.

of unity has begun to make us suspicious."[86] Juan Andrade of the POUM likewise declared in *La Batalla* on 9 December 1936: "Generic anti-fascism conceals political confusion."[87] Over the following months, radicals would clarify the terms of revolutionary unity, establishing the unsustainability of "generic anti-fascism" in the absence of consensus over issues such as public order, food supplies and socialisation, and attempting to win over grassroots members of rival organisations and the working-class women bearing the brunt of food shortages. By connecting fidelity to the revolution to the right of workers in the rearguard to bear arms and to the socialisation campaign then gaining momentum, radicals were able to generate new alliances around an alternative revolutionary programme to that of state reconstruction.

The possibility of a formal alliance on the basis of a revolutionary programme was revealed by the formation of the Frente de la Juventud Revolucionaria (Revolutionary Youth Front – FJR) in February 1937. Initial attempts to form a broadly anti-fascist Alianza Juvenil Antifascista (Anti-fascist Youth Alliance – AJA) had stalled over the question of whether the POUM's youth wing, the Juventud Comunista Ibérica (Iberian Communist Youth – JCI), could be included.[88] Fiercely opposed to this, the Juventudes Socialistas Unificadas (Unified Socialist Youth – JSU) was nevertheless insistent on admitting Catholic youth organisations into an anti-fascist umbrella organisation.[89] This was unacceptable to the libertarian youth, and an alternative unity platform on the basis of fidelity to the revolution was an organic outgrowth of the resulting stalemate.[90] The FJR gained momentum in the early part of 1937 and threatened to have serious implications, not least because it acted as a pole of attraction to a disaffected left wing of the JSU.[91] This led to the rare if not quite unprecedented phenomenon of anarchists appealing to the Socialist youth on the basis of the shared commitment which both libertarians and "authentic" Marxists had to the revolution. A speech of Santiago Carrillo, then a leading member of the JSU, was criticised in *Solidaridad Obrera* as "reformist hot air." The article went on to address the organisation's members:

---

86   *Acracia*, 28 January 1937.

87   Andrade, *La revolución española*, 37–8.

88   The JCI was to some degree more radical than its parent organisation, and had opposed the entry of the POUM into the Generalitat. See the Wilebaldo Solano file, Col·lecció Ronald Fraser, AHCB, 63. For an example of how the AJA failed to function at ground level, see Paz, *Viaje al pasado*, 71–2.

89   Helen Graham, "The Socialist Youth in the JSU: the experience of organisational unity, 1936–8" in *Spain in Conflict 1931–1939, Democracy and Its Enemies*, ed. by Martin Blinkhorn (London: Sage Publications, 1986), 86.

90   See "Las JJLL toman una firme decisión," FIJL F-DH 3 (2), Pavelló de la República (PDLR), and Garangou, *Les Joventuts Llibertàries*, 143–45.

91   See Graham, "The Socialist Youth," 92–9.

If the JSU are not socialists, communists or Marxists, what are they? The only thing to be seen with clarity in all of this is the desire to return... to the good times of the "Republic of workers of all classes." And this, socialist comrades, cannot be tolerated, must not be tolerated.[92]

Relations between the FIJL and the JCI during the civil war were, on the other hand, generally cordial. Alfredo Martínez, a member of the Regional Committee of the Catalan JJLL, spoke at a POUM rally in December 1936, while even anarchist purists such as Diego Camacho of the Los Quijotes del Ideal affinity group respected the integrity of individual POUM activists.[93]Martínez and the Secretary of the Catalan JJLL, Fidel Miró, were considered suspect by the purist "red-skins" of the Catalan youth for their apparent "reformism" and adhesion to the "circumstantialist" line of the CNT and the FAI.[94] Nevertheless, the solidarity displayed with the POUM as the campaign against the dissident communists gained momentum – a solidarity absent among the *comités superiores* of the CNT and the FAI – combined with a refusal to relegate the revolution to the requirements of the war, suggest that this characterisation lacks nuance. As early as November 1936, *Ruta*, then under Miró's editorship, declared that "if that unity serves only to defend the democracy in ruins or to bolster the Republic, it does not interest us in the least."[95] In February 1937, a National Plenum of the FIJL made the unity of anti-fascist youth conditional upon support for the revolution then underway. The JSU's bluff had been called, and the organisation refused to participate in the mass rally held by the JCI and JJLL that took place on 14 February in Barcelona on the initiative of the latter organisation. On 19 February, a pact establishing the tenets of the Revolutionary Youth Front in Cataluña was signed by representatives of the JJLL, the JCI, the youth sections of Mujeres Libres and the Syndicalist Party, along with various student organisations.

The first article of the pact recognised the revolution then underway in Spain and declared the mission of the FJR to be that of making both revolution and war. The pact also called for greater unity between the unions,

92   *Solidaridad Obrera*, 17 January 1937.

93   Paz, *Viaje al pasado*, 72. On improved relations between members of the CNT and the POUM, see also Adolfo Bueso, *Recuerdos de un cenetista II. De la Segunda República al final de la guerra civil* (Barcelona: Ariel, 1978), 185. The appearance of Martínez at the POUM rally is noted in the account published in the weekly review of the JCI, *Juventud Comunista*, 17 December 1936.

94   Paz, *Viaje al pasado*, 71. For a similar characterisation of Miró, see Peirats, *De mi paso*, 309. Peirats also dismissed the Catalan Regional Committee of the JJLL, to which both Miró and Martínez belonged, as "collaborationist" prior to May 1937, in Peirats, *Figuras del movimiento libertario*, 289.

95   *Ruta*, 7 November 1936.

the proportional representation of revolutionary forces in positions of leadership, a purge of the bureaucracy, and an army that faithfully reflected the "revolutionary aspirations of the combatants." It also affirmed its support for the socialisation of industry and land, and so while it stopped some way short of advocating a withdrawal of revolutionaries from government, the FJR thus aligned itself with those sectors of the Spanish revolutionary movement that saw socialisation and the greater cooperation, influence and initiative of the unions as a potentially key factor in consolidating the gains of the revolution.[96] As such, the bases of the FJR were a challenge to the JSU and, by extension, to anti-fascist unity as it was then constituted in the governing bodies of Republican Spain. By 1 March, the Catalan JJLL was reporting to the Peninsular Committee of the FIJL that the FJR had 40,000 members, and on 18 March it was reported that the founding of the FJR in the Levante region was imminent.[97]

In the manifesto that accompanied the pact, emphasis was placed on the importance of prioritising action over doctrinal disputes.[98] This was undoubtedly resented by those purist anarchists who believed that the JJLL should focus on propagandistic and educational work, leaving aside the "politics" of alliances. In *Ideas*, Amador Franco, pseudonym of Diego Franco Cazorla, a leading member of the Catalan JJLL, the Federación Estudiantil de Conciencias Libres (Student Federation of Freethinkers – FECL) and of the Irreductibles affinity group alongside José Peirats, sounded a note of scepticism:

> I have always considered the tendency towards alliances and the obligation to "fraternise"… as a fatalist imposition… I consider unity, as far as the youth is concerned, as something that does not require pacts or signatures… The Libertarian Youth is the hope for our idea and its practice if we know how to keep ourselves outside of useless pacts and continue our empowering labour.[99]

In April, a Regional Congress of the Catalan JJLL representing over 35,000 affiliates at the front and in the rear revealed a strong purist current urging that the organisation should proceed "as before 19 July," focusing on propaganda and education.[100] Fidel Miró had to survive a vote of confidence as

96   See "Bases de la Frente de la Juventud Revolucionaria," CDMH, PS Barcelona, 514/8.
97   See, respectively, "Informe de las JJLL al Comité Peninsular de la FIJL," CDMH, PS Barcelona, 514/8, and *Juventud Comunista*, 18 March 1937.
98   "Bases de la Frente de la Juventud Revolucionaria."
99   *Ideas*, 15 February 1937.
100   "Congreso Regional de las JJLL celebrado el día 17 de abril de 1937," CDMH, PS Barcelona, 239/03.

Regional Secretary while objections were raised with regard to participation in the FJR. In spite of such misgivings, the position of the Regional Committee was ratified. Even the FECL, a student body affiliated to the FIJL with strong purist associations (the aforementioned Amador Franco, along with Vicente Rodríguez García of the *Acracia* editorial board and the anti-collaborationist Ada Martí were all prominent members) was a signatory of the initial pact.

Meanwhile, radicals in the Catalan CNT greeted the FJR with enthusiasm even as its press also provided a platform for its discontents: "With an understanding of the moment that the 'elders' have not displayed," declared *Ideas* in a double-page spread, "the Revolutionary Youth has come together to signal what path to take."[101] A joint rally of the Catalan FAI and the JJLL was held in Barcelona in April, at which regular contributors to *Ideas*, Severino Campos and José Xena, shared a platform with Juan Santana Calero and Fidel Miró of the JJLL. The speeches denounced the counter-revolution and openly identified the PSUC with it.[102] Unsurprisingly, the POUM, which had taken up more radical positions following its exclusion from the Generalitat and practical illegalisation in Madrid, also looked on with interest at the development of events in the youth wings.[103] In April, Juan Andrade advocated the formation of a Workers' Revolutionary Front that would "stop the counter-revolution in its tracks and pose the problem of power by means of its own organs: committees of workers, peasants and combatants."[104] The possibility that libertarians would take the lead in establishing such a revolutionary front was the only hope for a party that lacked the numeric power to seize the initiative itself, and which had proved incapable of developing a means of influencing either the top or bottom levels of the CNT membership during the civil war.[105] The Catalan Regional Committee of the CNT reported in February that:

> The POUM has been wooing our organisation since its departure from the government, to the extent that it has proposed the entrance of whole sections into our organisation, something that we have not allowed on the understanding that anyone who wishes may come individually, but not as a collective.[106]

101   *Ideas*, 15 February 1937.
102   *Solidaridad Obrera*, 15 April 1937.
103   On the radicalisation of the POUM in this period, see Reiner Tosstorff, *El POUM en la revolució Espanyola* (Barcelona: Editorial Base, 2009), 97.
104   Andrade, *La revolución española*, 232.
105   This failure to find a means by which the POUM could effectively communicate with the CNT base was lamented by Ignacio Iglesias, a student and POUM militant in Sama de Langreo, Asturias. See the Ignacio Iglesias file, Col·lecció Ronald Fraser, AHCB, 67–8.
106   "Pleno Regional de locales y comarcales celebrado el día 4 de febrero de 1937," CDMH,

In spite of the reluctance of the *comités superiores* to associate with the POUM, the FIJL and the JCI were able to acknowledge a common, revolutionary, ground that was not shared by the Communist Party and its affiliate organisations. This was partly because, as Wilebaldo Solano, a leader of the JCI, would recall, they "were not councillors in the Generalitat... and they had lesser responsibilities."[107] Moreover, to the street-based activists of the JCI and the JJLL, the rationale of the Comintern position, adopted by the JSU, which was based on high politics and international diplomacy, seemed remote and irrelevant.[108] In this sense, by adopting such an openly anti-revolutionary position the JSU overplayed its hand, not only because it was unacceptable to the large anarchist youth organisation, but also because it alienated sections of its own membership. The FIJL denounced the leadership of the JSU that had held up to "public ridicule" the "theories of Marx and Lenin" and appealed directly to the base, the "truly Marxist and therefore revolutionary" young Socialists who had suffered the *bienio negro* and fought in Asturias: "you cannot accept this shameful affront to your doctrines and organisation... Ignore the siren calls of the defenders of bourgeois democracy, the seed of brutal fascism!"[109] The flysheet *Esfuerzo*, affiliated to the FIJL under the stewardship of Juan Santana Calero, who had arrived in Barcelona prior to the fall of his native Málaga, made plain this appeal:

> Young socialists! Those of you who are Marxists and therefore revolutionaries! React in time against the confusionist and counterrevolutionary policy of your leaders. Consider your responsibility before the international proletariat and before History. Young socialists! We want to march with you on the path of victory. For the triumph of the war and the revolution: LET US UNITE![110]

The acknowledgement that Marxists could also be true revolutionaries represented a shift in rhetorical emphasis for radical anarchism, and an adaptation to the political realities of the moment. It also informed the thinking

        PS Barcelona, 531/1.

107   Wilebaldo Solano file, Col·lecció Ronald Fraser, AHCB, 85.

108   On the relative ignorance of the JJLL in regard to such matters, see Paz, *Viaje al Pasado*, especially 123.

109   *Boletín de Información de la CNT-FAI*, 22 April 1937.

110   *Esfuerzo*, 3rd week of April, 1937. A similar appeal appeared in *Solidaridad Obrera*, 13 April 1937. *Esfuerzo* was, until the summer of 1937, printed in the form of a poster and plastered on the walls of Barcelona. This novel medium would be resuscitated by anarchists in the concentration camps of southern France at the beginning of their exile. See Chris Ealham, "Spanish Anarcho-Syndicalists in Toulouse: The Red-and-Black Counter-City in Exile," *Bulletin of Spanish Studies*, 91, 1–2 (2014): 101.

of radicals in the Catalan CNT who felt that an alliance of the trade unions could be effected from the bottom up.

Regardless of the pitfalls of this assumption, discussed above, negotiations between the two unions were in fact being carried out by their respective leaderships without the involvement of their wider memberships. The implications of this were made clear in an "urgent communiqué" to the Peninsular Committee of the FIJL, signed by Mariano Rodríguez Vázquez for the National Committee of the CNT on 8 March. Here it was implausibly stated that the reason for a delay in calling a National Plenum of the regional organisations was that there had not been any "fundamental problem to submit to discussion," the chief political problem facing the CNT being that of unity with the UGT. In that regard, the communiqué informed affiliates that a pact was imminent, as the Executive of the UGT had finally seen sense, but that "it is imperative that nothing occur that could cloud this favourable situation... It is necessary that you send communiqués and orient the organisation, in the sense that any clash or violence with the unions or affiliates of the UGT be avoided."[111] Viewed by radical *cenetistas* as a necessary step towards safeguarding the revolution, the pact between the unions was seen by the National Committee of the CNT as something to be engineered behind closed doors and then presented to a Plenum as a fait accompli, used in the meantime as a device for imposing internal discipline. "Let no-one forget," it continued, "that there could well be elements, even in our midst, interested in preventing the aspiration of all: THE REVOLUTIONARY ALLIANCE BETWEEN THE TWO UNIONS ... let no-one play the game of the mean-spirited and irresponsible."[112] If the revolution could indeed be safeguarded by such high political and bureaucratic practices, these were not the traditional methods of the CNT, whose members were increasingly entertaining more "irresponsible" options. That the libertarian youth would be at the forefront of this process was indicated at a rally of the JJLL the following month, when Miró affirmed that "the anarchists would return to the barricades of 19 July rather than give up the workers' revolution."[113]

Similar sentiments were being expressed in the anarchist women's organisation, Mujeres Libres (MMLL), which was also able to generate fruitful revolutionary solidarities in the spring of 1937. Although its members were all in the CNT, the organisation was not an officially recognised branch of the libertarian movement. Involved in a multiplicity of

111   "Circular urgente del Comité Nacional de la CNT al Comité Peninsular de la FIJL,"
       CDMH, PS Barcelona, 514/5.
112   Ibid.
113   *Solidaridad Obrera*, 15 April 1937.

autonomous projects made possible by the wave of expropriations in which its members had participated in the summer of 1936, and at one remove from the organisational discipline of the CNT and the FAI, the MMLL was a contributory factor in the radicalisation at the grassroots of Spanish anarchism in this period that has often been overlooked. This was detectable in the radical response to the fall of Málaga of its Secretary, Lucía Sánchez Saornil, for whom the military catastrophe revealed the bankruptcy of international and domestic parliamentary democracies: "And yet still they talk in Spain of democracy, and in its name they attempt to betray and subjugate us. No; the image of Málaga sacrificed digs into our hearts with nails of fire. Democracy, no; social revolution!"[114]

Sánchez Saornil was one of several contributors to the *Mujeres Libres* publication pushing a radical line and offering an immanent critique of the shortcomings of the libertarian movement. Lesser-known writers also offered lucid perspectives on the consequences of a stalled revolution, ranging from the sexism of comrades to the need for complete socialisation. With regard to the polemics around militarisation, one anonymous contributor lamented that:

> The notion of an army of iron, of a strong nation, of rigidity, of inflexibility, of a firm hand, all this has been internalised. It has burrowed deep, and our revolution has begun to stagnate, to stiffen, to turn to stone… The institutions born spontaneously of the people are being hacked at and chopped down by the cutting blade of discipline. Men that we saw scattered by the strong winds of 19 July now huddle behind that word, ready to stand up and grab the reins, to take up the whip… Discipline is all very well, but take care. Discipline and blind obedience are also the preconditions of slavery.[115]

Ana Piacenza, an Argentinian who had arrived in Spain alongside her partner José Grunfeld, gave an account of a women's demonstration in Barcelona that began in the local headquarters of the MMLL. The demand "less politics and more weapons for the front" was raised alongside calls for equality of sacrifice in the war effort. Piacenza, who wrote the article under the pseudonym Nita Nahuel, recorded that women had been subject to abuse on the demonstration from a man wearing a red and black neckerchief.[116]

114   Lucía Sánchez Saornil, *Horas de Revolución* (Barcelona: Publicaciones Mujeres Libres, n.d. [1937?]), 37.
115   *Mujeres Libres*, February 1937.
116   Ibid.

In the first part of 1937, women were at the forefront of the ongoing "war of bread" in Barcelona, during which the Councillor of Supplies in the Generalitat, Joan Comorera, and the supplies committees of the CNT blamed each other for a situation in which queues of working-class women waited for bread that was not always available, while those who could afford it resorted to the black market.[117] The subsequent anger of women in the city was used as a political football, with the partisan press, anarchist or otherwise, providing sexist explanations whenever that anger was directed at them. This provides the context for the abuse anarchist women experienced from an apparent "comrade," as reported in *Mujeres Libres*. Nevertheless, between the autonomous efforts of the MMLL and the defence committees to meet the needs of their constituents, solidarity with the women of the bread queues became an important feature of the revolutionary alliance of spring 1937.

The MMLL called for socialisation to end "speculation with the hunger of the people," and blamed the bread queues on the inefficiency and bankruptcy of traditional statist bureaucracy.[118] These connections had been forcefully revealed by an action of the *Patrullas de Control* in March. After the discovery of a warehouse full of largely rotten potatoes, these were made available to "the women of the town" under the protection of the *Patrullas* in an armed standoff with Assault Guards.[119] The MMLL grouping also acknowledged its support for the direct action that women had undertaken in Barcelona, invading markets and stalls to "take justice into their own hands."[120] In April, the official celebrations held to mark the anniversary of the founding of the Republic were disrupted when, as an American Trotskyist eye-witness observed:

> The food riots of the Barcelona working-class women drowned out the republican demonstrations of the Esquerra and the Stalinist and Socialist parties. From early morning until late at night in the market districts and in front of the Generalitat office massive demonstrations against the increase in food prices were staged. In some food markets the merchants' stocks were overturned and destroyed; in other markets fights developed against those who upheld the government's food policy."[121]

117   Guillamón, *La Guerra del pan*, 23–6.
118   *Solidaridad Obrera*, 16 April 1937.
119   Guillamón, *La Guerra del pan*, 378–9.
120   These events are discussed in detail in Guillamón, *La Guerra del pan*, 449–57.
121   Edward H. Oliver, *Sixth Anniversary of the Spanish Republic in Barcelona* (Chicago: Revolutionary Workers' League, 1937), 3.

Women queuing for groceries are confronted by inflated prices in an engraving by Gustavo Cochet, photographed by Mario Gómez Casas, reproduced by permission of the Museo Gustavo Cochet and the Ministerio de Innovación y Cultura de Santa Fe.

Foodstuffs that had been hoarded are distributed in the Barcelona neighbourhood of Sants after their discovery by the *Patrullas de Control*, 17 January 1937. Pérez de Rozas, Arxiu Fotogràfic de Barcelona.

The increasingly anti-statist nature of women's mobilisations around food supply was also noted by the review of the Women's Secretariat of the POUM, *Emancipación*:

> Now working-class women are beginning to realise that the working class no longer hold power as they did in the first months of the revolution... In the queues on the streets, the guardians of order are the same Assault Guards as before, with a rifle on their shoulder. The street protests against shortages have ended with the arrest of women workers, and demonstrations have been broken up by armed police... The greatest defenders of the revolution will be the thousands upon thousands of women workers when they understand that, once again, reformism wants to sacrifice the working class in the interests of the petite-bourgeoisie.[122]

The Women's Secretariat also called for socialisation and the formation of neighbourhood women's committees, while one contributor to its review highlighted the connection between "our day-to-day concerns" and "the great problems of the revolution": "for us, socialism is not a distant dream, but the only practical path to take in the struggle against poverty."[123] In many respects, the positions found in *Emancipación* mirrored those raised by the MMLL, and a similar process of radicalisation can be traced through its pages. Mary Low records how the Secretariat gave effective arms training to hundreds of women activists in Barcelona, and rapidly grew in size: "every day we requisitioned more rooms to house us all. Hundreds of women came every day to attend classes on socialism, child welfare, French, hygiene, women's rights, the origin of the religious and family sense, and to knit and sew and make flags and discuss, and read books. It was a great success."[124]

Given that the MMLL had been a signatory to the FJR and that the libertarian movement's most prominent advocate of joint work with the POUM, Alfredo Martínez, had also been an important contact in facilitating the union of the Women's Cultural Grouping in Barcelona with the *Mujeres Libres* group in Madrid, it is perhaps to be wondered at that the MMLL and the POUM's Women's Secretariat did not enter into an alliance.[125] However, while the Women's Secretariat called for a Women's Revolutionary Front in line with the example of the FJR, its review made no

122   *Emancipación*, 24 April 1937.
123   Ibid.
124   Low and Brea, *Red Spanish Notebook*, 190–1.
125   On the role of Martínez, see Ackelsberg, *Free Women*, 124.

explicit reference to the work of the anarchist women's organisation. Low, a friend of one of the editorial board of *Mujeres Libres*, admitted that the propaganda of the Women's Secretariat, as compared with that of the MMLL, was mostly "out of line, and sentimental... The anarchist women were more ambitious as far as posters were concerned. They attacked all kinds of problems with their slogans."[126] Street-level links between the POUM and the anarchist movement had been strengthened by the formation of the FJR and the continued participation of both organisations in the *Patrullas de Control*. However, within the POUM, an appreciation that it was the anarchists whose numerical superiority guaranteed them a vanguard role in the revolutionary struggle was not combined with sufficient sympathy for or knowledge of the libertarian movement's internal mechanisms. As we will see in the next chapter, this led to an inability to influence, or even to seriously attempt to influence, the grassroots of the CNT and the FAI, forcing the organisation to adopt a largely passive role in the events that determined its fate.

In March 1937, the POUM was encouraged by the emergence of a new grouping from within the ranks of the libertarian movement, intended to provide cohesion to the upsurge of revolutionary combativeness in this period. The Agrupación Amigos de Durruti (the Friends of Durruti Grouping – AAD) was formed in Barcelona, animated chiefly by journalists around the weekly *Ideas* and former members of the Gelsa section of the Durruti Column, and its early meetings were well attended. The AAD issued some 5,000 membership cards and gained pockets of support outside Cataluña, such as in Belver de Cinca and Pina de Ebro in Aragón.[127] The membership cards read: "We are enemies of the bureaucracy, privileges and military rank. We are revolutionary fighters. We aim at the immediate realisation of the social projects that the CNT-FAI defended in the glorious years of Confederal Cataluña."[128] News of the AAD's formation and its initial appeal were published in the newspaper of the POUM, *La Batalla*.[129] Juan Andrade was also favourably impressed: "The AAD has formulated its programme in posters pasted on all the streets of Barcelona... There are two points... that are also fundamental for us: All Power to the working class and democratic organs of the workers, peasants and combatants."[130] However, the apparent similarity of AAD and POUM aims at this juncture does not imply that the former was inspired by the latter, and when

126   Low and Breá, *Red Spanish Notebook*, 196.
127   See Casanova, *Anarquismo y Revolución*, 245.
128   Guillamón, *Los Amigos de Durruti*, 211.
129   Nin, *La revolución española*, 302–4.
130   Andrade, *La revolución española*, 248.

the AAD held a mass meeting in Barcelona in April, the POUM was not mentioned.[131]

The presence of former members of the Durruti Column in the AAD highlights the prominence of radical deserters from the front in the revolutionary alliance that emerged in the spring of 1937. Among them were several foreign volunteers who, as another important part of that alliance, would go on to play a vital role in the build-up to and during the May days in Barcelona. In April, a handful of members of the Gruppe Deutsche Anarcho-Syndikalisten im Ausland (Group of German Anarcho-Syndicalists in Exile – DAS) left the International Company of the Durruti Column in opposition to the implementation of militarisation, along with a group of heterodox Marxist and anti-Stalinist comrades who had become close to the anarchists in Spain, including the Swiss couple Clara and Paul Thalmann.[132] At the same time several Italian anarchists expressed their intention to leave the International Battalion of the Francisco Ascaso Column for the same reason.

About a dozen of the latter were named in an exchange of letters between Largo Caballero and the CNT at the end of April. The correspondence began when the Prime Minister stated that he had been informed by an unnamed source that they were "suspicious elements" who, along with many others, had, after being expelled from Spain, returned across the French–Catalan border at Portbou with "passports issued by the FAI" in order to enlist in "shock troops" in the rear.[133] Contrary to these claims, the Italians in question had arrived at the beginning of the civil war and immediately enlisted in militia columns. A subsequent exchange between Joan Peiró, Dionisio Eroles and the CNT's Committee for Statistics and Control saw this latter body deny absolutely the notion that the FAI issued passports and defended those named in Largo Caballero's letter, "comrades who have been active in the revolutionary movement for years and [who] have come here hounded by reactionaries the world over."[134] Largo's source was attempting to provoke police action on two fronts, at the border and against radical Italian refugees in Barcelona.

Anarchists had controlled important sections of the French–Catalan border since the beginning of the war. Contemporaneous to this exchange

---

131   Rosalio Negrete and Hugo Oehler, "Negrete and Oehler report back from Barcelona," *Revolutionary History*, 1, 2 (1988), http://www.revolutionaryhistory.co.uk/index.php/155-articles/articles-of-rh0102/4243-negrete-and-oehler-report-from-barcelona [accessed 1 December 2017].

132   See Nelles et al., *Antifascistas alemanes en Barcelona*, 165–6.

133   Letter from Largo Caballero to Joan Peiró, 24 April 1937, CDMH, PS Barcelona, 523/3.

134   Letter from the Vice-Secretary of the Defence Section of the CNT to Dionisio Eroles, 30 April 1937, CDMH, PS Barcelona, 523/3.

of correspondence, a police operation was underway in the border region of Cerdanya which would end the life of the influential anarchist activist Antonio Martín, discussed in the following chapter. This letter should be seen as providing a degree of cover for that operation, which was of a piece with the broader project of state reconstruction and not merely the result of a local dispute. Meanwhile, at the eastern end of the French–Catalan border at Portbou, an anarchist militia column patrolled the frontier. Its likely radical character is attested to by the superficial character of its "militarisation"; in March, German members of the column reported to the DAS in Barcelona that "for the time being we haven't noticed this militarisation at all, except that our formation has a captain and two sergeants, without military insignia and receiving the same pay."[135] The column contained a century named after the French anarchist Sébastien Faure, made up of French, German and Italian volunteers, which would be broken up after the May days. It was during these events that a police operation would begin against the Italian anarchist opponents of militarisation in the rear, most of whom, as Largo Caballero's letter had made clear, were stationed at the Espartaco barracks in Barcelona.

The internationalist nature of the radical alliance, and the internationalist stakes of its confrontation with the forces of state reconstruction, which had to do with border policy and the participation of foreigners in the revolutionary process, were becoming apparent. As an anti-fascist, anarchist refugee, Camillo Berneri's perspective on this aspect of the radical alliance is of interest. On 14 April 1937, he wrote an open letter addressed to Federica Montseny in which he called upon the anarchist minister to reconsider government collaboration. Moreover, he reaffirmed his opinion that the anarchists should prioritise a policy of Moroccan autonomy, and urged the defence committees to carry out a purge of the rearguard, stressing that "the fifth column is not only made up of members of fascist organisations, but of all the malcontents that desire a moderate republic."[136] Berneri was in close contact with volunteers at the front and with Spanish activists in Barcelona, and, as an ardent critic of Stalinism, advocated, in similar terms to the JJLL in this period, collaboration among "all sincere socialists."[137]

Berneri can thus be seen to embody several of the overlapping revolutionary solidarities that crystallised in the spring of 1937 around an emergent revolutionary programme. However, although Berneri would later be blamed for the rising in May, he was not a participant in the mobilisation and, in spite of the respect he enjoyed in anarchist circles, he was too far

135   Quoted in Nelles et al., *Antifascistas alemanes en Barcelona*, 148.
136   Berneri, *Entre la Revolución y las trincheras*, 23–8.
137   Ibid. 31.

removed from the inner organisational workings of the libertarian movement to influence it. In Barcelona in the spring of 1937, recalcitrant *milicianos*, anarchist refugees, purist opponents of state collaboration, advocates
of unity among authentic revolutionaries and women mobilising around the
issue of scarcity could rely on a network of organisations and expropriated
spaces in which to consolidate their burgeoning alliance. These included the
defence committees, the JJLL, the MMLL (all three of which maintained
lively and active neighbourhood centres), the FJR, the AAD, anarchist barracks and divisions in which the democratic and egalitarian functioning of
the original militias persisted in spite of militarisation, and a number of
sympathetic publications. Even so, to mobilise these different strands in a
joint effort, as happened in May, required a common organisational denominator. This would be provided by the Local Federation of anarchist affinity
groups (the FAI in Barcelona), under the stewardship of Julián Merino.

Merino was a veteran member of the FAI and an important organiser in
the Transport Workers' Union in the CNT who had fought against *treintismo* and been imprisoned both before and during the Republic in the years
prior to the civil war. He had been a FAI delegate to the defence committees
prior to July 1936, and had jointly led a raiding party onto boats in search
of weapons on the eve of the military revolt.[138] He had also been present as
a delegate of a militia column at the Plenum in Bujaraloz that had agreed
to the formation of the Regional Defence Council of Aragón.[139] His presence at the front in the autumn of 1936 suggests that his return to the rear
may have been due to his opposition to militarisation. Now Secretary of
the Local Federation of affinity groups, his presence in the meetings of the
regional *comités superiores* in Barcelona had disrupted their normal functioning and brought an insistent, radical voice to proceedings. In February he
had defended the refusal of the Gelsa section to militarise and was roundly
abused, called an "oddball... undermining the general sentiment of the
JJLL and the FAI."[140] He had also been the one to relate the episode of the
Patrullas de Control distributing confiscated potatoes to women in the bread
queues in March.

As a key union and defence committee delegate, Secretary of the
Barcelona FAI, long-standing opponent of "*treintismo*" with links to both
the bread queues and the revolutionary deserters opposed to militarisation

138   See Chapter Two.

139   See Joaquín Ascaso, *Memorias (1936–1938) hacia un nuevo Aragón* (Zaragoza: Prensas
        Universitarias de Zaragoza, 2006), 24.

140   "Reunión celebrada el día 12 de febrero de 1937 a las diez de la noche estando presentes
        el compañero Manzano [sic], de la columna Durruti, C.R de la FAI, Federación Local,
        JJLL y Comité Regional de Cataluña," CNT (España) Archives (IISG) CNT 85 C.

– indeed, possibly being among that number himself – Merino thus emerges as both the living embodiment of the different sectors of radical anarchism and one of those best placed to convert the radical programme of "socialisation and the people armed" into a concrete strategy. As we will see in the chapters that follow, in the May days and in the subsequent struggles, his ability to speak to both voluntarist and purist concerns, as well as to show practical solidarity to the hungry and to anarchist prisoners, would make him one of the outstanding figures of oppositional anarchism. If his varied connections make him seem an almost composite character, it should be borne in mind that I am not trying to establish Merino as a convenient "superman" capable of single-handedly bringing about the May days mobilisation: that revolutionary intervention was, like Merino himself, the product of a varied and complex movement whose anti-statist principles, among those sectors remaining outside of state collaboration, had been renewed in the period under discussion. This mobilisation would be supported by the new groupings formed in this period, the FJR, the MMLL and the AAD, but its organisational basis would emerge from the local FAI, which had shown its capacity, as at the beginning of the Republic, to unite voluntarist and purist anarchists behind a radical agenda.

Conclusions

From the winter of 1936 to the spring of 1937, the revolutionary gains of the previous July that remained in the territory of the Spanish Republic were threatened by the expanding parameters of the state. The relationship of Spanish anarchism to this process was complicated by the participation of its chief representatives in the anti-fascist alliance and the absorption of thousands of less well-known activists into administrative bodies and the front line. During this period, the *comités superiores* of the CNT and the FAI, in spite of their continued intention to intervene in government, were aware that the activity of their political opponents threatened to end the influence won for the organisations in July. In the first half of 1937, they attempted to bolster this influence through the campaign for socialisation. This attempt was only partially successful, however, on the one hand because it depended on the support of the UGT, and on the other because the process of socialisation was conceived of in different terms by the CNT hierarchy and its most active proponents on the ground.

Nevertheless, the energies unleashed by the socialisation campaign led to a surprising upturn in revolutionary activity and consolidation at the beginning of 1937, with notable examples including the Regional General

Council of the Economy established in L'Hospitalet and the founding of the Regional Federation of Agrarian Collectives in Aragón. The campaign also gave cohesion to apparently disparate issues such as scarcity in the rear and worker control of industry, itself resulting in an emerging alliance between radical anarchist workers and women in the bread queues of Barcelona, mediated by the MMLL and the *Patrullas de Control*. This should lead to a reconsideration of the apparent waning of the Spanish revolution in the winter of 1936, so lyrically attested to by Mary Low at the outset of this chapter. Rather than disappearing altogether, the socialisation campaign suggests that the revolution and its fate were moving from the immediately visible rupture that had taken place in the fields of experience and gesture to questions of structure. In that sense, while the decreasing visibility of women in "masculine" dress or headed to the front was significant, it should not obscure the fact that, at the same time, autonomous women's organisations were able to develop projects and strategies in expropriated premises, extending their influence and advancing a specific perspective that resonated with the emerging radical alliance both within and beyond the workplace.

While the libertarian movement was divided in its attitude to the revolution and the state, the attempt to evolve an alternative programme was also illustrative of the ambiguities and divisions in the movement's more radical wing. The creation of the FJR on the initiative of the JJLL in Barcelona revealed the potential for libertarians to take the lead in creating a revolutionary alliance to oppose and split statist anti-fascism. However, it was opposed by purists because it was "political," in the sense of involving political parties. Moreover, the report in *Mujeres Libres* of the aggressive response of an anarchist to a women's demonstration suggests that lingering chauvinist prejudices still had the potential to compromise the developing radical alliance. In spite of the persistence of such divisions, however, the first four months of 1937 had seen the consolidation of oppositional anarchism as an identifiable current within the libertarian movement. Radical anarchists had developed a programme based on a critical understanding of the revolutionary experience hitherto, and had seen new alliances and new organisational forms take shape. The MMLL, the JJLL, anarchist trade union delegates and the defence committees were united behind the demand for socialisation and the need for workers to retain their weapons. When police operations in Barcelona began to threaten the viability of this programme, the stage was set for the May mobilisation.

CHAPTER FOUR

May 1937:
From a Second July to the "Spanish Kronstadt"

The confrontation, known as the May days, that took place in Barcelona at the beginning of May 1937 was prompted by a police raid on the city's telephone exchange, the *Telefónica*. Since the summer, the *Telefónica* had been run jointly by a CNT-UGT committee and a delegate representative of the Generalitat. The *Telefónica*, site of the first great strike in Barcelona during the Second Republic, and which had only been taken in July at the cost of several lives, was of great importance to the CNT.[1] Run by a United States-based, and notoriously anti-union, company since the days of Primo de Rivera, the coming of the Second Republic had not brought its nationalisation, as had been promised by republicans and Socialists.[2] The system of workers' control put into operation there under the auspices of the CNT was therefore a living symbol of how the revolution had delivered where the Republic had failed. It was also a source of real power, as the workers at the exchange could monitor and even interfere with phone calls.[3] In a context in which the violence associated with state reconstitution had recently intensified, it was therefore little surprise when armed squads of Assault Guards were sent to the Plaça Catalunya on 3 May to take control of the *Telefónica* building. In fact, it was reported at a regional meeting of the CNT that day that this was the fourth time in recent weeks that such an attempt had been made by the security forces.[4]

A provocative act in itself, the assault on the *Telefónica* was clearly of a piece with the wider project of state reconstruction. The mobilisation that took place in response to it should therefore be seen in this context, and this chapter will accordingly discuss the events of May 1937 in Barcelona

---

1   See Graham, *The Spanish Republic*, 267.
2   See Gutiérrez Molina, *Valeriano Orobón Fernández*, 107.
3   Eduardo Pons Prades file, Col·lecció Ronald Fraser, AHCB, 66–7.
4   "Reunión extraordinaria que celebró el Comité Regional, con los demás comités responsables el día 3 de Mayo de 1937, en la ciudad de Barcelona," CNT (España) Archives (IISG) 85 C. Pons Prades recalled that the windows of the *Telefónica* building had been reinforced by the occupants in the days prior to the attack: Eduardo Pons Prades file, Col·lecció Ronald Fraser, AHCB, 68.

as a mobilisation of anti-statist anarchist workers.[5] The focus of the first part of this discussion will be on the immediate context that made a libertarian insurrection possible. The second section will analyse the nature, size and composition of the libertarian mobilisation, and what opportunities it appeared to offer radicals to implement their programme. This chapter will discuss the abandonment of the barricades in May as a reassertion of organisational hierarchies within the libertarian movement, enacted through a bureaucratic manoeuvre.[6] It will then proceed to analyse the impact of the events on the libertarian camp amidst the escalating repression of revolutionaries in the Spanish Republic.

Beginning again

The possibility of a "return to the barricades" had gained currency in the spring of 1937 as a consequence of reflections on the lost opportunity and errors of the previous July, which even Diego Abad de Santillán acknowledged had "revived" the state apparatus.[7] Such reflections became commonplace in the revolutionary movement in this period. Jaime Balius, in an article cited by Nin in *La Batalla*, affirmed: "We are the guilty ones; with the revolution in our hands we allowed the grandeur of the moment to frighten us."[8] Fidel Miró likewise lamented at a rally: "On 19 July we lacked sufficient vision to wipe out the vestiges of the failed political system."[9]

Perhaps the boldest of such declarations was made by Lucía Sánchez Saornil, who also emphasised the need to turn the tide of the counterrevolution through action:

[B]y keeping the government, the workers respected its old bourgeois

---

5   Due to considerations of space, this chapter will consider the events in May almost entirely insofar as they impacted upon the libertarian movement in Barcelona. For a wider perspective on the events, see Burnett Bolloten, *The Spanish Civil War: Revolution and Counterrevolution* (London: The University of North Carolina Press, 1982), 429–61; Graham, *The Spanish Republic*, 267–97; Manuel Aguilera, *Compañeros y Camaradas. Las luchas entre antifascistas en la Guerra Civil Española* (Madrid: Editorial Actas, 2012), 80–171. For accounts of comparable, concurrent disturbances that took place on a smaller scale in and outside of Cataluña, see Peirats, *The CNT, Vol. 2*, 132–6; and Casanova, *Anarchism*, 147–8.

6   The very recent publication of Agustín Guillamón, *Insurrección. Las sangrientas jornadas del 3 al 7 de mayo de 1937* (Barcelona: Descontrol, 2017), further reinforces the interpretation of the mobilisation offered here. It differs in certain respects, however, especially with regard to why the demobilisation took place.

7   "Acta del Pleno Regional de grupos anarquistas de Cataluña, celebrado el día 6 de diciembre."

8   *La Noche*, 2 March 1937.

9   *Solidaridad Obrera*, 15 April 1937.

structure and the weight of the bureaucratic apparatus that had hitherto surrounded it. They did not notice that they were leaving the greatest enemy of the revolution standing... The state began the strangulation of the revolution. Nevertheless, all is not lost if the unions know how to act with determination... and [if they] defend their right to the management of the economy we will be able to save ourselves.[10]

A radical critique was thus crystallising around a common identification of a missed revolutionary opportunity, while the energy and combativeness generated by the socialisation campaign had led to a belief that mistakes could be rectified through a return to the traditional direct action tactics of anarcho-syndicalism. That this might impact on a war effort to which anarchists were being enjoined to sacrifice their principles was evidently not lost on Sánchez Saornil, who defiantly addressed such concerns in her article: "And to those who shout at us that the war must come before everything, we reply: For the war everything, except liberty. Viva la Revolución!"[11]

While the distance of Barcelona from the front lines and the depth of anarchist implantation in the city made it the likeliest setting for a "second July," there were also signs of discontent and restlessness further afield. In March, the FAI members behind the Valencia-based review *Nosotros* affirmed that

in this Republic of workers ruled by the bourgeoisie, there is only conservatism and a desire to choke the revolution underway in Spain... comrades, we will not cease to defend freedom and attack everything suggestive of dictatorship, whether white, brown or red.[12]

On the Andalusian front line, Alfonso Nieves Núñez distributed a letter at the end of April from the imprisoned anarchist commander Francisco Maroto denouncing the lack of solidarity he had received from the *comités superiores*. The arrest of Maroto had followed a confrontation with Gabriel Morón, the Civil Governor of Almería, and caused consternation among libertarians throughout Republican Spain.[13] Nieves Núñez, on behalf of the affinity group *Los Intransigentes*, added the following postscript:

10   *Mujeres Libres*, April 1937.
11   Ibid.
12   *Nosotros*, 23 March 1937.
13   The unlikely case concocted against Maroto was accompanied by a campaign on the part of the Communists demanding that he be given the death penalty, which he duly was, although the sentence was annulled in 1938. He was murdered by the Francoists following the fall of the Republic. On the Maroto case, see Amorós, *Maroto*, 125–66, and a contrasting account in Quirosa-Cheyrouze y Muñoz, *Almería, 1936–37*, 159–69.

A new fascism stabs us in the back. We must react against it. A single clamour: FREEDOM FOR MAROTO, FREEDOM FOR ALL REVOLUTIONARY PRISONERS. If we need to begin again to achieve this, as on 19 July, LET US BEGIN![14]

The question of how to "begin again" was debated by the Local Federation of the Barcelona FAI at the second session of a Plenum of affinity groups on 12 April 1937.[15] Significantly, given their importance to the radical alliances discussed in the previous chapter, the Federation's Secretary, Julián Merino, had invited the city's defence committees, the JJLL and the German refugee grouping, the DAS, to send delegations to the meeting, a move he justified as "bringing together the living forces of anarchism."[16] At this Plenum, a majority of delegates favoured the withdrawal of anarchists from the Generalitat, and in what appears to have been a tense atmosphere, replacement executive bodies were proposed with a variety of different names. The representative of the Local Federation of the JJLL suggested that if further collaboration proved impossible, the anarchists constitute a revolutionary Convention.[17] Francisco Caudet, of the affinity group *Constancia y Desinterés*, proposed that the withdrawal of the CNT and the FAI from government be accompanied by the nomination of a Central Committee on the part of the defence committees.[18] The anarchist defence committee from the Barcelona suburb of Gràcia known as *Grupo 12* advanced a programmatic proposal similar in aims and tone to that of the Friends of Durruti (AAD), involving withdrawal from government, complete socialisation and the creation of a revolutionary anti-fascist committee to coordinate the armed struggle against fascism.[19] The Plenum, which Jacinto Toryho, then editor of *Solidaridad Obrera*, declared to be unauthorised when it became clear that the collaborationist positions had been defeated, is suggestive of a coalescence of voluntarist positions among members of the JJLL, anarchist refugees, the defence committees and the anarchist affinity groups of Barcelona.

The radical positions advanced at this Plenum may also provide a clue as to the content of the programme of the AAD. Pablo Ruiz, who as a part

14   See "Comité Nacional Circular N° 7," 3 May 1937, CNT (España) Archives (IISG) 46 B.
15   The proceedings are presented and analysed in minute detail in Guillamón, *Los Comités de Defensa*, 196–221.
16   Ibid. 214.
17   Ibid. 200–1.
18   Ibid. 201. In the minutes, the name of the delegate is given as Caudet, while the affinity group is referred to only as *Constancia*. However, I have located a FAI membership card bearing the complete name: CDMH, PS Barcelona, 1793/1.
19   Guillamón, *Comités de Defensa*, 208–9.

of the Gelsa section had left the Durruti Column in opposition to militarisation, attended the Plenum and was a leading member of the grouping. A central plank of the AAD programme was the formation of a revolutionary Junta, composed of "workers of the city and country and combatants," which would replace the government of the Republic. At the end of April 1937, this programme appeared on posters plastered on walls around Barcelona.[20] Apart from the proposal of a revolutionary Junta, the programme reflected libertarian concerns regarding public order and militarisation, while advocating socialisation of the economy and union control of supplies.[21] Marxists in Spain greeted the AAD programme with enthusiasm, a fact that may have contributed to limiting the attraction of the grouping within the CNT and the FAI, as purist anarchists were troubled by the seemingly "Bolshevik" tone of the group's pronouncements.[22] Peirats averred that "the reason that the AAD had little influence could be due to the slight importance of its components, the intervention of the POUM in its centre and the Marxist flavour of certain of its slogans."[23] While this statement is inaccurate as regards the intervention of the POUM and overzealous in its dismissal of the grouping's importance, it is illustrative of the purist reservations that would hamstring the AAD's attempts to serve as a pole of regroupment within the libertarian movement.

Nevertheless, as the April Plenum demonstrates, the emergence of the AAD and its call for a revolutionary Junta were not isolated phenomena but part of a broader process within the anarchist movement whereby the need for an alternative policy to state collaboration was widely accepted. Within days of the Plenum, the mouthpiece of the JJLL published an article by Ada Martí, a journalist associated with anarchist purism, which also proposed the formation of a "Junta de Defensa." Contrasting the potential dynamism of such a body with the protracted crises of the Generalitat, Martí averred that a Junta "composed of the unions, will put an end, once and for all, to the consultations, pleas and demands of all parties – regardless of whether their programmes and representatives are political or 'apolitical.'"[24]

While the agreements arrived at by the Barcelona FAI in April, which were not published in *Solidaridad Obrera* or *Tierra y Libertad*, were to an extent reflected in Martí's article and in the programme of the AAD, of greater significance was the manifesto that resulted as a direct consequence

20   *Los Amigos de Durruti*, 220–1.
21   Ibid.
22   See the recollections of a member of the Los Quijotes del Ideal affinity group, Diego Camacho: Paz, *Viaje al pasado*, 120–1.
23   José Peirats, *Los anarquistas en la crisis política española* (Editorial Alfa: Buenos Aires, 1964), 249.
24   *Ruta*, 17 April 1937.

of these discussions, which was presented on 24 April in the name of the Local Federation of the FAI, the defence committees and the JJLL. This document would establish a practical basis for action which, because it emerged from within the heart of the libertarian movement with no hint of external Marxist influence, represented a voluntarism that was palatable to purist anarchists, and was indicative of the continuing capacity of anti-statist anarchism to give an organisational expression to radical discontent. By some distance the most radical programmatic statement to have emerged from oppositional anarchism up to that point, the manifesto was neverthe-less the logical outgrowth of an oppositional critique that had centred on the error of state collaboration and a socialisation campaign at loggerheads with the process of state reconstruction.

The manifesto proposed the withdrawal of anarchists from official posts and a return to the "revolutionary and anti-state terrain," comprehensive socialisation and, most intriguingly, the "constitution of a local revolution-ary committee for the coordination of the armed struggle against fascism and the counterrevolution, in all its forms."[25] It therefore conferred a man-date on those who would be central to the revolutionary mobilisation of May 1937. We might even speculate that the delay between the Plenum and the publication of the paper may be explained by further conversations among Barcelona anarchists as to the viability and composition of such a committee.[26] The novelty of this local revolutionary committee resides in its emerging constitutionally from a regular Plenum yet having a mission that bypassed the authority of the *comités superiores*. This was an innovation of mid-level delegates and activists that seemingly squared the circle of strug-gling against the state and on behalf of the revolution while remaining part of an organisation with a foot in both camps. It is therefore worth paying attention to those who authored the manifesto.

At the Plenum, the composition of the manifesto had been entrusted to a working group composed of Iglesias, Francisco Caudet of the affin-ity group Constancia y Desinterés, and the delegates of the affinity groups Móvil, Luz y Cultura and Cultura y Acción. If the Iglesias referred to here was Abelardo Iglesias, of the *A* affinity group, strongly associated with the defence of state collaboration, it would appear improbable that he had much to do with the confection of the manifesto.[27] Little is known about

---

25   Guillamón, *La Guerra del pan*, 489–91.

26   Guillamón goes so far as to speculate that Julián Merino, Pablo Ruiz and Juan Santana Calero were all likely members of this committee: Guillamón, *Insurrección*, 296. How-ever, the only corroborative evidence in this regard relates exlusively to Merino.

27   A common name, the Iglesias delegated to the working group charged with composing the manifesto could also feasibly refer to another Iglesias who would urge anarchist insurrection as late as October 1937 (discussed in the following chapter).

the affinity group Móvil although its likely radicalism is attested to by its later opposition to the legalisation of the FAI.[28] The closeness of the group Constancia y Desinterés to the defence committees is implied by the nature of its proposal to the Plenum, discussed above. Of the components of Luz y Cultura we know that one, Joaquina Dorado Pita, was a member of the defence committee of the city centre and of the JJLL in the suburb of El Poble-sec, and would participate in the fighting in May.[29] By her own account, it was nearly always Dorado Pita who represented the affinity group at meetings of the FAI.[30] She was also secretary to Manuel Hernández in the socialised carpentry industry of Barcelona, replacing him when he departed for the front. Eduardo Pons Prades, a worker in the same industry, recalled that Hernández was a member of the AAD.[31] A picture is thus emerging of a working group, brought together by shared membership of the FAI, with close links to the JJLL, armed women in the rearguard, the defence committees and the AAD, four of the most important components of the mobilisation in May. This number rises to five when we consider that the group was mandated to draw up the manifesto by a Plenum in which the anarchist refugees of the DAS had participated.

Julián Merino was also involved in the writing of the manifesto as the delegate of the affinity group Cultura y Acción. This explains why the initial suggestion of the defence committee Grupo 12 to constitute a "revolutionary anti-fascist committee to coordinate the armed struggle against fascism" became radicalised to also incorporate the struggle against the counterrevolution in the rear. The belief that anarchists were having to fight on two fronts was expressed with increasing frequency during this period. In his autobiography, Ramón Liarte, an activist in the Catalan JJLL, records a conversation with Camillo Berneri from the spring of 1937 in which the Italian activist warned his "young friends" that "fascism is only one sector of the counterrevolution," to which Liarte replied in agreement: "the civil war has two fronts… and the revolution must triumph at both."[32] Mariano Viñuales, a CNT delegate in the Popular Tribunals of Cataluña, declared in an interview in April that "for the proletarian revolution to succeed, it is

---

28   This is discussed in the following chapter. The names of three members of the Móvil group have been recovered from membership cards: Antonio Alex, a textile worker based in Gràcia, José Casanovas and Pascual Prades: CDMH, PS Barcelona, 1793/1.

29   See Iñiguez, *Esbozo de una enciclopedia*, 191; Vega, *Pioneras y revolucionarias*, 226.

30   Vega, *Pioneras y revolucionarias*, 159.

31   Eduardo Pons Prades file, Col·lecció Ronald Fraser, AHCB, 76. Dorado Pita would also be the lifelong partner of Liberto Sarrau, a member of the Los Quijotes del Ideal affinity group.

32   Ramón Liarte, *Entre la Revolución y la Guerra* (Barcelona: Picazo, 1986), 212.

necessary to wipe out the politicians *on all fronts.*"[33] At the January Plenum of unions in Barcelona referred to in the previous chapter, the delegate for the Maritime Transport Workers' Union, almost certainly Merino, had lamented that the CNT was only able to conceive of the "anti-fascist front," ignoring the "anti-Confederal front" that was then in operation.[34]

Emblematic of this "anti-Confederal front" were two events in Cataluña that served to heighten tension in the region in the period immediately prior to the May days. On 25 April, police responding to a request for assistance from UGT members at the Trefilería Barcelonesa factory, where the majority of the workforce backed socialisation, arrived on horseback, surrounding the factory while an assembly of workers was taking place, causing it to break up.[35] Then, on 27 April, Antonio Martín, a veteran CNT member and a key figure of the organisation in the border town of Puigcerdà, was killed. A former member of the CCMA, Joan Pons Garlandí of the ERC, then a delegate to the Interior Security Council of the Generalitat (the JSI), the body responsible for public order in Cataluña, described in his memoirs, written just after the war, how trusted Catalan "patriots" had been sent to nearby Bellver to take advantage of the first opportunity to end the power of Martín in the area. This opportunity arrived when Martín and others from Puigcerdà and the town of La Seu d'Urgell were ambushed at a roadblock, during which "a patriot, known as The Shirtless, renowned throughout the region for his marksmanship, situated in a strategic spot, fatally wounded [Martín]."[36]

The murder of Martín followed that of Roldán Cortada, an activist of the PSUC and a former member of the CNT who had signed the *treintista* manifesto. It has been suggested that Cortada was murdered by the CNT, as the organisation had recently been informed of his role in preparing an attack on "the FAI."[37] According to sources in the POUM, Cortada was in fact an opponent of the PSUC's sectarian policies.[38] In any case, the murder of the PSUC member prompted a police investigation centred on the

33   *Mi Revista*, 1 April 1937.
34   Guillamón, *La Guerra del pan*, 206.
35   See Carme Vega, Anna Monjo and Mercedes Vilanova, "Socialización y hechos de mayo: una nueva aportación a partir del proceso a Mauricio Stevens (2 de junio de 1937)," *Historia y Fuente Oral*, 3 (1990): 95.
36   Joan Pons Garlandí, *Un republicà enmig de faistes* (Barcelona: Edicions 62, 2008), 150–2. On the background and aftermath of this episode, see the recent work by Antonio Gascón and Agustín Guillamón, *Nacionalistas contra anarquistas en la Cerdaña (1936–1937)* (Barcelona: Descontrol, 2018).
37   François Godicheau, *No callaron: las voces de los presos antifascistas de la República, 1937–1939* (Toulouse: Presses Universitaires du Mirail, 2012), 37.
38   See Victor Alba and Stephen Schwartz, *Spanish Marxism versus Soviet Communism* (New Brunswick and London: Transaction Publishers, 2009), 186–7. Ramón Liarte also considered the murder to have been part of a set-up: Liarte, *Entre la Revolución y la Guerra*, 239.

anarchist stronghold of L'Hospitalet.[39] It also led to a redoubling of calls from the PSUC to disarm the rearguard.[40] In spite of its calls for calm throughout this period, *Solidaridad Obrera* nevertheless made an urgent appeal with regard to the subject of arms on 2 May, on the same day that a young member of the Catalan JJLL was killed in Barcelona by gunfire emanating from the local HQ of the Catalan nationalist party, Estat Català.[41] The appeal, anomalous in the trajectory of *Solidaridad Obrera* under the editorship of Jacinto Toryho, contradicted the tendency of official CNT directives since the previous autumn:

> The guarantee of the revolution is the proletariat in arms. To attempt to disarm the people is to position oneself on the other side of the barricades. Whether Councillor or Commissar, an order of disarmament cannot be dictated against the workers, who are struggling against fascism with more generosity and heroism than all the politicians of the rearguard... Workers: Let no one disarm you under any pretext! This is our slogan: Let no one disarm you![42]

That such a combative editorial could be published in *Solidaridad Obrera* suggests that it was beginning to dawn on even the *comités superiores* of the CNT that the arms its members disposed of were fundamental to the power of the organisation as a whole, and that its plans to recover lost influence through control over the economy would count for little if factories were left at the mercy of the police. As much as was intimated by an editorial in *Tierra y Libertad*, which affirmed the "impossibility of leaving in the hands of the state the destiny of our revolution, the revolution begun, driven and defended by the workers in arms."[43] Given the role that the *comités superiores* would go on to play during the May days, we might wonder whether such combative language was merely a bluff intended to ease state pressure on their members. This radicalisation of the slogans of the CNT perhaps encouraged the illusory hope that the *comités superiores* would not disown a new revolutionary mobilisation. The May days would also prove, however, that the radical anarchists were not bluffing when they posed the possibility that "the gesture of the 19 July" would "have to be repeated."[44] There was no ambiguity or subtlety in the challenge the Local Federation of the

39   See *Solidaridad Obrera*, 1 May 1937; and Bolloten, *The Spanish Civil War*, 431.
40   Ferran Gallego, *La crisis del antifascismo. Barcelona, mayo de 1937* (Barcelona: Random House, 2008), 391.
41   See Paz, *Viaje al Pasado*, 136–7.
42   *Solidaridad Obrera*, 2 May 1937.
43   *Tierra y Libertad*, 1 May 1937.
44   *Esfuerzo*, second week of April 1937.

JJLL in Barcelona made to the police chief Eusebio Rodríguez Salas: "we will continue to be armed… and whosoever attempts to disarm us without respecting our documentation will have to do so over our dead body. And we will see who emerges victorious."[45]

The programme that had emerged in opposition to state reconstruction in Spain had been encapsulated in the slogan of *Ideas*: "Socialisation and the people armed!" When police on horseback broke up an assembly of workers well-disposed to socialisation in April 1937, the slogan's obverse – the mutually constitutive relation between state force and hierarchical relations in production – could be perceived. In the months prior to the May days, the role of Republican police in defending private or state property from anarchist projects had become more clear, while the process by which anarchist volunteers could be transformed into an anti-fascist police force through the *Patrullas de Control* had seemingly gone into reverse. With the *Patrullas* under the jurisdiction of the defence committees and those same committees tasked with participation in the coordination of a "revolutionary committee" to fight both fascism and the "counterrevolution," it was entirely logical that any further attempt by police to obliterate workers' power in Barcelona would provide the spark required for the armed enactment of the oppositional programme. The frontiers of the anarchist city would once again be marked by barricades, the successful defence or conquest of which would bring to a definite end the revolutionary interregnum begun in July 1936.

The mobilisation of the "anti-state"

The assault on the *Telefónica* building on 3 May was resisted by the CNT workers inside. An uneasy standoff then took place, both inside and outside the building, in the Plaça de Catalunya. A meeting of the Regional Committee of the CNT was held to discuss developments, where it was noted that if the Generalitat did not rectify the situation, "our people" were prepared to take to the streets. In this regard, the intervention of the representative of the Local Federation of the FAI, who suggested that those present keep in mind the "project for the organisation of the defence groups," is suggestive. However, Manuel Escorza, head of the CNT's Investigation Services, declared:

We are granting this occurrence an importance which it does not merit.

45   See the leaflet, JOVENTUTS LLIBERTÀRIES. FEDERACIÓ LOCAL DE BARCELONA, "Una provocación más' (Barcelona, 1937) PDLR, Fons DH, DH 6 (4) 1- Joventuts Llibertàries (FIJL – FAI).

It is a mundane affair, a premature action that has not been thought out in the least... What remains to be seen is whether we really control our membership.[46]

The meeting concluded with the agreement that the organisation demand the dismissal of the police chief, Rodríguez Salas.[47] When this demand was refused, the basis for a de-escalation of the situation disappeared. The Catalan nationalist Manuel Cruells was of the opinion that the "bloody week of May" would have been avoided were it not for the incomprehensible intransigence of President Companys at that moment.[48] However, why and how the city had become "a sea of barricades" by the following day requires further explanation.[49]

The mobilisation has been described as "spontaneous" by both eyewitnesses and participants.[50] Certainly, the rapid response of the revolutionaries on the streets of Barcelona was not the result of directives from the anarchist press or the *comités superiores* of the CNT. In the prevailing atmosphere of high tension, it was observed: "The political atmosphere was charged with electricity and everyone was waiting for the inevitable spark."[51] To the Americans, Charles and Lois Orr, it seemed that "the workers... went out into the street *en masse*... all quite spontaneously, not only without any leadership, but actually against their leaders, and against all newspapers."[52] However, while the combination of tension and provocation contributed to a rapid escalation that surprised onlookers, the May mobilisation cannot be said to have been spontaneous in the way that this term is normally understood.

A simple explanation for the events, amply attested to by eyewitnesses, participants and subsequent histories, is that the neighbourhood defence

46   "Reunión extraordinaria que celebró el Comité Regional."

47   Ibid.

48   Manuel Cruells, *Mayo Sangriento. Barcelona 1937* (Barcelona: Juventud, 1970), 55–6.

49   The phrase comes from Helmut Kirschey, "A las barricadas. Memorias y reflexiones de un antifascista," in *Barcelona, mayo 1937. Testimonios desde las barricadas*, ed. by C. García, H. Piotrowski, S. Rosés (Barcelona: Alikornio ediciones, 2006), 174.

50   See the letter of Jaime Balius to Burnett Bolloten, 24 June 1946, reproduced in Guillamón, *Los Amigos de Durruti*, 155. Eyewitness observations on the supposed "spontaneity" of the events can be found in Albert Weisbord, "Barricades in Barcelona," available at the internet archives of Albert and Vera Weisbord: http://search.marxists.org/archive/weisbord/Barricades.htm [accessed 1 December 2017]; and Adolfo Carlini (Domenico Sedran), "Un bolchevique-leninista de España os cuenta toda la verdad sobre las Jornadas de Mayo" in *Barcelona, mayo 1937*, 91.

51   Clara and Paul Thalmann, "La sublevación en Cataluña" in *Barcelona, mayo 1937*, 112.

52   Postcard written by Charles Orr to his mother on 8 May 1937, reproduced in *Letters from Barcelona: An American Woman in Revolution and Civil War*, ed. by Gerd-Rainer Horn (London: Palgrave Macmillan, 2009), 161. The Orrs were left-socialists working for the POUM in Barcelona.

committees of the libertarian movement mobilised their forces. How this was brought about is discussed below. What is less clear is why the defence committees felt sufficiently emboldened to act, at this moment, *apparently* beyond the margins of organisational discipline. A clue as to why this happened is provided by the intervention of the delegate of the Local Federation of the FAI at the meeting of the CNT's Regional Committee discussed above. It seems likely that the "project for the organisation of the defence groups" to which the delegate referred was the formation of the "central committee" discussed in the previous subsection, which the combined representatives of the local FAI, JJLL and defence committees had considered necessary in order to carry forward the fight against both fascism and the counterrevolution. Merino, the regular delegate for the Local Federation of the FAI at regional meetings of the libertarian movement in Cataluña, was not present on 3 May, and it is possible that his absence was due to activity preparing the ground for the mobilisation.

What can be concluded is that the Local Federation of the FAI considered a project of aggressive, revolutionary self-defence to have been mandated by a regularly constituted Plenum, and that this was likely brought up at the meeting of 3 May to indicate to those present the option of an armed mobilisation. The reference to the defence committees at this meeting, although vague and inconclusive in itself, is one among several links between the mobilisation of May and the radical measures proposed in April by a combination of the defence committees, affinity groups and the JJLL through the Barcelona FAI. These links are important because they indicate how the action could be said to have emerged through the traditional decision-making processes of the anarchist movement, and were not conceived of by the participants as contravening organisational discipline.

The neighbourhood defence committees of the CNT were initially alerted to the raid on the *Telefónica* directly via telephone by workers in the building in contact with the headquarters of the various committees.[53] Sara Berenguer, a member of the neighbourhood defence committee of Les Corts, recalled in her autobiography:

> As the alarm went up in response to that shameless attack on the *Telefónica*, the Confederal neighbourhood committees intervened energetically… The activists of the neighbourhoods called us on the telephone every minute to find out about our situation and to let us know of their own initiatives.[54]

53   This explanation was offered by the leading POUM activist Jordi Arquer, in the Jordi Arquer file, Col·lecció Ronald Fraser, AHCB, 140.
54   Sara Berenguer, *Entre el sol y la tormenta* (Barcelona: Seuba Ediciones, 1988), 88.

As in July 1936, the only libertarian mobilisation of comparable scale to have taken place in Barcelona, the core delegates who represented these neighbourhood defence committees informed the wider network of activists by telephone, who were instructed to present themselves with their weapons at their local defence committee headquarters. Diego Camacho, an activist of the JJLL in the neighbourhood of Clot, recalls being informed of events by telephone at his place of work by Juan Turtós Vallès, a member of the JJLL of Clot and a delegate member of the neighbourhood defence committee.[55] The shop steward at Camacho's workplace, having confirmed the information with the local trade union committee, assembled the workers who then voted to go on strike and report to their neighbourhood defence committees and union sections.[56] Members of the DAS were telephoned at the occupied German embassy on the central avenue, the Passeig de Gràcia, and told to construct a barricade to control the street.[57] Members of the *Patrullas de Control* in the neighbourhood of Sants were told that the *Patrullas* no longer counted for anything, and that their unit of around fifty members was now responsible only to the local defence committee.[58] Albert Weisbord, an independent dissident communist from the United States who was in Barcelona at the time, remarked on the prominent role of the *Patrullas*, who probably numbered around 890 members: "The Patrolmen, armed with submachine guns, go from barricade to barricade, investigating every house and rooftop to ferret out any surprise the enemy might try to spring."[59] The CNT's National Committee would later claim that the *Patrullas de Control* had not participated in the events of May, a claim that has been taken at face value in the historiography.[60] It is likely that the functioning of the *Patrullas* as adjuncts of the defence committees during this period is at the root of this confusion.[61]

55   Paz, *Viaje al Pasado*, 141. Juan Turtós Vallès was a member of the defence group Orto who had participated in the fighting in July. See Iñiguez, *Esbozo de una enciclopedia*, 606; and "Juan Turtós Vallès – Anarquista del Grupo Orto," http://puertoreal.cnt.es/bilbi-ografias-anarquistas/3415-juan-turtos-valles-anarquista-del-grupo-orto.html [accessed 1 December 2017].

56   Paz, *Viaje al Pasado*, 143.

57   Kirschey, "A las barricadas," 174.

58   See "Entrevista amb Joan 'Remi,'" 97 and 126.

59   Weisbord, "Barricades in Barcelona." On the figure of 890, see José Luis Ledesma, "Una retaguardia al rojo. Las violencias en la zona republicana" in *Violencia Roja y Azul. España, 1936–1950*, ed. by Francisco Espinosa (Barcelona: Crítica, 2010), p.198

60   For example, in Godicheau, *No Callaron*, 38. Their role is also played down in Guillamón, *Barricadas en Barcelona*, 150.

61   In addition to the testimony of Joan "Remi," a hostile witness also reported that the *Patrullas* responded to the orders of the defence committees. See the intercepted exchange between the leading Communist Vicente Uribe and an unnamed interlocutor, recorded at 12.15 am on the morning of 7 May, "Dossier elaborat per Josep Tarradellas, relatiu

As a result of the frenetic activity of the defence committees, around 7,000 libertarian revolutionaries were mobilised behind the barricades.[62] In addition to Spanish anarchists, barricades were mounted by members of the POUM and also by foreign revolutionaries in Barcelona, such as the German DAS and Italian anarchists who had left the front but who had regrouped in Barcelona in order to form a new battalion.[63] It should also be borne in mind that, in addition to the thousands of activists on the streets and guarding buildings, many anarchist activists on the periphery of the city remained confined to their neighbourhoods without actively participating in the events in spite of a readiness to do so if necessary.[64]

The mobilisation was backed up by a degree of popular support among working-class non-combatants, indicated by a successful general strike throughout the city. In a report on the May days prepared for the internal discussion bulletin of the Barcelona POUM prior to the planned celebration of the local party Congress, which in the event never took place, Josep Rebull affirmed: "The movement was greeted with sympathy by the working class in general in the first days – proof of this is the breadth, rapidity and unanimity of the strike – and left the middle classes in a state of watchful neutrality, influenced, naturally, by terror."[65] There is also anecdotal evidence of wider community participation in the building of barricades. Albert Weisbord observed that "the large crowds that gathered around [the barricades] clamoring for action left no doubt that the overwhelming mass of workers were wholeheartedly behind the vanguard and were only awaiting the orders of their respective organizations to march forward."[66] Orwell also recalled popular participation in barricade-building: "long lines of men, women and quite small children were tearing up the cobblestones, hauling them along in a hand-cart that had been found somewhere, and staggering to and fro under heavy sacks of sand," a testimony corroborated by the report of Edi Gmür, a Swiss Communist volunteer in Spain.[67] Orwell also

als Fets de Maig i a la posterior repressió del POUM," Fons ANC1–1/Generalitat de Catalunya (Segona República).

62   See the convincing estimates in Manuel Aguilera Povedano, "Los hechos de mayo de 1937: efectivos y bajas de cada bando," *Hispania*, 73, 245 (2013), 789–816. Here the total numbers of combatants is suggested to be between 7,000 and 7,500 on the revolutionary side.

63   Aldo Aguzzi, "Un anarquista italiano en las Jornadas de Mayo," in *Barcelona, mayo 1937*, 155–7.

64   See Paz, *Viaje al pasado*, 154.

65   See Josep Rebull, "Las Jornadas de mayo," http://es.internationalism.org/book/export/html/3244 [accessed 1 December 2017].

66   Weisbord, "Barricades in Barcelona."

67   See, respectively, Orwell, *Orwell in Spain*, 108, and Edi Gmür, "(En Barcelona, después de disfrutar de un permiso en Valencia)," in *Barcelona, mayo 1937*, 184.

states that, in the POUM headquarters, "the office upstairs was ceaselessly besieged by a crowd of people who were demanding rifles and being told that there were none left."[68]

Such a degree of enthusiasm and willingness to participate does not mean that working-class support for the rising was unanimous. Diego Camacho was unsure of popular support in his neighbourhood, noting that people "seemed shocked, as if wondering whether we hadn't all gone crazy. It was difficult to know if they approved or disapproved of seeing rifles on the street once more."[69] Nevertheless, the mobilisation clearly indicates considerable popular backing for the revolution and "its people" in opposition to the state. Orwell's account continues to be the subject of polemic, but it seems likely that his contemporary interpretation of events was widely shared:

> The issue was clear enough. On one side the CNT, on the other side the police. I have no particular love for the idealised "worker'… but when I see an actual flesh-and-blood worker in conflict with his natural enemy, the policeman, I do not have to ask which side I am on.[70]

In a similar vein, the review of the POUM's Women's Secretariat affirmed after the events:

> Our place has to be at the side of our class. When the workers are dying with arms in hand at the barricades, we must immediately realise that this is because they are defending the life or death interests of the working class.[71]

In any case, that such a widespread sentiment of class solidarity, which was not new to the city, could result in an apparently successful mobilisation against the Republican state was remarkable when one bears in mind that thousands of the CNT's most seasoned militants had left Barcelona for the front, and that its *comités superiores* had nothing to do with it. To that extent, therefore, the May events demonstrated both a degree of support for the anti-state programme defended by the radical anarchists and the fact that many workers did not question the continued viability of the anarchist project even in wartime.

Excluding foreign participants, who may have accounted for up to eleven per cent of the combatants, the libertarian mobilisation was

68   Orwell, *Orwell in Spain*, 106.
69   Paz, *Viaje al pasado*, 143.
70   Orwell, *Orwell in Spain*, 106.
71   *Emancipación*, 29 May 1937.

composed of members of the JJLL, the Barcelona defence committees, the *Patrullas de Control*, FAI affinity groups, militia on leave, the MMLL, the AAD and specific unions of the CNT.[72] It should be noted that these groups had an overlapping membership, and that foreign participants also fell into these categories. Members of the JJLL were also members of the CNT and, if they had joined the youth organisation prior to the revolution, would also have belonged to the FAI. Joan "Remi," for example, belonged to all three organisations and was also a member of the *Patrullas de Control*. Sara Berenguer was a member of her neighbourhood defence committee, the JJLL and the MMLL. Ada Martí, an active participant in the May days, also belonged to these three organisations and, as a member of the Agrupación Los de Ayer y Los de Hoy and a future contributor to *El Amigo del Pueblo*, was probably also a member of the AAD.[73]

The participation in the events of members of the MMLL meant the visible return of one of the most important features of the July days: armed women on the barricades.[74] Their presence not only added to the sensation, summed up in *La Batalla*, that "The spirit of July has once more taken possession of Barcelona," but also confirmed that the socio-cultural aspect of state reconstruction – the "normalisation" of the rearguard – was no more complete by May than was the project to regain a monopoly of violence.[75] This should be borne in mind when we note Sara Berenguer's recollection: "It seemed to me that the effervescence of the first days had returned."[76] Comparisons with the July days were widespread during the street fighting, and were indicative

72   The figure of eleven per cent of revolutionary combatants in May being of foreign origin is estimated from the number of foreign victims and is provided in José Luis Oyón, *La quiebra de la ciudad popular. Espacio urbano, inmigración y anarquismo en la Barcelona de entreguerras, 1914–1936* (Barcelona: Ediciones del Serbal, 2008), 474. The number of foreign victims on the libertarian side included at least five Italians and one Portuguese, although it should be noted that two of these Italians, Camillo Berneri and Francesco Barbieri, were not combatants but were arrested at home and then murdered. It is also known that several German anarcho-syndicalists participated in the fighting, and in this regard, the name of one anarchist victim about whom nothing is known, Elias Werna, is suggestive. For a list of the victims of the May days along with their organisational affiliation, see Manuel Aguilera Povedano, "Lista de víctimas de los Hechos de Mayo de 1937 en Barcelona," Miguel Aguilera Povedano blog (2013), http://wp.me/p2FTqL-8V [accessed 1 December 2017].

73   Los de Ayer y Los de Hoy was formed by veteran members of the CNT at the beginning of the civil war and was affiliated to the Local Federation of the FAI. It was intended to bridge the generational divide between older and younger activists in the movement. According to Negrete and Oehler, it had agreed to adhere to the AAD at a meeting in Barcelona on 1 May: Negrete and Oehler, "Negrete and Oehler report back from Barcelona."

74   See the recollections of participants in Vega, *Pioneras y revolucionarias*, 222–8.

75   *La Batalla* cited in Bolloten, *The Spanish Civil War*, 432.

76   See Berenguer, *Entre el sol*, 88.

A woman streetfighter depicted in an engraving by Gustavo Cochet, photographed by Mario Gómez Casas, reproduced by permission of the Museo Gustavo Cochet and the Ministerio de Innovación y Cultura de Santa Fe. The caption, 'What courage!', is a reference to a print contained in Goya's *Disasters of War.*

that the struggle was understood by revolutionary combatants as a point of rupture, the opportunity to "begin again" sought by radicals.[77]

Aside from membership of the CNT, which applied to the vast majority if not all the libertarian combatants in May, the most common organisational denominator within this movement has generally been taken to be the JJLL. The prominence of the JJLL in the fighting was emphasised by friends and foes alike. In the aftermath of the events, *Solidaridad Obrera* was moved to publicly defend the JJLL, which it described as "the target for the rage of many people who are either ignorant or frankly counterrevolutionary."[78] At a National Plenum later in the month, the delegate for the Catalan Regional Defence Committee stated that the JJLL had "borne the brunt" of the struggle in Barcelona.[79] It has been suggested that the preponderance of the JJLL in the May fighting was owing to the determination of younger libertarians to experience what they had missed out on in July, desirous of imitating the vanguard role played by more experienced revolutionaries in those days. With many of the combatants of July now at the front or dead, as well as several others now incorporated in the administration of the state, it was the turn of the youth to show their mettle.[80] This hypothesis is not substantiated by the evidence at our disposal. The average age of the victims from among the libertarian combatants whose age is known is 35.[81] The JJLL, in spite of its name, did not in reality function as an organisation of only younger members of the libertarian movement.[82] In its origins, the Catalan JJLL had operated as the cultural, educational and propagandistic wing of the FAI. Aside from which, the mobilisation was systematic and disciplined, and cannot be attributed to the eagerness of the activists who took part. Youthful exuberance and impetuosity were not absent from the May days, nor were they determinant factors. The prominence of the JJLL can instead be explained by its status as a specifically anarchist "umbrella" organisation in Barcelona within which membership of affinity groups, defence committees and the MMLL often overlapped. Its place alongside these bodies in the vanguard of Catalan anarchism during the war is indicated by the joint Plenum of the FAI, JJLL and defence committees discussed in the previous subsection.

77   See Orwell, *Orwell in Spain*, 126, and "Reunión extraordinaria que celebró el Comité Regional."

78   *Solidaridad Obrera*, 8 May 1937.

79   See "Actas del Pleno Nacional de Regionales, Extraordinario, del Movimiento Libertario, celebrado los días 23 y sucesivos de mayo de 1937," CNT (España) Archives (IISG) 46 B.

80   Aguilera Povedano, "Los hechos de mayo de 1937," 795.

81   See Aguilera Povedano, "Lista de víctimas de los Hechos de Mayo."

82   See Jesús L. Santamaría, "Juventudes Libertarias y Guerra Civil (1936–1939)," *Studia Histórica*, 1 (1983): 217.

The "comités superiores de defensa"

At several removes from the escalating tension at its base, the National Committee of the CNT was taken by surprise by events. Jordi Arquer, a leading member of the POUM, was in Valencia when news of the May days arrived. He was able to speak to Joan Peiró, who was none the wiser about what was taking place in Barcelona.[83] The perspective of the National Committee was expressed by Joan Manent Pesas, then Ministerial secretary to Peiró, who remembered that "from a governmental point of view, for us it was catastrophic, so much so that it was as if we were going to lose the war the next day."[84] Despite *Solidaridad Obrera* describing the attack on the *Telefónica* as a "monstrous provocation" on 4 May, it made no gesture of support for those of its readers behind the barricades.[85] At this point, state power in the city was effectively confined to the centre and, with the artillery at the hill of Montjuïc in the hands of the CNT and trained on the Generalitat, the revolutionaries held the upper hand. As much was enthusiastically conveyed to a meeting of representatives of the Catalan libertarian movement by Merino on the morning of 4 May, in spite of Valerio Más, Regional Secretary of the Catalan CNT, warning those in attendance of the danger facing the movement if the situation was allowed to continue.[86] By contrast, Merino reported that, from his point of view, "our position is un-improvable... The fact that we have been able to take the city and to take Civil Guards prisoner should give an idea of the state of our morale; that is to say, that of our comrades."[87]

This apparent slip of the tongue would likely have revealed to those present the extent of Merino's involvement, if his detailed knowledge of the situation had not already done so. Severino Campos later recalled that Merino convoked a meeting at the Casa CNT-FAI during the May days.[88] García Oliver remembered seeing Julián Merino in the Casa "giving orders on a telephone reserved for the Regional Committee," and it seems incontrovertible that Merino was a member of the Regional

---

83   See the Jordi Arquer file, Col·lecció Ronald Fraser, AHCB, p.74

84   Joan Manent Pesas file, Col·lecció Ronald Fraser, AHCB, 57.

85   *Solidaridad Obrera*, 4 May 1937.

86   "Reunión extraordinaria celebrada el día cuatro de mayo de 1937, por el Comité Regional y los demás comités responsables de Cataluña," CNT (España) Archives (IISG) 85 C.

87   Ibid.

88   See Gimenólogos, *En busca de los Hijos de la Noche*, 567. Campos testifies that this meeting took place on 5 May. Owing to his apparent confusion between the two meetings that took place on 4 and 5 May, Guillamón concludes that Merino must have convoked the meeting on 4 May: Guillamón, *Insurrección*, 494.

Defence Committee, the organisation coordinating the defence committees.[89] Matías Suñer Vidal, a member of the *Patrullas de Control* and of the FAI who participated in the fighting, testified that at this time he was "at the orders of a secret revolutionary committee… that directed military operations against the PSUC," naming as members of this committee Julián Merino, Lucio Ruano and José Manzana.[90] We might assume that this was one of the *comités superiores de defensa*, which the anonymous participant in the mobilisation Joan "Remi" identifies as the coordinator of events.[91] Merino, as the former FAI delegate to the Catalan Regional Defence Committee, was well placed to re-establish this body, and had in effect been mandated to do so by the working group nominated at the April Plenum of the Barcelona FAI. Lucio Ruano was the pseudonym of the Argentinian anarchist Rodolfo Prina. Ruano had been a part of the action group that murdered the Catalan nationalist former police chief Miquel Badía and his brother in April 1936, and his presence at a meeting during the May days is confirmed by the account of Campos.[92] For reasons that I will establish below, I consider it unlikely that Manzana was a member of the Regional Defence Committee on 4 May.

Whether or not this committee had called the meeting on 4 May, there the "governmental point of view" was far from dominant, and several delegates raised possibilities that went beyond the resignation of those responsible, which was considered a minimum requirement for the cessation of hostilities by the delegates of the unions and the representative of the defence committees. Other delegates stressed their opposition to negotiations with the Generalitat. The delegate from Gerona declared that

> it is useless to hold joint rallies: we are like the spider and the fly. We have to go all out [to finish with] the Government. If we allow our

89   García Oliver, *El eco de los pasos*, 421.

90   See "Suñer Vidal, Matias' (2016), http://militants-anarchistes.info/spip.php?article 13135 [accessed 1 December 2017].

91   "Entrevista amb Joan 'Remi,'" 130.

92   See Agustín Guillamón, "Justo Bueno (1907–1944)" (2014), http://grupgerminal.org/ ?q=system/files/JustoBueno-1907-1944-Guillamon.pdf [accessed 1 December 2017]. Ruano had been sentenced to death by a meeting of the CNT-affiliated Metalworkers' Union on 27 January 1937, for crimes of robbery and murder committed in the Aragonese countryside while temporarily leading the Durruti Column after the death of its founder. His tenure as Durruti's replacement on the Aragón front had also brought accusations of arbitrary shootings and plunder. His eventual murder, carried out on 15 July, appears to have taken place with the common consent of the regional *comités superiores* and even his friend and fellow action group member Justo Bueno. His girlfriend, his brother and his brother's girlfriend were killed alongside him. For further biographical information, see Gimenólogos, *En busca de los Hijos de la Noche*, 557–69.

governmental activity to get in our way we will never be able to operate freely.

The delegate from the Health Workers' Union expressed the conviction that

> we have been too tolerant. The order of the day is to liquidate these provocations, so that nobody dare contradict the organisation. With the facts as they stand we are convinced that if the Government is to for once take a step back then it will be due to fear.[93]

The delegate from the Food Supplies Union found it "paradoxical that we are about to enter talks with those who less than a few hours ago were calling us mutinous and uncontrollable."[94] The meeting ended, as one delegate noted, with two positions in evidence, which although not explicitly stated had to do with whether the CNT would be prepared to head up the mobilisation, with the implication of bringing down the Generalitat, or whether it would continue to negotiate with its governmental partners. While the negotiations continued, the meeting ended with the more radical option hanging in the air.

That same day, *La Batalla*, the daily newspaper of the POUM, called on the working class to form committees for the defence of the revolution.[95] This was to be the closest that the POUM would come to taking the initiative during the events, as the party was understandably unwilling to act independently of the CNT. Representatives of the POUM met with the regional CNT leadership at the beginning of the fighting, on the night of 3 May. Their proposal, to form a joint revolutionary leadership and "destroy the internal enemy," was politely rebuffed.[96] Juan Andrade, of the POUM executive, also made contact with the Regional Committee of the FAI during the events, and towards the end of the fighting urged a coordinated military action that would at least secure a better bargaining position for the revolutionaries, but this was also rejected by the anarchists.[97] Although unlikely to

---

93   "Reunión extraordinaria celebrada el día cuatro de mayo."

94   Ibid.

95   See Weisbord, "Barricades in Barcelona."

96   See Bolloten, *The Spanish Civil War*, 433, from which the reference to destroying the internal enemy is taken (Bolloten is quoting Julián Gorkin, a member of the POUM's executive committee). See also the Wilebaldo Solano file, Col·lecció Ronald Fraser, AHCB, 42–4.

97   Juan Andrade, "La revolución española y el POUM," in *Juan Andrade (1897–1981). Vida y voz de un revolucionario*, ed. by Pelai Pagès, Jaime Pastor and Miguel Romero (Madrid: La Oveja Roja, 2008): 90.

have been decisive, Andrade's decision to approach the Regional Committee of the FAI, as opposed to the more radical Local Federation which was directly involved in the events, was indicative of the distance of the POUM from the internal radicalisation of the anarchist movement in Barcelona.

The mobilisation in defence of the revolution had revealed to the participants the opportunity to deliver a comprehensive blow to the counterrevolution in the city. Clara and Paul Thalmann, stationed behind a barricade at the open-air flower market on La Rambla on the first night of the fighting, recalled that the workers there were convinced that "now the end had arrived for the Stalinists in Cataluña."[98] Moving from the defensive to the offensive had further implications, however: would the victorious revolutionaries impose their programme? The situation in May brought back to the surface the questions the libertarians had debated in July, that of collaborating with the state or "going for everything."[99] "The question of whether or not it was necessary to take power had never been discussed so much in the headquarters of the CNT and the FAI," remembered Severino Campos.[100] By May, however, the experience of what one member of the JJLL described as "forty-eight hours of revolution and ten months of counter-revolution" had given a clearer, if not a definitive, idea of what "going for everything" could mean in the context of civil war and revolution: socialisation of industry and distribution, unity based on loyalty to the revolution, and the people armed.[101] It was clear that these ends could not be attained while the government was left standing.

A labyrinth of barricades now divided the "governmental point of view" of the National Committee of the CNT from that of the activists of Barcelona. Appealing over the radio for calm on 4 May, García Oliver, who had arrived in Barcelona on a peace-making mission, declared that "even if I had a rifle or a bomb in my hand, I would not know against whom to fire, because all those fighting are my brothers."[102] This speech was so far removed from what the young militants who idolised him expected to hear that rumours proliferated that the Minister of Justice had been taken hostage and forced to make the speech under duress.[103] As far as the *comités superiores* were concerned,

---

98   Thalmann, "La sublevación en Cataluña," 114.

99   This is discussed in Helmut Rüdiger, *Ensayo crítico sobre la revolución española* (Buenos Aires: Imán, 1940), 23; Paz, *Viaje al pasado*, 143; and García Oliver, *El eco de los pasos*, 429.

100   Guillamón, *Insurrección*, 495.

101   *Ideas*, 20 May 1937. The quote is from an article by Francisco Pérez, a member of the JJLL in Tamarite (Aragón).

102   García Oliver, *El eco de los pasos*, 426.

103   See Peirats, *The CNT Vol. 2*, 123–4. For the disbelieving and indignant reactions to the speeches over the radio of the CNT and the FAI representatives, see Fraser, *Blood of Spain*, 379 and 382; the "García" file, Col·lecció Ronald Fraser, AHCB, 19; Bonomini, "Semana sangrienta" in *Barcelona, mayo 1937*, 153.

however, the combatants had allowed themselves to be provoked by their adversaries and, incorrectly believing themselves to be defending the CNT, were in fact risking a military disaster for which the organisation would be blamed.[104] This stance put the exhortations to workers to resist disarmament of a few days earlier into perspective, and, whether or not such slogans were merely hot air, the incompatibility of maintaining a position of even nominal resistance to state reconstruction while participating in that same process was brutally exposed by the events of May. Any contemporary hopes that these same committees would lead the libertarian movement in an offensive against the counterrevolution were thus to be disappointed.

On 4 May, the Regional Defence Committee drew up its plans for the military defeat of the forces of the state in Barcelona. The Italian anarchist Ernesto Bonomini, then sharing a house in the city with Camillo Berneri, reported that, at the end of the second day of fighting, the defence committees decided to mount a final assault on the enemy positions, whereupon "the comrades in the castle at Montjuïc immediately put themselves at the orders of the Committee, and at the agreed hour were prepared to bombard the Generalitat, the police station and the Hotel Colón [Headquarters of the PSUC Central Committee]."[105] The defence committees in the suburbs were told to ready themselves to march on the centre of the city and occupy centres of government and the premises of the PSUC.[106] In Gràcia, on the initiative of the neighbourhood defence committee, an agreement for coordinated action was established between the POUM, the CNT defence committees, the JJLL, the JCI and the DAS.[107] According to Joan "Remi," this plan

> did not come from the Regional Committee or the Local Federation but from the Regional Committee of defence groups [the Regional Defence Committee]... which had nothing to do with the Regional Committee of the [CNT]... The defence groups were something separate, and they'd reached the limit of their patience.[108]

By the following morning, the delegate of the Regional Defence Committee present at a meeting of representatives of the Catalan libertarian movement

104   See the official report compiled by the National Committee in the aftermath of the events and published as an appendix in Brademas, *Anarcosindicalismo y revolución*, 255–63; also García Oliver, *El eco de los pasos*, 420.

105   See Ernesto Bonomini, "Semana sangrienta," 151.

106   Ibid. for the general outline of the plan. On the column organised in Sants, see "Entrevista amb Joan 'Remi,'" 98; and for Gràcia, the Wilebaldo Solano file, Col·lecció Ronald Fraser, AHCB, 48–9.

107   See the Wilebaldo Solano file, Col·lecció Ronald Fraser, AHCB, 54.

108   "Entrevista amb Joan 'Remi,'" 103.

was evidently under pressure from those behind the barricades to sanction a plan of attack: "We can't put up with any more. We will be in serious danger if we don't act quickly. We can't hold back the neighbourhoods any longer, they want an all-out attack and nothing else."[109]

It may well have been Merino who made the suggestion at this meeting that a "Council of Defence" be formed. While the possibility that this delegate was suggesting the formation of an alternative authority to that of the Generalitat is seductive, it is impossible to verify. The word used is "Consejo," evoking the Defence Council of Aragón, which Merino was involved in founding. Nevertheless, it is also plausible that what was being suggested was the broadening of the existing Regional Defence Committee, which is what in fact took place. Nor is it clear who was speaking, as the delegate appears in the minutes as "F.L.," which could stand for the Local Federation of Affinity Groups (Merino), or the Local Federation of Unions. Also discussed was the resolution brought by Gregorio Jover, a veteran *cenetista* and former member of the Nosotros affinity group, who was at that point lieutenant colonel of a division on the Aragón front, back in Barcelona briefly on account of the unfolding crisis. Those in his division had voted to march on Barcelona in support of the mobilisation. In a further example of how democratic procedure at the front was trumped by bureaucratic procedures in the rear, this possibility was rejected by the delegates at the meeting.[110]

The meeting, which according to Campos's account had been called hastily and was attended by those it was possible to round up at short notice, ended with the significant decision to nominate a Defence Committee, to "augment the existing local body."[111] The new members selected were José Manzana and José Xena, to be aided by the CNT Councillor for Defence in the Generalitat, Francisco Isgleas, and, while he remained in Barcelona, Gregorio Jover. This corroborates the account given by Suñer Vidal, of a central defence committee containing Merino, Ruano and Manzana, but suggests that Manzana had not been a member until after this meeting. Following the failure of the *comités superiores'* radio appeals to make an impact on the combatants, the broadening of the Regional Defence Committee suggests an attempt by the regional *comités superiores* to co-opt it, in tacit recognition that it was its authority, not that of the *comités superiores*, that was respected on the barricades. As Joan "Remi," put it, "on 5 May we stayed put,

---

109   "Reunión extraordinaria celebrada por el Comité Regional de Cataluña con asistencia de casi todos los compañeros más responsables de la organización," CNT (España) Archives (IISG) 85 C.

110   Ibid.

111   Ibid. Campos's recollections are cited in Guillamón, *Insurrección*, 494.

right? ... Because for us, regardless of what García Oliver or whoever else might say, it was only for the defence committees to give the order that it was over."[112] Although this manoeuvre is not alluded to in the historiography, it would seem likely that these heavyweight additions to the defence committee hierarchy played a significant role in the subsequent demobilisation of the rising.[113] The meeting ended with the agreement that the new committee was to be granted "WIDE POWERS TO ACT AS REQUIRED."[114]

Meanwhile, perhaps as a consequence of the plans of the defence committees to move on to the offensive, members of the AAD saw an opportunity to advance their programme. Delegates from the *Agrupación* had already met with representatives of the POUM executive committee on 4 May, agreeing that the best that could be hoped for from events was an orderly withdrawal following the abandonment of the barricades by the governmental forces and assurances that no repression would be visited upon the combatants.[115] On 5 May, however, members of the grouping drew up and distributed a leaflet behind the revolutionary barricades, urging the combatants to remain at their posts. It demanded the execution of those responsible for the provocation, the socialisation of industry and the replacement of the Generalitat with a revolutionary Junta in which the POUM, having fought alongside the revolutionaries, would be represented.[116] The leaflet was later disowned in the strongest terms by the Regional Committee of the CNT, which described its content as "absolutely intolerable." Furthermore, as the Councillors of the Generalitat had collectively resigned and been replaced by a temporary "unity" government of the anti-fascist forces that day, "everyone must accept its decisions given that we are all represented within it."[117] The leaflet of the AAD was only distributed with great difficulty. Balius would later state that some people lost their lives while distributing it, while the manner in which it was received by the combatants evidently varied from the enthusiastic to the hostile.[118] The

112   "Entrevista amb Joan 'Remi,'" 130.

113   The meeting is referred to in Guillamón's recent work. However, he considers this augmented defence committee to have been tasked only with the defence of the "Casa CNT-FAI" building: Guillamón, *Insurrección*, 226.

114   "Reunión extraordinaria celebrada por el Comité Regional de Cataluña con asistencia de casi todos los compañeros más responsables de la organización." Capitalisation of words as they appear in the minutes.

115   See Guillamón, *Los Amigos de Durruti*, 70.

116   See AGRUPACIÓN "AMIGOS DE DURRUTI," "Trabajadores," PDLR, Fons DH, DH 6 (1), 4- Amigos de Durruti (CNT-FAI). The leaflet is reproduced in Guillamón, *Los Amigos de Durruti*, 78.

117   See the report attached to a FAI communiqué dated 1 June 1937, "FAI Comité Peninsular Secretariado. Circular 28–1937," CNT (España) Archives (IISG), 49 A. See also *La Noche*, 6 May 1937.

118   See the letter of Jaime Balius to Burnett Bolloten, 24 June 1946, reproduced in Guillamón, *Los Amigos de Durruti*, 155.

newspaper of the *Agrupación*, *El Amigo del Pueblo*, would later claim (with sexist bias) that the leaflet was received "with jubilation" by "the men of the barricades."[119] By contrast, Clara and Paul Thalmann, who helped distribute the leaflet, recalled: "Everywhere we were received with distrust... In many places we came across a brusque refusal, they rejected us."[120]

The AAD was not the appropriate formation to take on a vanguard role at this time, and it was probably not the intention of its chief animators that it should do so, in spite of the hopes of the international, heterodox leftist milieu that had gravitated towards it.[121] The question at issue was whether the revolutionaries of the defence committees would be able to follow through with their plans, not only in flagrant opposition to the desires of the *comités superiores*, three of whose chief representatives, Rodríguez Vázquez, García Oliver and Montseny, were now in Barcelona, despatched from Valencia by Largo Caballero to call for calm, but also in spite of the new additions to the Regional Defence Committee. Time was of the essence. While Eduardo Pons Prades remembered that nobody among the libertarians doubted that "in the end we would make ourselves the masters of Barcelona," the reality was that hunger and fatigue would come into play the longer a state of watchful deadlock was maintained.[122] As much had been predicted on 4 May by "Aurelio" (probably Aurelio Fernández in spite of it being unusual to have delegates identified by their first names in the minutes of meetings):

This is going to end in chaos, through fatigue. They'll go at it today, tomorrow as well, but in a few days tiredness will conquer everyone, if not the lack of ammunition. The movement must be directed: does that suit the CNT or not?[123]

The following day it was reported that the CNT activists in the *Telefónica* building had not eaten since the events began.[124]

On 5 May, the anarchist emissaries of the Republican government in Valencia were locked in negotiations with the Generalitat.[125] Pressured

119   See *El Amigo del Pueblo*, 12 June 1937.
120   See Thalmann, "La sublevación en Cataluña," 116.
121   Aside from the Thalmanns, this milieu also included Moulin, the pseudonym of Hans David Freund, who assumed leadership of the Trotskyists in Spain during the May days and had maintained some contact with the AAD.
122   Eduardo Pons Prades file, Col·lecció Ronald Fraser, AHCB, 77.
123   "Reunión extraordinaria celebrada el día cuatro de mayo."
124   "Reunión extraordinaria celebrada por el Comité Regional de Cataluña con asistencia de casi todos los compañeros más responsables de la organización."
125   See the National Committee report in Brademas, *Anarcosindicalismo y revolución*, 258; and Santillán, *Por qué perdimos la Guerra*, 167.

by the *comités superiores* to await their outcome, the Regional Defence Committee held back the improvised columns preparing to march on the centre from the suburbs.[126] The members of these columns belonging to the POUM were advised by Nin of the impossibility of proceeding without the cooperation of the CNT.[127] Similarly, the attack that party activists stationed at the POUM headquarters had planned on the nearby Café Moka, which had been occupied by Assault Guards, failed to materialise.[128] Meanwhile, the commander of the Tierra y Libertad Column, stationed at the Espartaco barracks alongside a number of Italian anarchists, was ordered by the Regional Committee of the CNT not to proceed with its planned assault on the PSUC-dominated Carlos Marx barracks.[129]

In an effort to break the deadlock, the JJLL in Gràcia launched an extraordinary appeal, addressed "to the authentic revolutionaries":

The continuous provocation brought about by the politicians and the armed police bodies has had as its consequence a new rising of the workers affiliated to the CNT, FAI, JJLL and POUM… It would be a vile joke to play on the comrades who have fallen in the bloody struggles against these animals if we were to accept a new trap laid by the politicians, when it is us workers with arms in hand who must have the final word. If the comrades sealed off in our committees do not have sufficient energy to push on ahead, we must relieve them and delegate a Revolutionary Committee capable of doing so. Comrades, it's now or never! Let's do away with the armed police bodies that offer no guarantees as to the revolutionary future. Let's do away with the political parties that attempt to inoculate our cause with their poison. Let us not wait another moment. While some remain on the barricades defending the revolution with arms, others must proceed rapidly to the socialisation of wealth and the means of production. We won't accept ambiguities. Either we get rid of the armed police, politicians and other enemies of the working class or they will get rid of us… Let us learn from what we've lived through and not leave a single institution standing that represents the hateful past. Revolutionaries! Forward with the social revolution above everyone and everything else![130]

126   "Entrevista amb Joan 'Remi,'" 130.
127   See the manifesto written by Andreu Nin in the aftermath of the events and distributed around the working-class districts of Barcelona, in Nin, *La revolución Española*, 336.
128   Orwell, *Orwell in Spain*, 117.
129   See Aguzzi, "Un anarquista italiano," 160.
130   "Las Juventudes Libertarias de Gracia a los auténticos Revolucionarios," Fons ANC1–1/Generalitat de Catalunya (Segona República).

As with the leaflet produced by the AAD, this proclamation from the JJLL in Gràcia is notable for its acknowledgement of revolutionary solidarity with the POUM and its recognition of the mobilisation as an opportunity to implement the radical programme and rectify the half measures of July that had left standing the institutions of "the hateful past." It is also notable for its derision of the *comités superiores*, "sealed off" from events. However, while the solution of these "authentic revolutionaries" was to replace these committees, to do so they required, at the very least, the backing of the defence committees that had initiated the rising.

At that point, those behind the barricades were anxiously awaiting word from what Joan "Remi" intriguingly refers to as the "*comités superiores de defensa*" – that is to say, the committees that coordinated the defence committees at a local and regional level.[131] "Remi" explains his use of the plural by stating that there existed "the Regional Defence Committee and the Local Federation of defence groups"; it is quite possible that the former refers to the new appointees nominated on 5 May and the latter to the committee containing Merino and Ruano. In any case, those coordinating the rising were under a great deal of pressure, and had no doubt been made aware by the new members nominated by the *comités superiores* that any autonomous initiative would be disowned by the organisation. As Wilebaldo Solano affirmed with regard to the defence committees and their relationship to the *comités superiores*:

> It is highly difficult that this kind of position... crystallises and affirms itself. There is discontent. There is unease. There is even opposition... But from that to a clear rupture... there is a big difference... What is more is the question of pride in the organisation. They were capable of criticising the organisation, of criticising their leaders. But the moment arrived at which the criticism halted. The definitive step was not taken.[132]

Josep Rebull, a local member of the POUM, would state that the failure of the revolutionaries to take the Generalitat by force could only be explained by such "psychological factors."[133] Neither of these activists of the POUM

---

131   "Entrevista amb Joan 'Remi,'" 130.

132   See the Wilebaldo Solano file, Col·lecció Ronald Fraser, AHCB, 127.

133   Rebull, "Las Jornadas de mayo." Rebull, isolated on the extreme left of the POUM, attempted during the May days to persuade the executive committee of his party to undertake an independent military initiative to secure a better bargaining position for the revolutionaries. This attempt came to naught. See Agustín Guillamón, "Josep Rebull de 1937 a 1939: la crítica interna a la política del CE del POUM durante la Guerra de España," *Balance. Cuadernos de historia del movimiento obrero*, 19 and 20 (2000).

would have been aware, however, of the more salient fact that the body co-ordinating the defence committees in Barcelona had been compromised by a bureaucratic manoeuvre at the meeting of 5 May. Of the four new Regional Defence Committee members, Isgleas was a Councillor in the Generalitat and Manzana a front-line officer who had overseen the militarisation of the Durruti Column. While the position of Xena and Jover was more ambigu-ous, it is probable that by the afternoon of 5 May, Merino and Ruano (and any other initial members of the committee) were not acting with a free hand, regardless of whether they were assailed by doubts or not. To judge by his subsequent behaviour, discussed in the following chapters, it would seem that Merino was untroubled by such "psychological factors," although he would later admit to bitterness as to the lack of courage shown by his comrades.[134]

The orders of the defence committees to hold back were not uniformly accepted throughout the revolutionary ranks and arguments reportedly raged in the Espartaco barracks and in the "Casa CNT-FAI" itself.[135] In spite of the combative manifestos put out by the JJLL and the AAD, how-ever, the backing of the defence committees was crucial to the success of the mobilisation, and it is unlikely that any initiative external to those bodies was ever considered. Even the leaflet of the AAD issued on 5 May should not be seen in that light. While the line it expressed was clearly contrary to the pacifying appeals of the *comités superiores*, the AAD did not believe itself capable of carrying out its programme alone, but instead wanted to win support for that programme within the movement in order to influ-ence the policy of the organisations. It was later affirmed, in the by-then underground organ of the *Agrupación*: "We were not going to attempt an isolated action or persevere with conduct that we could not sustain with the resources of the *Agrupación* alone."[136] Juan Andrade, who had contact with members of the AAD, later recalled that "[the AAD] did not want to be any-thing more than an internal opposition within the FAI."[137]

By Thursday 6 May, with the arrival of well-armed Assault Guards from Valencia imminent, the slow abandonment of the barricades had begun. The Catalan flag replaced the black and red flag of the CNT flying over the *Telefónica* building.[138] But the May days did not represent a victory for Catalan nationalists as such, as the effective autonomy enjoyed by the region since July came to an end with the arrival of the Assault Guards and the assumption

134   See the following chapter.
135   See Aguzzi, "Un anarquista italiano," 160, and Rüdiger, *Ensayo crítico sobre la revolución española*, 23.
136   *El Amigo del Pueblo*, 12 June 1937.
137   Andrade, "La revolución española y el POUM," 88.
138   Orwell, *Orwell in Spain*, 121.

of central governmental control over public order.[139] Orwell observed that, in the wake of the May days, the flag of the Spanish Republic became visibly prominent in Barcelona for the first time during the civil war.[140] The anarchists' contestation of the state's monopoly of violence was dealt a severe blow when, on Friday 7 May, it was announced that the *Patrullas de Control* had placed themselves at the orders of the central government. That same day, *Solidaridad Obrera* appeared in a special edition of two pages, declaring the struggle to be over and reproducing appeals for calm and serenity from Mariano Rodríguez Vázquez and Federica Montseny.[141]

Consequences

The bleak prediction of the radicals regarding the consequences of inaction proved correct. While the *comités superiores* of the CNT had done what they could to hold back their members, their opponents had taken advantage of what opportunities they had to strengthen their position.[142] At a meeting of the Regional Committees of the CNT and the FAI on 13 May, Severino Campos, speaking for the latter body, declared: "When we obeyed the cease-fire, they came against us so violently that we suffered many losses."[143] The corpses of twelve members of the Catalan JJLL from the Sant Andreu neighbourhood were dumped in the cemetery at Cerdanyola. They had been tortured to death on 4 May.[144] Important anarchist critics of the Communist Party and its policy had been murdered. The most famous case was that of Camillo Berneri, shot on 5 May along with his comrade and compatriot, Francesco Barbieri. Berneri had published scathing critiques of Soviet Union policy, particularly with regard to its continued commercial relations with Nazi Germany and persecution of anarchists, in the Spanish heterodox leftist review *Orto* as far back as August 1933.[145] He had also

139   See Graham, *The Spanish Republic*, 279–83.
140   Orwell, *Orwell in Spain*, 123.
141   *Solidaridad Obrera*, 7 May 1937. The placing of the *Patrullas* at the service of the government took place on Thursday 6 May, according to the CNT's own report. See Brademas, *Anarcosindicalismo y revolución*, 261.
142   See the report of the National Committee of the CNT in Brademas, *Anarcosindicalismo y revolución*, 261; Paz, *Viaje al pasado*, 163 and 171; Aguzzi, "Un anarquista italiano," 160–1; Santillán, *Por qué perdimos la Guerra*, 166.
143   See "Reunión del Comité Regional de Cataluña, estando presentes todos los Comités responsables, celebrado en el día 13 de Floreal del año 1937," CNT (España) Archives (IISG), 39 A.
144   See Aguilera, *Compañeros y camaradas*, 124–5.
145   See Camillo Berneri, "Moscú y Berlín," in *Orto (1932–1934) revista de documentación social*, ed. by Javier Paniagua (Valencia: Biblioteca Historia Social, 2001), 989–93.

publicly defended the POUM and, in an article completed just before his murder, declared the attacks of the PSUC on the POUM to be "an act of sabotage against the anti-fascist struggle."[146] As his residence was situated next to a PSUC-controlled barricade, once it had been registered and his identity confirmed, his fate was sealed.[147] In an *ex post facto* justification for his death, the PCE's official history of the war would later imply that Berneri had inspired the anarchist mobilisation, shamelessly describing him as the "chief theoretician of the 'putschist' policy."[148]

For women attempting to acquire groceries, whose radicalisation had been a key precursor to the May mobilisation, defeat brought further humiliation. In her eyewitness report on the events, the Glaswegian anti-parliamentary communist Jane Patrick included the following observation from the third day of fighting:

> The Generalitat issue the Ration Cards. Many women came here this morning who had been at the Generalitat to have their cards renewed. Because they were FAI members, the Generalitat refused to renew them. The Government officials said, with a sneer: "Viva la FAI," and when the women replied: "Yes, Viva la FAI!" the officials threw the cards back at them and said "Then get your ration cards from the FAI."[149]

In the aftermath of events, George Orwell observed mounted Assault Guards who were keeping order while queues of women waited to buy olive oil and who "sometimes amused themselves by backing their horses into the queue and trying to make them tread on the women's toes."[150]

On 7 May, the Local Federation of the JJLL met to exchange impressions of what had occurred. Although there was agreement on the need to adopt procedures appropriate to underground activity, there was no such accord as to the import of the events. Diego Camacho remembered: "I had a Bolshevik conception of the revolution. I thought that... having failed to assault the Palace of the Generalitat and put the Stalinists of the PSUC to the sword, we had been defeated."[151] The young libertarian was, however, struck by the optimism of Diego Ruiz Arnau, an anarchist doctor then in his mid-fifties, who considered that the people had "demonstrated

146   Camillo Berneri, "En defensa del POUM," http://2014.kaosenlared.net/component/k2/item/19975-en-defensa-del-poum.html [accessed 12 December 2017].
147   See Guillamón, *Los Comités de Defensa*, 238–40.
148   *Guerra y Revolución en España 1936–1938, Vol. 3*, coord. by Dolores Ibárruri (Moscow: Editorial Progreso, 1971), 20.
149   *The Barcelona Bulletin*, 15 May 1937.
150   Orwell, *Orwell in Spain*, 141.
151   Paz, *Viaje al pasado*, 174.

their resolve to confront the counterrevolution."[152] Eduardo Pons Prades was also optimistic that the revolutionaries' show of strength would alter the course of events.[153] This echoed the attitude that the CNT's Regional Committee had displayed in its meeting with the POUM, that the counterrevolutionaries would be given pause now that the workers had "shown their teeth."[154] At a meeting of the *comités superiores* immediately after the events, discussed below, Josep J. Domènech, the former Supplies Councillor of the Generalitat and then Public Services Councillor, in a comment that reflected the complacency and ingenuity of the leading stratum of the CNT-FAI at this time, affirmed that, with "tact and good sense," the *Telefónica* would soon be returned to the control of the CNT, because the new occupants knew nothing of telephones![155] However, the disappearance on Friday 7 May of Alfredo Martínez, member of the Regional Committee of the JJLL and Secretary of the FJR, was the first sign that the cessation of hostilities would not imply an end to the repression, which was given a particularly grisly aspect by the convergence of a triumphal imposition of "order" on the part of the police and the instructions given to Stalinists worldwide to exterminate "Trotskyists."[156] In this regard it is worth noting that Martínez had been the JJLL member "who had worked hardest in the creation of the FJR," and had spoken at a POUM rally in December.[157]

On the night of 8 May, an enlarged meeting of the Catalan libertarian movement took place in Barcelona.[158] Present were many of the leading figures of the libertarian movement, including Rodríguez Vázquez and Montseny, yet to return to Valencia. Earlier that evening, members of the Barcelona city police had opened fire at a car carrying Montseny, injuring her secretary and another passenger. Even as the meeting took place, police were surrounding the home of Dionisio Eroles, the CNT delegate for public order in the Catalan Government and one of those responsible for the *Patrullas de Control*. Five of Eroles's bodyguards had been taken out of their homes and shot.[159] It was therefore in an atmosphere of high tension that

152   Ibid. 173–4.

153   See the Eduardo Pons Prades file, Col·lecció Ronald Fraser, AHCB, 71.

154   See the Wilebaldo Solano file, Col·lecció Ronald Fraser, AHCB, 42–4.

155   See "Reunión extraordinaria del comité regional de Cataluña con asistencia de la camarada ministra de sanidad, el comité nacional y demás comités y camaradas responsables de la organización. Celebrada el día 8 de Floreal de 1937," CNT (España) Archives (IISG), 39 A.

156   Martínez's disappearance was reported in *Solidaridad Obrera*, 12 May 1937. On Stalin and the campaign against "Trotskyism," particularly with regard to Spain, see Elorza and Bizcarrondo, *Queridos Camaradas*, 333–4 and 345–6.

157   *Solidaridad Obrera*, 15 May 1937.

158   "Reunión extraordinaria del comité regional de Cataluña."

159   See "Conferencia celebrada per 'Hugues' entre el ministre de sanitat i Marian Vázquez

the meeting revealed the fault lines that the events of the previous days had brought to the surface in the Spanish libertarian movement. In that context, the leading figures of the organisations continued in their role as "firefighters," attempting to calm spirits and stressing the need to avoid being provoked by the forces of law and order.[160] This attitude was summed up early on in proceedings by Rodríguez Vázquez, who stated: "All problems have to be resolved one by one, with calmness and serenity, sacrificing part of our ideological concepts for the good of the common cause."[161]

Conflict arose at the meeting over the responsibility of the *comités superiores* for the repression that the newly arrived Assault Guards were unleashing in the Catalan region. The leadership had assured CNT members that the crisis would pass with the removal of the officials responsible for the assault on the *Telefónica* building, yet the area around the French border, until recently recognised as a zone of libertarian influence, had been "invaded," according to the delegate Arenas, with the apparent acquiescence of the *comités superiores*. This delegate was Miguel Arenas Rodríguez from La Seu d'Urgell.[162] A heated argument took place between José Xena and the delegates of the border region.[163] Xena, who had provided the only vote in favour of "going for everything" at the famous Regional Plenum of 21 July 1936 discussed in Chapter Two, had apparently maintained a position of radicalism from that point on. From May, however, we find him continuously demanding internal organisational discipline, part of a wider dynamic by which intermediate cadres whose relationship to state collaboration had been ambiguous increasingly found themselves facing down lower-level activists from the suburbs and provincial towns. His first such test may have been in imposing demobilisation from within the expanded Regional Defence Committee, discussed above.

Further disagreements arose over the question of disarmament and the release of prisoners taken by libertarians during the fighting. On the question of disarmament, José Manzana, another member of the expanded Regional Defence Committee, stated:

amb ministers de justicia i governació amb referencia a la tramesa de forces de seguretat a Catalunya," Fons ANC1-1, Generalitat de Catalunya (Segona República).

160 The apellation "fire-fighters' had been used on the barricades: see "Entrevista amb Joan 'Remi,'" 127.

161 "Reunión extraordinaria del comité regional de Cataluña."

162 Gascón and Guillamón, *Nacionalistas contra anarquistas*, 363 and 445–6. In the first edition of this book, I incorrectly suggested that the delegate was Juan Giménez Arenas, known as the "Quijote of Banat." For a short biography of the latter, see "Juan Giménez Arenas – anarquista conocido como el Quijote de Banat," http://puertoreal.cnt.es/bilbiografias-anarquistas/4337-juan-gimenez-arenas-anarquista-conocido-como-el-quijote-de-banat.html [accessed 1 December 2017].

163 "Reunión extraordinaria del comité regional de Cataluña."

This morning we have spoken to the neighbourhood committees and
these are resisting as far as possible… the voluntary hand-over of weapons. Naturally, if we impose ourselves they will do so, but that would be
unjust given that we have spent twenty years inculcating rebelliousness
and disobedience in the masses and cannot all of a sudden demand that
they be obedient and disciplined… it is not right that a weapon that is
worth a life and the sacrifice of several comrades be handed over like
this.[164]

The delegate for the Defence Section of the CNT explained the reluctance of the neighbourhood defence committees to release their prisoners,
four hundred of whom had in fact been released the previous day by the
defence committee of the Sants neighbourhood, without assurances that
the same magnanimity would be shown the imprisoned comrades of the
CNT.[165] This produced a heated debate with Miguel Barrachina, who had
been a member of the defence committee of Gràcia in July 1936, who insisted on the need to obey the agreements taken by the organisation. To
this the exasperated delegate for the Defence Section declared that "for
the agreements to be obeyed they must be approved beforehand in consultation with the comrades."[166] It was clear, however, that, for the *comités superiores*, further debate was to be avoided, and no further guarantees
from the government or the PSUC were to be sought, still less wrested by
force.

While there can be no doubt that the leading cadres of the CNT
saw the May insurrection as a disaster and a return to normality as desir-
able, their insistence on releasing prisoners with no sign that their enemies would follow suit is hard to explain. The priority of the organisation
was to avoid culpability for a collapse of the anti-fascist front. The order
of the day was to avoid provoking further disharmony, an attitude which
extended to discouraging relatives of those who had been killed in the
fighting from attending their funerals, for fear that they might "mount
some sort of demonstration."[167] This was combined with complacency as
to the power and political will of their rivals, particularly those in the security forces and in the PSUC. Sure that the provocative manoeuvre of May
had "failed," the National Committee of the CNT evidently trusted that

164   Ibid.
165   *Solidaridad Obrera*, 7 May 1937.
166   "Reunion extraordinaria del comité regional."
167   Ibid. See also the advice given to those grieving in *Solidaridad Obrera*, 7 May 1937. The
       approach of the CNT to the deaths of its members during the May fighting presents
       a remarkable contrast with the previous tendency to make martyrs of the fallen. See
       Casanova, *Anarchism*, 150.

the show of strength on the streets would deter their opponents from further provocations.[168]

Relevant in this regard is the discussion of the AAD at the meeting, whose leaflets were described as "weapons launched by the true disturbers of order" to create "discord among those who must always be united." Such intemperate language far exceeded what the *comités superiores* were prepared to use in reference to the agents of state reconstruction, even behind closed doors. Yet more revealing, however, was the admission that the organisation would have to mount a campaign of propaganda to counter the AAD "because the ideas that they express in these leaflets are well received in our ranks."[169] Earlier that day, the AAD had distributed a manifesto that affirmed the revolutionary nature of the May days and which castigated the *comités superiores*: "The treachery is of an enormous scale. The two essential guarantees of the working class, security and defence, are offered on a plate to our enemies."[170] The leaflet went on to affirm that the *Agrupación* remained on a war footing and that its "indomitable spirit" would be maintained.

On 12 May, a plenary meeting of individual union leaderships authorised the Local Federation of unions in Barcelona to track down the leadership of the AAD and to demand an explanation from them for the leaflets printed during and after the May days. The following day, at an enlarged meeting of the Catalan Regional Committee, at which representatives from all branches of the libertarian movement were present, a campaign of slander was begun against Jaime Balius, a leading figure within the AAD and by then something of a veteran of the CNT. Attendees were warned that "we must have the upmost care insofar as [the AAD] is concerned, because it is said that the secretary of the group is an old communist."[171] At a time when it was frequently averred that the AAD was composed of *agents provocateurs*, the subtle insinuation that Balius might still be serving the interests of "communists" was a carefully chosen slur designed to cause the group the maximum possible discredit. Prior to 1931, Balius had been active in the ranks of Catalan nationalism. At the outset of the Republic he briefly passed through the dissident communist Bloc Obrer i Camperol (Workers' and Peasants' Bloc, later to merge with the Izquierda Comunista de España [Spanish Communist Left] to form the POUM), which at the time was still a part of the CNT. His

---

168   See the report in Brademas, *Anarcosindicalismo y revolución*, 261–3.

169   "Reunion extraordinaria del comité regional."

170   See AGRUPACIÓN "AMIGOS DE DURRUTI," "Trabajadores," PDLR, Fons DH, DH 6 (1), 4- Amigos de Durruti (CNT-FAI). The leaflet is reproduced in Guillamón, *Los Amigos de Durruti*, 223–7.

171   See "Reunión del Comité Regional de Cataluña, estando presentes todos los Comités responsables, celebrado en el día 13 de Floreal del año 1937," CNT (España) Archives (IISG), 39 A.

subsequent public repudiation of nationalism and unambiguous adherence to anarchism cannot have been unknown to those who now tried to use traditional anarchist antipathy to Marxism against one of those who had openly advocated an aggressively anti-Stalinist policy within the CNT.

The suggestion that the AAD contained *agents provocateurs* appeared in the CNT's response to the leaflet distributed by the AAD during the May days.[172] *El Amigo del Pueblo*, the mouthpiece of the AAD, appeared for the first time later that month in a heavily censored edition, which attempted to announce the beginning of a battle over the meaning and purpose of the CNT and the FAI with the headline "We are not provocateurs! We are the same as ever! Durruti is our guide! His flag is our flag! No one will take it from us! Long live the FAI! Long live the CNT!"[173] Pressed to provide the Local Federation of unions with a list of the *Agrupación's* members, the AAD instead responded with a letter insisting that their ideas should be debated at assemblies of unions and CNT activists.[174] This, of course, was out of the question. At the end of the month, it was publicly declared that the AAD had been expelled from the CNT.[175]

The second week of May had seen the appearance of Santana Calero's flysheet, *Esfuerzo*, in Barcelona. Aside from the manifesto of the AAD, this was probably the first libertarian publication after the May events to offer an unequivocal defence of the mobilisation, likening the revolution's defenders in Barcelona to those who fought fascism at the front and those who had defeated the mutiny in July.[176] The edition called for the release of the revolutionary prisoners and the "revolutionary defence of the workers against their enemies" and was also noteworthy in maintaining its pre-May attempts to divide the JSU and urging revolutionary unity.[177] This strategy was not limited to Cataluña, as demonstrated by articles highlighting the lack of internal democracy in the JSU and its consequently anti-revolutionary policy in the organ of the CNT in the province of Granada, *Hombres Libres*.[178] This position was, to an extent, echoed in a joint manifesto of the Catalan CNT, FAI

172   See *La Noche*, 6 May 1937.

173   *El Amigo del Pueblo*, 20 May 1937.

174   "FAI Comité Peninsular Secretariado a las Regionales. Circular 28–1937," CNT (España) Archives (IISG), 49 A.

175   *Solidaridad Obrera*, 28 May 1937. Most individual members of the AAD were never successfully expelled from the organisation as the specific union branches to which they belonged, as well as the local organisations of the JJLL, refused to ratify the decision of the *comités superiores*. For further discussion of the AAD in the aftermath of the May events, see Guillamón, *Los Amigos de Durruti*, 79–94; Amorós, *La revolución traicionada*, 242–8 and 251–8.

176   *Esfuerzo*, second week of May, 1937.

177   Ibid.

178   *Hombres Libres*, 7 May 1937.

and JJLL, made public on 11 May. Although lacking the stridency of *Esfuerzo*, this manifesto appealed to workers of the UGT to distance themselves, on the basis of class unity, from counterrevolutionary politicians.[179] This tactic was to recede in all branches of the libertarian movement, however, and was to suffer an immediate blow at the Regional Congress of the JJLL. This fracturing of revolutionary solidarities is discussed further in Chapter Six.

Meanwhile, the governmental crisis ended when Largo Caballero refused to move against the POUM in the absence of any evidence linking them to the initial mobilisation in May. This precipitated the withdrawal of the Communist ministers, who were followed by the rest of the cabinet, with the exception of the CNT ministers, the UGT representative Ángel Galarza and Largo Caballero himself. In the resulting negotiations, Rodríguez Vázquez made it clear on behalf of the CNT that the organisation would not participate in any government over which Largo Caballero did not preside. On 17 May it was officially announced that Juan Negrín would be the new Prime Minister. Negrín was a member of the PSOE who had already come into conflict with the CNT in his role as Finance Minister in the outgoing cabinet.[180] Largo Caballero had been ousted from government, and with him went his allies in the CNT.[181] On 18 May, *Solidaridad Obrera* declared on its front page: "A Counterrevolutionary Government has been formed."[182]

In this context of defeat and repression, the Thalmanns met to exchange impressions with the Trotskyists Erwin Wolf, Moulin and Grandizo Munis, who represented the miniscule Bolshevik-Leninist organisation in Spain (the *Sección Bolchevique-Leninista de España*).[183] While Munis and Wolf, who had not been in Barcelona during the events, were optimistic about the possibilities for a revolutionary advance, Moulin was circumspect. For the Thalmanns, by contrast, no optimism was warranted: "The May uprising,

179   Published in *Ruta*, 14 May 1937.
180   See the recollections in the Joan Manent Pesas file, Col·lecció Ronald Fraser, AHCB, 50.
181   On the government crisis, see the accounts from different perspectives given in Bolloten, *The Spanish Civil War*, 462–73; Graham, *The Spanish Republic*, 299–307; Enrique Moradiellos, *Don Juan Negrín* (Barcelona: Ediciones Península, 2006), 245–9. The latter's interpretation of events is indicated by his loaded description of the CNT's exit from government as "desertion": Moradiellos, *Don Juan Negrín*, 249.
182   *Solidaridad Obrera*, 18 May 1937.
183   The Bolshevik-Leninists were affiliated to Trotsky's Fourth International organisation. Wolf had been Trotsky's secretary in his Norwegian exile. Both he and Moulin would be murdered by Stalinist agents within months. Munis would survive the war, breaking with the Fourth International over its attitude to the Second World War. A lifelong Marxist, he delivered the eulogy at Trotsky's funeral, wrote an influential history of the Spanish revolution, and, after returning clandestinely to Spain during the Barcelona tram strike in 1951, spent five years in Franco's jails.

in which we have participated, was the Spanish Kronstadt," a defeat for the revolution that would prove to be definitive.[184] As the suppression of the Kronstadt revolt has historically been defended by the Trotskyist movement, the Thalmanns' remark left Munis apoplectic. Grinding his teeth, he declared his interlocutors to be "puerile anarchists" and "clowns." Nevertheless, in terms of representing a defeat for working-class participation and control that represented a point of no return on the trajectory of the revolution, the Thalmanns' analogy was to prove both prescient and apposite.[185]

The severity of the situation facing the libertarian movement was beginning to dawn on the *comités superiores*, but in spite of the demands of the delegate of the Regional Defence Committee at a meeting on 19 May for "urgent measures" to be taken, the Regional Committee of the CNT insisted once more that "no strikes or violent action" were to be undertaken under any circumstances.[186] The veteran activist Vicente Pérez Combina approached the heart of the matter when he stated that "we are the masters of the economic situation, but the economy is useless if alongside it we have no arms... Do not think that we will be respected if we are disarmed."[187] As the May days had demonstrated, however, it was one thing to possess arms, another to use them. Before any coordinated approach to the question of arms, and the attendant questions of power and the fate of the revolution could be broached, radicals would have to force a reckoning *within* the ranks of the libertarian organisations.

Conclusions

The May rising in Barcelona was predicated on the prior crystallisation of a vanguard grouping around the neighbourhood defence committees, the JJLL, the MMLL, anarchist refugees, and deserters opposed to militarisation, organised in defence of a radical programme and mandated by a Plenum of the Barcelona FAI to struggle against "the counterrevolution."

184   Kronstadt is a naval base thirty kilometres west of St Petersburg, whose name has become synonymous with the uprising which took place there in 1921 in the name of soviet democracy, and which was bloodily suppressed by the Bolsheviks, with the personal approval of Lenin and Trotsky. In an article written during his French exile in 1971, Balius would also affirm that "May 1937 is the Spanish Kronstadt." See Guillamón, *Los Amigos de Durruti*, 65. The comparison is also made in Richards, *Lessons of the Spanish Revolution*, 186.

185   For the account of this meeting, see Thalmann, "La sublevación en Cataluña," 119–20.

186   "Reunión celebrada el día 19 de mayo de 1937, estando presentes los comités: Regional de Cataluña – JJLL-FAI-FL- y DR – Presidentes de sindicatos y cargos representativos," CNT (España) Archives (IISG), 95 B.

187   Ibid.

Following this Plenum, a Regional Defence Committee was set up by Julián Merino. The mobilisation this Committee effected in response to the police assault on the *Telefónica* building was so successful that it briefly appeared likely that the "error" of July that oppositional anarchists had identified would be rectified, and the seat of Catalan government, left standing during the short summer of anarchy, would be toppled in this springtime of the radicals. Nevertheless, the rising failed. The radical programme was not carried through to its ultimate conclusion. Worse for the components of the revolutionary alliance, by showing the limits of the hand they could yet play, they not only failed to mount a thoroughgoing offensive against their adversaries, but also left themselves open to further repression by the state.

It was not ideological scruples that had prevented the military victory of the revolutionaries, but acquiescence to the assertion of organisational hierarchies within the libertarian movement. The hypothesis presented here is that the radical anarchists rose on account of the mandate granted by the Barcelona FAI to undertake armed resistance to the "counter-revolution." In that sense, we can only appreciate why both the mobilisation and the demobilisation occurred through an understanding of the participants as committed members of organisations whose internal mechanisms they respected. Whether the radicals would have been as prepared to accept the decision to demobilise had they known that the *comités superiores* of the movement had, behind closed doors, altered the composition of the Regional Defence Committee, is highly questionable. Nevertheless, the addition of four prominent CNT members to this Committee at the regional meeting of 5 May is a significant discovery that enhances our understanding of how this demobilisation was enacted.

Hitherto, explanations for the demobilisation have tended to depend on appeals to the "psychological factors" discussed above. Without wishing to dismiss their importance, such explanations fail to overcome the logical inconsistency in this argument: that it was the defence committees who ordered both the mobilisation and the demobilisation. Can the abrupt change of tack from planning an all-out assault one day to ordering a demobilisation the next be explained by doubt and organisational loyalty? Perhaps, but it ought to be remembered that the coordinators of the initial mobilisation were respectful of the organisational norms of the libertarian organisation and believed the action to have been mandated by constitutional means.

Alternative explanations – such as that of Helen Graham, that García Oliver and the *comités superiores* of the libertarian movement "saw the bigger picture: not only... in terms of the overriding imperatives of the war... but also in terms of the overall balance of firepower *within Republican Spain*," and that of Guillamón, that the rising was defeated "by the radio broadcasts of the *comités superiores*' – fail to account for the fact that the plan of attack drawn up by the defence committees on 4 May remained on the table after García Oliver's arrival and widely derided appeal.[188] Even allowing for the existence of important "psychological factors" and residual respect for the increasingly "sealed off" *comités superiores*, it seems likely that the decision on 5 May to alter the composition of the Regional Defence Committee was decisive in tipping the balance. Merino and others coordinating the rising may have found themselves outnumbered, their recommendations contradicted, by the new additions with one foot in the Regional Defence Committee and one in the *comités superiores*. It is possible that this was not a conscious manoeuvre on the part of the regional *comités superiores*, but it would not need to have been in order to have an impact, and it follows an established pattern of ad hoc, bureaucratic resolutions taken behind closed doors undermining the initiative and resolve of those on the street. On the other hand, if it was a conscious manoeuvre, then it was a logical one: the *comités superiores* recognised the limitations of their own influence over those on the barricades and took appropriate measures to instead change the composition of the Regional Defence Committee, whose authority certainly was still respected by the broader activist base, as is confirmed by the testimonies of Joan "Remi" and Matías Suñer Vidal.

The May days had demonstrated that the architects and promoters of the radical programme in Barcelona were far from isolated from the wider membership of the libertarian movement, and remained capable of mobilising broader community support. The participation of the CNT in government, and the maturation of anti-fascism as an emerging dominant ideology in Republican Spain, had not precluded the continued success of the anarchists' anti-state project in Barcelona. When García Oliver entered the Casa CNT-FAI and caught sight of Merino occupying a telephone booth, animatedly making and taking one call after another, it was clear that both the governmental and radical wings of Spanish anarchism continued to stake a claim to the authority and resources of the libertarian movement. Following these events, it became evident to the *comités superiores* that such coexistence was no longer possible.

May was the point at which the ambiguous nature of the CNT's position was resolved definitively in favour of state reconstruction, even though the events precipitated the organisation's exit from government. The mobilisation, which was partly coordinated from underneath the noses of the *comités*

188   Helen Graham, "'Against the State': A Genealogy of the Barcelona May Days (1937)," *European History Quarterly*, 29, 4 (1999) 485–542 (521); Guillamón, *Insurrección*, 343.

superiores inside the Casa CNT-FAI, also revealed to this leadership stratum that a tightening of internal discipline was required. In this process, formerly voluntarist anarchists would be relied upon as enforcers, in particular García Oliver, but also, as the regional meeting of 8 May revealed, those whose position as regards state reconstruction had hitherto been ambiguous, such as Xena and Eroles. For the anti-statist radicals, by contrast, the success of the mobilisation vindicated the radical programme and convinced several voluntarists, not least Merino, of the capacity of the radicals to take on and defeat the state. In spite of the fact that they had ended in defeat, therefore, the radical perspective following the May events would be reaffirmed through a renewed effort to break with state collaboration, backed up with the threat of a return to the streets. While the context of increasing pressure from without and increasing polarisation within the libertarian movement presented new and difficult challenges to the radicals, the truly definitive nature of the defeat that May represented would only become clear after several more months of anarchist struggle against the state.

CHAPTER FIVE

The Spanish Revolution in Retreat, May–December 1937

After the events of May 1937, the space in which the oppositional currents of Spanish anarchism could operate was greatly circumscribed by a combination of violent police and military repression, the increasingly bureaucratised and hierarchical nature of the libertarian movement, and the extension of the draft in the Republican rear. Ever greater numbers of activists were absorbed by a war whose course gave little cause for optimism: Bilbao fell in June, Santander in August and Asturias in October. Meanwhile, in the rear, thousands of anarchists and POUM militants were jailed, above all in Cataluña. Between May 1937 and the end of summer 1938 around 4,000 anti-fascists were imprisoned for varying lengths of time in Cataluña alone, the majority of whom were members of the CNT.[1] George Orwell reported in articles for the *New English Weekly* in July and September 1937:

> When I left Barcelona in late June the jails were bulging; indeed, the regular jails had long since overflowed and the prisoners were being huddled into empty shops and any other temporary dump that could be found for them. But the point to notice is that the people who are in prison now are not Fascists but revolutionaries; they are there not because their opinions are too much to the Right, but because they are too much to the Left.[2]

Local centres of the JJLL, the neighbourhood defence committees and those frequented by foreign revolutionaries were subject to police raids, registers and closure. The targets of such actions were thus those same centres through which the anarchist vanguard had renewed itself after July 1936,

1   See the database of names compiled by François Godicheau, "Los Hechos de Mayo de 1937 y los 'presos antifascistas': identificación de un fenómeno represivo," *Historia Social*, 3, 44 (2002), 39–63. The *comités superiores* tended to play down the quantity of CNT members in prison, but José Xena admitted at the Extraordinary Congress of the IWMA in December that "one and a half thousand" were in jail as he spoke. See "Actas del Congreso de la AIT celebrado en París," PDLR, Fons SA 5/5 (2).
2   Orwell, *Orwell in Spain*, 216.

143

and via which the libertarian mobilisation in May had been effected. Outside of Barcelona, in the Catalan provinces, anarchists complained of "reigns of terror" being installed in areas formerly dominated by the CNT.[3] In August, the Regional Defence Council of Aragón was dissolved by government decree, whereupon troops of the 11th Division of the Popular Army under the Communist Enrique Lister broke up the region's collectives and arrested hundreds of libertarians.[4]

Nevertheless, in Barcelona, where members of the defence committees were aware of how close they had come to gaining a victory over their opponents, the May events had not been accepted as a definitive defeat by the activists who had initiated them. In fact, we might surmise from the combative nature of the threats and statements issued over the months that followed that they remained confident of their capacity to mobilise their forces. An editorial in *Ideas* gave an indication of persistent voluntarism among Catalan anarchists:

> Workers! You have the opportunity to be free. For the first time in social history the arms are in our hands; do not release them... Always remember that it is planes, cannon and tanks that the fronts need to quickly overcome fascism... what all the politicians want is to disarm the workers... and take from them everything they have conquered at the cost of so much blood, of so many proletarian lives... Disarm those who want to disarm you.[5]

Within the Barcelona FAI, the exit of the libertarian movement from spheres of government was considered to be an opportunity to employ extra-legal measures in defence of the revolution, while armed insurrection continued to be invoked as a viable option at Plenums as summer turned to autumn. Meanwhile, resentment at the pacifying role of the *comités superiores* in May continued to fester. "Am I to consider counterrevolutionaries to be my brothers?" wondered the Argentinian painter Gustavo Cochet – some of

3   This expression was used in a CNT report of 25 June in relation to Puigcerdà. See CDMH, PS Barcelona, 842/4, which contains similarly disturbing accounts from Amposta, Tortosa and Torelló.

4   Lister himself claimed that somewhere in the region of 120 libertarians were arrested. See Enrique Lister, *Nuestra Guerra. Aportaciones para una Historia de la Guerra Nacional Revolucionaria del Pueblo Español 1936–1939* (Paris: Colección Ebro, 1966), 155. In fact, the figure was probably initially 475; see Casanova, *Anarquismo y Revolución*, 273. On the dissolution of the Defence Council of Aragón, see ibid. 264–97; Bolloten, *The Spanish Civil War*, 525–31; Díez Torre, *Trabajan para la eternidad*, 216–20; Walther L. Bernecker, *Colectividades y revolución social. El anarquismo en la guerra civil Española, 1936–1939*, trans. by Gustau Muñoz (Barcelona: Crítica, 1982), 427–30.

5   *Ideas*, 20 May 1937.

whose engravings depicting revolutionary Barcelona have been reproduced in this book – in a contribution to *Ideas*, indicative of the bitterness that the demobilisation had generated:

> "Cease-fire!" was the cry... Very well, but what conditions were established for the cease-fire to take place? We were not defeated and we could have won, we had force and reason on our side, we had courage and the consciousness of a revolutionary duty. I repeat: what conditions were demanded?[6]

These factors, added to the apparent return to bourgeois normality in the Republican rearguard, embodied in the privileges of a minority at a time of generalised scarcity and the release of rightists and clergy from Republican jails, fuelled a continuous critique of the *comités superiores* that would persist into 1938.[7]

What remained at issue was the ongoing commitment to anti-fascist collaboration that had served to undermine the mobilisation in May. Considering this policy to have been responsible for the abandonment of the barricades, the radicals' strategy over the summer of 1937 was to attempt to force the libertarian organisations to change course. The radical majority in the Local Federation of Anarchist Affinity Groups (the Barcelona FAI) under its strategically minded Secretary, Julián Merino, attempted to have its anti-collaboration positions adopted at the Regional level.[8] Such a withdrawal from state collaboration could only be countenanced if serious consideration was given to the question of whether to continue collaborating in the anti-fascist war effort, and on what terms, and whether to forcibly confront the authorities of the Republican state, regardless of the impact this might have on the same. As this chapter will discuss, the radicals did not shirk from confronting these questions but were nevertheless incapable of forcing through the change of direction they considered necessary. Wary of being ejected from their posts, the *comités superiores* attempted to introduce structural changes to the FAI that would undermine the authority of the radical Local Federations. Consequently, the radicals would be exhausted by having to simultaneously defend themselves from police

6   Ibid.
7   Complaints about the release of fascist prisoners from their detention on Calle Santaló were aired at regional meetings of the CNT. See "Reunión del Comité Regional celebrada el día 8 de Julio de 1937," CNT (España) Archives (IISG) 39 A.
8   The debates within the Catalan FAI in this period have been referred to by historians but have not been discussed in as much detail as below. See Godicheau, *La Guerre D'Espagne*, 332–5; Amorós, *La Revolución Traicionada*, 315–9 and 324–6. A recent exception to this rule is Guillamón, *La represión contra la CNT*, especially 198–231.

operations and offer solidarity to prisoners, while fighting an internecine battle with those they called the "neo-anarchists" over the functioning and purpose of the FAI.

Militarism, nationalism and the "war that is not for true freedom"

In an article intended to admonish anarchist activists for their faulty priorities, *Amanecer*, the strongly pro-collaboration review of the CNT's Catalan School for Activists, reported on a rally held on 4 June 1937 in the Olympia theatre in Barcelona to pay homage to the defenders of Madrid and the Basque country. There, a delegate speaker who had arrived from the Spanish capital asked the assembled throng: "'Do you want to win the war?' and the crowd, one hundred per cent revolutionary, barely answered the question. One person shouted out 'What we want is to win the revolution!'"[9] Enthusiasm for the war was on the wane among anarchists. Previously, the social content of the war had been emphasised by the radicals, in opposition to the characterisation of the conflict as a war of national liberation fought in defence of democracy. The FAI veteran José Alberola had articulated the radical perspective in a speech given in March 1937: "It is said that we must renounce our ideas in order to win the war. If what they call war was nothing more than that we would have to be deserters. But it is principally a social conflict."[10] By the summer of 1937 there were ample signs that this perspective could no longer be sustained, not least because of the participation of sectors of the anarchist movement in the recasting of this "social war" as one of national independence.

Anarchists in Spain and abroad linked the "error of participation" in government to a concomitant degeneration in the ideology professed by prominent activists. An article in *Terre Libre*, the mouthpiece of the Francophone Anarchist Federation, averred that some could no longer claim to be anarchists because "they promote *l'union sacrée*, patriotism, nationalism and so on."[11] As we have seen, however, anarchist collaboration in the reconstruction of the Republican state drew on pre-existing ambiguities within the movement that were identifiable not only in its gradualist, but also its purist and voluntarist sectors. There were thus parallels

9   *Amanecer. Órgano de la Escuela de Militantes de Cataluña*, May–June 1937.
10   Alberola, *Interpretación anarquista de la revolución*, 13.
11   *Terre Libre*, May 1937. The article was almost certainly authored by Voline (pseudonym of Vsevolod Mikhailovich Eikhenbaum), who had been instrumental in setting up the first soviet of St Petersburg in 1905 and who had later fought in Nestor Makhno's anarchist army of the Ukraine during the Russian civil war, before being expelled from the Soviet Union in 1921.

between the rhetoric of Montseny in 1931 and 1936, when the Republic was defended as the "progressive" and more "civilised" alternative facing the Spanish working class. Nevertheless, it is evident that war and state collaboration served to accelerate the process by which concepts of nationhood and an intermingling of the categories of "people" and "proletariat" became prevalent in Spanish anarchist discourse.[12]

Relevant in this regard is the presence on the editorial board of *Solidaridad Obrera* of Salvador Cánovas Cervantes, a proponent of a "racial" understanding of Spanish anarchism who had been ejected from the CNT after standing for election during the Second Republic.[13] A particularly egregious example of this trend was provided by an editorial in *Solidaridad Obrera* on 26 May 1937, the front page headline of which read: "Our revolution must be Spanish!"[14] Although a thinly veiled attack on Soviet intervention in Spain, the nationalist rhetoric employed in this article stressed the "Iberian, independent and national" character of the Spanish proletariat, "unconnected to any foreign influence," and opposed the "purely Spanish, purely Iberian, purely peninsular" position of the CNT and the FAI to those of the "parties of exotic origin" in Spain, a position "which can be summarised in the phrase: *Spain for the Spanish.*"[15] Such positions were characterised as "national anarchism" by Alexander Schapiro, an anarcho-syndicalist veteran of the Russian revolution, writing in *Le Combat Syndicaliste*: "To eulogise racism and disparage 'exoticism' are two simultaneous and complementary phenomena that indicate, to say the least, an anti-revolutionary state of mind."[16]

Traditionally, such anarchist antipathy towards nationalism had gone hand in hand with anti-militarism, a commitment that was also tested in this period.[17] Illustrative of this antipathy was a leaflet authored by Liberto

12   See Angel Smith, "Los anarquistas y anarcosindicalistas ante la cuestión nacional," in *Izquierdas y nacionalismos en la España contemporánea*, ed. by Javier Moreno Luzón (Madrid: Editorial Pablo Iglesias, 2011), 145–6.

13   See Xosé M. Núñez Seixas, *¡Fuera el invasor! Nacionalismos y movilización bélica durante la Guerra civil Española (1936–1939)* (Madrid: Marcial Pons, 2006), 71–2; Martin Baxmeyer, "'Mother Spain, We Love You'!: Nationalism and Racism in Anarchist Literature during the Spanish Civil War (1936–1939)," in *Reassessing the Transnational Turn: Scales of Analysis in Anarchist and Syndicalist Studies*, ed. by Constance Bantman and Bert Altena (New York: Routledge, 2015), 205.

14   *Solidaridad Obrera*, 26 May 1937.

15   Ibid.

16   A translated copy of Schapiro's article, "¿Nacional-Anarquismo?," was included in a dossier of offending articles and persons relating to anarchists in France that was compiled by the National Committee of the CNT over the summer: "Informe sobre las actividades de las organizaciones y de algunos anarquistas franceses, en relación con la lucha antifascista española," CDMH, PS Barcelona, 523/13.

17   On the connection between Spanish anarchist anti-nationalism and anti-militarism, see

Sarrau on behalf of the Los Quijotes del Ideal affinity group, which, according to Diego Camacho's recollections, denounced both Juan García Oliver's "militarist outbursts" and Federica Montseny's "ravings on 'national anarchism.'"[18] Already, at a Regional Congress of the JJLL on 17 April 1937, the delegate from Puigcerdà had lamented the consequences of the military "pose" adopted by García Oliver.[19] This was in reference to a speech in March at which the then Minister of Justice had urged those entering officer training in the Republican army "to bear in mind that enlisted men 'should cease to be your comrades and become the cogwheels of our military machine.'"[20] The delegate noted the opprobrium with which French comrades had greeted such language, providing further evidence of the international nature of the critique of state collaboration, which in turn contributed to the worsening of relations between the *comités superiores* and the CNT's critics at home and abroad.

At a tempestuous Plenum of the IWMA in Paris on 11 June, the CNT delegates were made to suffer what they regarded as the indignity of attacks on their conduct from miniscule and in some cases barely operative sister organisations.[21] Moreover, they were unable to prevent the anti-collaborationist motions passed at this meeting being reported to oppositional anarchists in Spain.[22] The indignities continued. At a fund-raising rally held in Paris later that month, scuffles broke out in the crowd when García Oliver and Montseny were met with shouts of "Murderers!" and "What about Camillo Berneri?"[23] Schapiro, who in Paris had alleged that the CNT "had dragged its history and its principles through the mud," accused the CNT of helping to construct, through its "so-called 'anti-fascist' alliances... a red fascism to fight the white one."[24]

The political character of the Republican rearguard was causing similar unease in Spain. In June, delegates from the Durruti Column attended a meeting of the Regional Committee of the Catalan CNT, where they stressed that the anarchist combatants were "sacrificing their health and their life for an ideal, which they believe they will see implanted very soon on the Iberian Peninsula, and now they find that they have enemies both at

Smith, "Los anarquistas y anarcosindicalistas," 142.

18   Cited in Díaz, *Víctor García*, 25.

19   "Congreso Regional de las JJLL celebrado el día 17 de abril de 1937."

20   Quoted in Bolloten, *The Spanish Civil War*, 328.

21   "Notas sobre el último Pleno de la AIT que acaba de celebrarse en Paris," CNT (España) Archives (IISG) 46 B.

22   See Paz, *Viaje al pasado*, 214.

23   See "Comité Nacional (Circular n° 12) A la Regional de Cataluña," CDMH, PS Barcelona, 463/5.

24   Respectively, "Notas sobre el último Pleno de la AIT," *Le Combat Syndicaliste*, 23 July 1937.

the front and in the rear."[25] As had occurred prior to May, the Barcelona FAI under Merino attempted to synthesise and amplify such radical concerns. At the end of June, the Local Federation issued a communiqué in which the war was characterised as being "not for true freedom," and libertarian unease as to the meaning of the war, the fate of the revolution, and the militarist and nationalist positions adopted by the *comités superiores* was again in evidence at a Regional Plenum of Anarchist Affinity Groups of Cataluña in July.[26] During the second session, Merino urged the FAI to confront its enemies in the rearguard, "forgetting for a moment that fascism is in Aragón."[27] This frank admission that, in order to regain hegemony in the rear, Spanish anarchists would need to temporarily "forget" the war against fascism, was complemented in the following session by the analysis of Simón Tapia Colman, who was to become a musician of world renown during his post-war Mexican exile, who was speaking as a delegate of the affinity group *Hispania*:

> There is absolutely nothing for us to do in this war, since it has been transformed from a workers' war into an imperialist war. We must say that we are prepared to lose everything except our anarchist movement, which cannot compromise before a bourgeois war. We must set a deadline for the Government to make an immediate rectification, otherwise we must withdraw all support from the war effort.[28]

This was thus the second intervention at the Plenum to call for attention to be diverted from the war effort to face the enemy in the rearguard. It is further remarkable for its qualification of the war as "imperialist" in nature, which also resonated with radical anarchists abroad. On 31 July, the veteran French anarchist André Prudhommeaux wrote that "our Spanish comrades have become cannon fodder for a cause that is not theirs... an imperialist war."[29] The intervention of Tapia Colman shows that such an analysis was not restricted to foreigners or fringe groups, and indicates an ongoing mutual influence among radical anarchists inside and outside

25   See "Pequeña reunion celebrada entre una Delegación, de la División de Durruti, y algunos compañeros del Comité Regional, Comisión de Guerra y Comité de Relaciones del frente y de la retaguardia," CNT (España) Archives (IISG) 39 A.

26   "Federación Local de Grupos Anarquistas de Barcelona, Circular N° 11," Federación Anarquista Ibérica Archive (IISG) 49 A.

27   "Acta del pleno regional de grupos anarquistas de Cataluña celebrado el día 1 de julio de 1937 y sucesivos," Federación Anarquista Ibérica Archives (IISG) 17 B.

28   "Acta del pleno regional de grupos anarquistas de Cataluña."

29   The article was published in *L'Espagne Nouvelle* and included in "Informe sobre las actividades de las organizaciones y de algunos anarquistas franceses."

Spain. The reference to losing "everything except our anarchist movement" is a clear allusion to the phrase wrongly but widely attributed to Durruti, that Spanish anarchism "renounced everything except victory," echoing in turn Lucía Sánchez Saornil's defiant "for the war everything, except liberty," discussed in Chapter Four.

These sentiments were to be echoed later that month in *Anarquía*, a new underground – or "clandestine" – publication produced by the Barcelona FAI, which was not submitted to the state censor, and which declared that "everything can be done except that which endangers our principles."[30] Tapia Colman evidently placed the integrity of the movement above the anti-fascist war effort, a position that was immediately hailed by another delegate, on this occasion that of the affinity group Rebeldes, who declared that, for Tapia Colman's proposal to have an effect, it was necessary to

> arrive at the agreement that those in official positions withdraw from them, as the way that the war is going endangers us. The moment has arrived to confront our political enemies, and not to allow, as has happened up to now, the organisation to prevent us from saying the truth about the war.[31]

Such characterisations of the war as were voiced at this Plenum were to find an echo in the days and weeks that followed. At a meeting of the Catalan region of the CNT on 5 July, a delegation from the Aragón front complained of the effect on morale that the political intrigue and frivolity of the rearguard had on the comrades on the front line. Pujol, the delegate from the Metalworkers' Union, used this opportunity to link the character of the war with the question of the revolution and the purpose of the libertarian movement:

> To my mind the war has been corrupted. It is no longer the struggle of the libertarians against oppression. It has been converted into a struggle between two fascisms, the red and the black, and that is why the Confederal combatant is alienated: He sees clearly that he is fighting for a cause that is not his own... In my opinion it is necessary to hold not a limited meeting of this or that Committee but a meeting of the

30   *Anarquía*, 12 July 1937. On the invention of the Durruti quote, see Paz, *Durruti*, 727. The phrase was used by the *comités superiores*, who also attributed it to their fallen comrade. See Federica Montseny's speech of 21 July 1937, *El mitin del Olympia en Barcelona 21 de Julio de 1937* (Barcelona: Talleres Gráficos Bosch, 1937), 22; "La FAI al pueblo: 'Renunciamos a todo, excepto a la victoria,'" statement of the Peninsular Committee of the FAI, 1 October 1937, CNT (España) Archives (IISG) 49A.

31   "Acta del pleno regional de grupos anarquistas de Cataluña."

entire organisation in Spain, so that it might determine whether the war should be continued with or not, and we must initiate the true revolution.[32]

The same delegate would report a week later of a generalised reluctance to mobilise for the front among workers in his industry, an attitude that was attributed to the absence of Confederal divisions organised according to libertarian characteristics.[33]

Considering the war to be for a cause that was "not their own," "not for true freedom" or even that was fought on behalf of "red fascism," the radical wing of the libertarian movement thereby rejected the priorities of the *comités superiores*, who considered the anti-fascist war to take precedence over the revolution, and the armed defence of the latter to be undesirable, or even impossible.[34] The representatives of these committees responded to this challenge with both rhetoric and methods familiar from times of war. At the Regional Plenum of the FAI in July, the delegate of Diego Abad de Santillan's Nervio group, José María Lunazzi, an Argentinian teacher known as El Gringo, denounced the aforementioned characterisations of the conflict as "sowing defeatism, creating confusion and encouraging activities that represent treachery to the war against fascism, upon the victory of which we must build a new world."[35] It was also upon accusations of "defeatism" that the purist anarchist publication *Frente y Retaguardia* was shut down by the *comités superiores* at the end of the year.[36] Such interventions shed light on what the delegate of the Rebeldes group had meant when he referred to the organisation preventing anarchists "from saying the truth about the war."

Still more troubling for the libertarian conscience than the censorship by the *comités superiores* of what they regarded as "defeatism" was the

32   "Reunión del Comité Regional celebrada el día 5 de julio de 1937. Presidida por el compañero Laborda," CNT (España) Archives (IISG) 39 A.

33   "Reunión del Comité Regional de Cataluña celebrada el día 12 de julio de 1937, estando presentes casi todos los miembros del mismo," CNT (España) Archives (IISG) 39 A.

34   At a meeting of the National Committee on 30 June, the National Secretary of the CNT, Mariano Rodríguez Vásquez, had affirmed that the organisation in Cataluña was not capable of "resorting to force"; see "Reunión del Comité Nacional del 30 de Junio de 1937," CNT (España) Archives (IISG) 68 C.

35   "Acta del pleno regional de grupos anarquistas de Cataluña."

36   See the letter to the Liaison Committee of Lleida from the Defence Section of Cataluña, 16 December 1937, which urged that future publication of the review was to be prevented "at all costs," CDMH, PS Barcelona, 512/8. Nevertheless, within a month a new clandestine publication, *El Incontrolado*, had appeared, written by young libertarian soldiers, which was similar in content and tone. On *El Incontrolado*, see Godicheau, "Periódicos clandestinos," 194–5, which does not, however, link its appearance to the suspension of *Frente y Retaguardia*.

willingness of the same to accept the use of courts-martial to impose military discipline on anarchist combatants. This became evident when, on 15 July, a battalion of the 25th and 26th Divisions, operating on the Aragón front, refused orders to enter into battle. The Regional Committee of the CNT in Aragón declared that it would "accept the sentence pronounced," provoking the opposition of radicals in Cataluña. Again it was Pujol, the delegate of the Metalworkers' Union, who raised a protest at the meeting of the Regional Committee, declaring that he was "unwilling to give his approval to this grave event about to take place" and asking that his opposition be noted in the minutes:

> It is not for the Organisation to take on the role of executioner of those who have perhaps acted according to the dictates of their conscience, which opposes all authoritarianism and discipline, [an attitude] that we ourselves have inculcated in them![37]

Pujol's intervention was seconded by the delegate from the construction industry, while that of the Local Federation of unions suggested that the case was related to the fact that the libertarian combatants had to face two enemies, one in the front and one in the rear. A delegate from the Liaison Committee drew the attention of those present to the "contradiction" implied by comrades who had accepted militarisation now wishing to reject military discipline, a cynical remark given that militarisation had been imposed in the teeth of much anarchist opposition. The meeting eventually agreed to urgently contact the authorities in Valencia and Aragón requesting clemency.[38]

Such appeals to authority were a compromise between the acceptance of military discipline on the part of the *comités superiores*, who would even threaten to impose martial discipline on oppositional anarchists in the rear in the summer of 1937, and the tactics being advocated in the Barcelona FAI. At the Regional Plenum of that organisation in July, radical interventions abounded. During the third session, the affinity group Amor y Verdad urged the withdrawal from official positions, a boycott of and systematic opposition to the state and the "return to a new 19 July."[39]

37   "Reunión del Comité Regional de Cataluña efectuada el día 19 de Julio de 1937, estando presentes las delegaciones siguientes: Luz y Fuerza, Sanidad, tres miembros del Comité de Enlace, Alimentación, Construcción, Fabril, JJLL, FL, dos de la CAP, Artes Gráficas, Distribución y Siderometalúrgica," CNT (España) Archives (IISG) 39 A.

38   Ibid.

39   "Acta del pleno regional de grupos anarquistas de Cataluña." The Amor y Verdad affinity group was based in the Catalan municipality of Gironella, where prior to the war it had been active in opposition to "*treintismo*"; see the introduction, by Josep Cara

The group was represented at the Plenum by the delegate José Viladomiu, a founder member of both the FAI and the CNT in Gironella, who had fought in the Tierra y Libertad Column before abandoning the front in March 1937 in opposition to the militarisation of the column.[40] Just as the radicalisation of the Barcelona FAI prior to the May days was influenced by the return to the rearguard of recalcitrant elements of the anarchist columns, so the radical policies advocated by Catalan anarchists in this period, and their refusal to subordinate the fate of the revolution to the demands of the war, was likewise informed by the presence among them of respected figures who had made plain their own priorities through the abandonment of the front line.

As José Alberola had indicated, the revolutionary, social content of the war had been integral to radical anarchist participation. Once this became harder to perceive, anti-nationalism and anti-militarism returned to the forefront of libertarian politics, informed by both the strident denunciations of veteran anarchists exiled in France and the reports and deserters arriving in Cataluña from the front. "Forgetting for a moment" that fascism was in Aragón, anarchists in the FAI attempted to reassert the revolution in the rear in order to revive the revolutionary content of the war.

The "anarchist ship back on course"?

Many anarchists saw the CNT's ejection from the Republican government as an opportunity to rectify its previous stance and for the libertarian movement to adopt a more combative posture. A National Plenum of the libertarian movement held at the end of May 1937 arrived at apparently radical agreements, which affirmed that the libertarian organisations "would not collaborate directly or indirectly" with the new "Government of the counterrevolution" and would instead carry out "propaganda criticising [its] work." In spite of this, however, the Plenum itself was a somewhat subdued affair. Although the apparently radical outcome ratified opposition to and non-collaboration with the government, of more significance was the ongoing concern for internal discipline and refusal to countenance any further mobilisation "on the street."[41] The delegate for

Rincón, Jordi Jané Roca and Josep Quevedo García to *Luz y Vida. Una publicació obrera de Gironella. Edició Facsímil, 4/11/1932–24/11/1933* (Barcelona: Ajuntament de Gironella i Centre d'Estudis Josep Ester Borràs, 2003), 13–21.

40   See Iñiguez, *Esbozo de una enciclopedia*, 630–1.

41   See "Acuerdos del Pleno Nacional de Regionales celebrado los días 23 y sucesivos de mayo de 1937" included in "Circular 25–1937" from the Peninsular Committee of the FAI, Barcelona, 31 May 1937, CNT (España) Archives (IISG), 49 A.

the Central region did envisage the possibility that, with the agreement of the organisation nationally, comrades in Cataluña and Valencia could "move fully against the repressive governmental action," but this intervention found no echo among the other delegates, least of all those from the regions in question. Crucially, the agreement not to collaborate did not extend to a withdrawal of the multiple councillors and municipal delegates of the libertarian movement working in various branches of state administration. Furthermore, it was based on a calculation that the UGT, under the influence of Largo Caballero, would continue in an attitude of hostility to the new government. The flaws in this calculation were becoming apparent even as the Plenum took place, and allowances were made in the agreements to revise the non-collaboration stance should the UGT position change.[42] No critique or reflection on the experience of collaboration itself was made, and the criticism voiced by the Catalan delegates of the National Committee's handling of the crisis were limited to the ingenuity with which the latter had tied the fate of the organisation in government to the person of Largo Caballero.[43]

Barely had the agreements of the National Plenum not to collaborate with Negrín's government been publicised when, on 3 June, the National Committee of the CNT found itself obliged to issue a note to the press denying that it had offered its support to his administration.[44] The previous day, the CNT mouthpiece *Solidaridad Obrera* had published on its front page the news that the National Secretary of the organisation, Mariano Rodríguez Vázquez, had met with the new Prime Minister of the Republic, under the headline "Before the difficulties of the moment, the CNT offers its support to the Government."[45] In its denial of the following day, the National Committee insisted that the meeting had only dealt with the possible conditions required for any future collaboration.

Such ambiguity met with the scorn of several notable anarchists in France. The revolutionary syndicalist publication *Le Combat Syndicaliste*, commenting on the apparent contradiction between the agreements of late

42   The National Committee highlighted "the fact that strong nuclei of the UGT have manifested their adhesion to the current Government, against the position that the Executive adopted from the first moment." See "Actas del Pleno Nacional de Regionales, extraordinario, del Movimiento Libertario, celebrado los días 23 y sucesivos de mayo de 1937," CNT (España) Archives (IISG), 46 B.

43   Ibid.

44   *Solidaridad Obrera*, 3 June 1937. The National Committee reported to a National Plenum that it had received the impression from Negrín that there was little enthusiasm within the new government in regard to possible collaboration from the CNT; see "Acta del Pleno Nacional de regionales celebrado los días 2 y sucesivos de junio de 1937," CNT (España) Archives (IISG) 46 B.

45   *Solidaridad Obrera*, 2 June 1937.

May and the behaviour of the *comités superiores*, stated that the latter "must be made aware that this revolution will be defended, in spite of them, against their errors and against their deficiencies."[46]*Le Combat Syndicaliste* was the journal of the French affiliate organisation of the IWMA, the Confédération Générale du Travail – Syndicaliste Révolutionnaire (General Confederation of Labour – Revolutionary Syndicalist – CGT-SR), formed in 1926, whose secretary, Pierre Besnard, was a well-known veteran of the movement and the then General Secretary of the IWMA.[47] An attitude of ambivalence towards state collaboration was also in evidence among veteran libertarians on the Aragón front, where attempts on the part of the newly created Comisión Asesora Política (Political Advisory Commission – CAP) to have telegrams sent from majority libertarian divisions of the army protesting the CNT's ejection from the Generalitat met with short shrift.[48] The CAP, discussed in more detail in the following chapter, had been set up at a Regional Plenum of the Catalan libertarian movement in June with the aim of coordinating the branches of the movement in the region. The delegate it had sent to the front reported that lieutenant colonel Gregorio Jover had declared himself "very happy that the CNT were no longer collaborating and therefore would not even consider sending telegrams of protest."[49]

The greatest challenge to the libertarian movement's continued commitment to state collaboration came from the stance adopted by the Local Federation of the FAI in Barcelona. This body felt compelled to respond to a statement issued on 14 June by a joint Plenum of the Catalan regional CNT unions and FAI affinity groups which favoured continued collaboration in the Catalan Generalitat on the terms that had operated hitherto.[50] The response, which was probably written by Merino, called for a Regional Plenum of affinity groups to discuss such matters and made a thoroughgoing critique of governmental collaboration and the rhetoric with which libertarians had justified this policy:

46   *Le Combat Syndicaliste*, 11 June 1937.
47   The size of the CGT-SR in 1937 was probably around 5,000 members, while *Le Combat Syndicaliste* had a circulation of around 6,000, although it is likely that it was read by "two or three times that number"; see David Berry, *A History of the French Anarchist Movement, 1917 to 1945* (Oakland: AK Press, 2009), 151.
48   See "Reunión del Comité Regional y demás comités responsables celebrado el viernes día 2 por la tarde del mes de julio de 1937," CNT (España) Archives (IISG) 39 A. The CNT's ejection from the Generalitat is discussed in the following chapter.
49   Ibid.
50   See "Dictamen que presenta la ponencia nombrada por el pleno regional de sindicatos de la CNT y federaciones de grupos de la específica, celebrado en Barcelona el día 14 del corriente, para dictaminar el tercer punto del orden del día," Federación Anarquista Ibérica Archives (IISG) 17 B.

In order to collaborate we not only interrupted the impetuous rhythm of the struggle against the rotten apparatus of the State, but also, overwhelmed and mesmerised by the degenerate atmosphere of the political world, we, the irreconcilable enemies of that oppressive mechanism, were "obliged" to accept the paradoxical and ironic "mission" of re-evaluating its functions as a regulatory apparatus of human activities and repressor of individual and collective liberties, and were thereby "nobly" condemned to sterility and to the failure of our struggles and possibilities in the interests of a washed-out and outmoded anti-fascism and a war that is not for true freedom.[51]

The communiqué clearly identified state collaboration as the factor by which libertarians had become the agents of their own repression. Following the May days, during which Merino had played a key role, there was a feeling that a reorientation of the FAI could steer the CNT away from its postures of collaboration and compromise. The statement of the Local Federation was the opening salvo in this battle of ideas, and Merino would be among the most vocal advocates of a more combative policy within the Catalan FAI over the following months.

Anarquía, the clandestine mouthpiece of the Local Federation, echoed Gregorio Jover in welcoming the CNT's exit from government, commenting in its third issue that "at least [the organisation] will be able to breathe fresh air."[52] The fourth edition went further, considering the moment to be particularly propitious for the movement to reassert its traditional anti-statism:

In opposition, and even underground, the CNT, returning to the anarchist fold – albeit a return forced by circumstances – can, once again, be itself, propagate its positions from the unions, moralise its atmosphere, which has become somewhat strained in these times of collaboration, purge its ranks and recover the respect and sympathy of the workers... through a new and clear activity, free from alien and disturbing influences that destroy or falsify it.[53]

If, the author continued, this prognosis was to prove over-optimistic, if the "anarchistic personality" of the CNT's leaders had been "completely lost amidst the cosy complacency of the ministerial or councillor's armchair," then other, "new and upstanding activists" would have to take their place,

51   "Federación Local de Grupos Anarquistas de Barcelona, Circular N° 11."
52   *Anarquía*, 12 July 1937.
53   *Anarquía*, 18 July 1937.

and put the "anarchist ship back on course towards the longed for free-dom."[54] The editorial of the same edition made clear both the practical and ideological reasons for opposing state collaboration, in terms suggestive of Merino's involvement:

> We contest collaboration on the grounds of both principles and in-terests. Principles, because through collaboration we struggle against our own ideals. Interests, because even the most ardent supporter of collaboration must have been convinced that we have gained nothing by it and lost much... Through collaboration, in addition to granting prestige to the forms of Government... it has been made clear that our convictions are not very firmly rooted in our consciousness. The worst of all is that: after the fact of collaboration; after many comrades and the Committees have sung its virtues, with what moral authority, with what force can they now combat it?[55]

In other words, the renovation of anarchism and the affirmation of anarchist ideas would require the renovation of the *comités superiores* if such an affir-mation was to have any credibility.

Similar conclusions could be drawn from an article published at the end of the previous month in *Frente y Retaguardia* by Vicente Rodríguez, a prominent member of the JJLL, who had until June co-edited *Acracia* with José Peirats. Rodríguez critically evaluated the notion that the limitations of the Spanish revolution revealed a fundamental flaw in anarchism itself, affirming on the contrary: "The regime of collectives and socialisation has only failed when obstacles have been deliberately placed in its way by pol-iticians and bourgeois elements, who have been respected by a revolution that has not known how to arrive at its ultimate consequences."[56] It was the dilution of anarchism, rather than the ideas themselves, which had led to the current impasse:

> The current situation in Spain corroborates our affirmations. Liberty will not be achieved through authoritarian means... Anarchism stuck inside authoritarianism, had necessarily to fail... The failure of authori-tarianism as the solution to the vital problem of society is the most pal-pable evidence that we anarchists can give to affirm that only a federalist regime animated by mutual aid and solidarity... will provide the true solution to the social problem... We can also affirm that the failure of

54   Ibid.
55   Ibid.
56   *Frente y Retaguardia*, 26 June 1937.

certain individuals who have distanced themselves from the fundamental principles of anarchism does not imply the failure of the ideas that such people claim to represent... Have the ideas failed? No; men have.[57]

The Catalan section of the JJLL would also make plain this critique within the national Plenums of the FIJL. There they would be joined by representatives from the Aragón front such as Amador Franco, who declared at a Regional Congress of the JJLL of Aragón in July that:

> if we commit the error of continuing this [political] policy, of accepting its constitution, its customs, its collaboration, we will soon find ourselves trapped in a spider's web that will prevent us from making any gesture in defence of our dignity.[58]

In reference to the agreement of the CNT and the FAI to wage a propaganda campaign against the Communist Party, one of the Catalan delegates to the National Plenum of the FIJL held in Valencia at the beginning of August affirmed the need for any such campaign to be framed within a wider renunciation of collaboration, in a clear echo of the arguments advanced in *Anarquía*, cited above: "if after uncovering the abuses and errors of the Government we then reveal our own desires to collaborate we would be doing nothing more than contradicting our anarchist theories."[59]

Against such appeals, however, the Peninsular Committee of the FIJL declared that the question of whether or not the libertarian movement collaborated in governments was beyond the prerogatives of the FIJL and should be left to the judgement of the CNT and the FAI.[60] In any case, the Catalan section was in a minority within the national youth organisation, and its strategic or ideological interventions were necessarily limited. Rather, it was frequently restricted to defending the right of the section to maintain a line that was at variance with the rest of the FIJL. Clearly, there was a degree of unity among the "purist" anarchists of the JJLL and the Local Federation of the Barcelona FAI with regard to state collaboration. Sidelined within the FIJL, the anarchists of the Catalan and Aragonese JJLL had the opportunity to take their arguments to the Regional Plenum of the FAI, where the potential for cooperation between voluntarist and purist anarchists must have been apparent.

57   Ibid.
58   Quoted in Fernández Soria, *Cultura y libertad*, 58–9.
59   "Actas del pleno de regionales de la FIJL celebrado en Valencia los días 2 y 3 de agosto de 1937," CDMH, PS Barcelona, 237/01.
60   Ibid.

The categories of voluntarism and purism were not fixed, but can be usefully applied to the different approaches of radical anarchists to the question of state collaboration. At this time, the purist tendencies could be seen to affirm the integrity of anarchist principles, in the statements of the Catalan JJLL and in the pages of its mouthpiece *Ruta* – now edited by Peirats – and *Frente y Retaguardia*, whereas the voluntarist current, which in the summer of 1937 found a voice in *Anarquía* and the publication of the AAD, *El Amigo del Pueblo*, placed greater emphasis on the working class as the agent of revolution and on the need for anarchists to exit the organs of the state and return to the unions and affinity groups. The editorial of *Anarquía* cited above suggests that Merino was consciously attempting to provide a bridge between the voluntarist and purist wings of radical anarchism that would enable strategic cooperation. The wording of the Local Federation's communiqué calling for a Regional Plenum also seems to have been carefully chosen in this respect: making state collaboration the chief target of its polemic, it also affirmed that it was necessary to "maintain the purity of anarchist principles" and to elaborate a proactive response to the failures of state collaboration. The communiqué called upon all anarchist opponents of state collaboration to recognise an ally in the Local Federation, and set the tone for the stormy debates at the Regional Plenum when it took place:

> It is necessary that the healthy reaction that... has begun against these procedures [of state collaboration] spreads throughout our organisations and strengthens our resolve to pulverise our eternal adversaries with the unity, action and power of our movement... It is indispensable that we react with firmness once and for all against this morbid apathy that breaks our morale and wounds our own interests... Out with political collaboration, everyone to the affinity groups and the unions... You must keep in mind... that while the union organisations and many affinity groups of the region consider that we must and can collaborate, we the Affinity Groups of Barcelona maintain different criteria.[61]

That discontent was widespread among Catalan anarchists throughout the summer of 1937 is evidenced by the embattled tenor of the meetings of the committees. At a meeting of the Regional Committees of the libertarian movement on 9 June it was admitted that "the criticisms made against the Committees are the same for everyone, the hostile mood against us is everywhere gaining momentum."[62] This mood was also, albeit rarely, explicitly expressed in the anarchist press. On 8 July, *Anarquía* published a short article for which it was subsequently censured by the Peninsular Committee of the FAI, which read, in part:

> In the name of the Law, the "guardians of order" commit outrages, loot the unions, destroy the constructive labour of the CNT and the FAI, tread on and tarnish the revolutionary economy, manifested in the collectives, broken up by the uniformed hordes. And all this with the consent of the... responsible Committees of the CNT. For shame! ... An end must be put to this chaos.[63]

At a meeting on the following day, the affinity group Germinal agreed to write to the Local Federation demanding that the author responsible for this article be sanctioned and that the publication's title and use of the FAI's name be rescinded. The affinity group further agreed to push for Merino's removal as Secretary of the Local Federation, confirming that he was associated with the publication of such critiques.[64]

The *comités superiores* saw it as their duty to check the hostile mood. On 22 June, the new Regional Secretary of the Catalan CNT, José Juan Domènech, reported back from a meeting with the Catalan President Lluís Companys, that:

> what worried him [Domènech] most was the atmosphere of hatred that was growing in the wake of these [repressive post-May days] events, to such an extent that he feared that the day was coming when the Committees would be unable to hold back the natural desire for revenge among those affected.[65]

---

62   "Reunión del Comité Regional celebrada el día 9 de junio de 1937, estando presentes los demás comités responsables," CNT (España) Archives (IISG) 95 B.

63   *Anarquía*, 8 July 1937. Following the intervention of the *comités superiores*, the subsequent issue claimed that the article had been published by mistake and that it was not "in the spirit of *Anarquía* to attack any responsible Committee" and that, on the contrary, its pages were open to any member of said committees; see *Anarquía*, 12 July 1937. In the meantime, at the Peninsular Plenum of the FAI held in Valencia earlier in the month, the delegate of the National Committee of the CNT had brought the Plenum's attention to the appearance of the publication, a "libellous broadsheet," which questioned the policies of the "Confederal committees." The Plenum subsequently instructed the Catalan Regional Committee of the FAI to disavow the publication. See "FAI Comité Peninsular, Circular 36–1937, Barcelona 12 de Julio de 1937," Federación Anarquista Ibérica Archive (IISG) 49 A and *Memoria del Pleno Peninsular*, 52.

64   See "Acta de la reunión del grupo 'Germinal' celebrada el día 9 de Julio con asistencia de cinco compañeros," CDMH, PS Barcelona, 1312 / 2.

65   "Reunión del Comité Regional de Cataluña, celebrada el día 22 de junio de 1937. Estan-

The Local Federation of Anarchist Affinity Groups, by contrast, declared that "for the good of the movement" this hostile mood should make itself felt where it might have most impact, urging in the communiqué discussed above that an end be put to the "street and café criticisms of the *compañeros* and the Committees," because "everything that has to be said can and must be said in the unions, in the activist meetings, and in the meetings of the affinity groups."[66]

The fruits of this perspective were seen at the Regional Plenum of Catalan Anarchist Affinity Groups held from 1 to 3 July at the Casa CNT-FAI. This assembly would reveal the depth and extent of the radical critique of the policy of the libertarian organisations that was being advanced by anarchists at this time. It would also reveal, however, how seriously this opposition was taken by the *comités superiores*, which mobilised its most recognisable and respected figures to prevent the strategy advanced by the radicals from resulting in any concrete agreements or activity. The communiqué through which the Local Federation had convoked the Regional Plenum of July had made government collaboration the fundamental issue to be discussed at the Plenum. There, several affinity groups proposed radical alternatives to the policy, and Merino's position was further elucidated, alluding to both the undemocratic methods by which the policy of collaboration had been arrived at and its ineffectiveness in advancing the libertarian cause:

The comrades were duty bound to recognise that Companys, Largo Caballero and Azaña could not stop being bourgeois. That is why we said before a much disputed majority, that this was not the way... In the economic sphere, the CNT and the FAI have made progress that has not been consolidated, because in the governments of Valencia and Cataluña our ministers have done nothing to consolidate it.[67]

The initial exchanges at the opening session of the Regional Plenum reflected disquiet at the situation the anarchists found themselves in. Suffering repression at the hands of "a microscopic enemy that had become gigantic," the question of who was to blame for this state of affairs resulted in the censure of the Regional Committee of the FAI and, opposed to this, a wider self-criticism that affirmed that "the responsibility belongs to everyone, and each of us must accept our part."[68]

do presentes los demás Comités responsables," CNT (España) Archives (IISG) 39 A.
66   "Federación Local de Grupos Anarquistas de Barcelona, Circular N° 11."
67   See "Acta del pleno regional de grupos anarquistas de Cataluña."
68   The quotes here are from the delegates of the affinity groups *Cultura y Acción* (Merino) and *Amigos*, respectively.

During the second session of the Plenum the attendees became more specific in their critique and in proposals for a change of direction. The delegate from Pla de Besós lamented that the FAI, on uniting itself with the CNT, had changed its character and that "in this way, we have made ourselves accomplices in the absorption of anarchism by the union organisation."[69] This was a widely felt position, and was to become a central issue among the anarchists of Barcelona over the remainder of 1937. The complaint was confirmed in its essentials by Severino Campos on behalf of the Regional Committee, who reported that the joint regional conferences of the libertarian movement to which the FAI had been invited had in fact sidelined the latter organisation, with the representatives of the CNT dictating events. Then, when Catalan delegates spoke at a national level, the National Secretary of the CNT had refused to acknowledge the separate character of the regional FAI, as the Catalan libertarian movement was now supposed to speak through one voice.[70]

Towards the end of the second session of the Plenum, Julián Merino, speaking as the delegate of the Cultura y Acción affinity group, made a lengthy intervention that also located the problems of Spanish anarchism in the fact of the FAI's reduced role:

> We have doubts as to the efficacy of this Plenum… It would seem that there is a deliberate interest in preventing the FAI from arriving at fixed positions with regard to questions of importance. We have taken the wrong road… If we were to go over the mistakes made in Spain, this Plenum would go on forever. Mistakes that no one has wanted to put right. As Campos said, the anarchist movement is influenced by hidden powers… We have always posited the FAI as the vanguard of the CNT, but since 19 July it has trailed behind the Confederation.

69   "Acta del pleno regional de grupos anarquistas de Cataluña." Pla de Besós was the name given to the Barcelona suburb of Sant Adrià de Besòs for the duration of the civil war. Its delegate at this Plenum was Antonio Bonilla Albadalejo, who had fought in the Durruti Column and contributed to the AAD mouthpiece, *El Amigo del Pueblo*. See "Antonio Bonilla Albadalejo – anarquista de la columna durruti," http://puertoreal.cnt. es/bilbiografias-anarquistas/4329-antonio-bonilla-albadalejo-anarquista-de-la-colum-na-durruti.html [accessed 4 December 2017]. Bonilla was one of those most convinced that José Manzana had been responsible (whether deliberately or not) for the death of Durruti. See Gimenólogos, *En busca de los Hijos de la Noche*, 405–6.

70   "Acta del pleno regional de grupos anarquistas de Cataluña." This outcome confirms the observation made in the previous chapter as to the role of the Liaison Committees between the different libertarian organisations in the "bolshevisation" of the movement. The Regional Committee of the FAI had included observations to this effect in its report prior to the Plenum; see "Comité Regional de GGAA de Cataluña. Informe que presentamos a los grupos de nuestra actuación a partir del primero de abril del año en curso," CDMH, PS Barcelona, 1335/10.

Offering a voluntarist solution to the situation, Merino continued:

> We are not enamoured of grandiloquent gestures or crazy actions, but of restoring prestige to the movement... Due to a lack of political vision we have enabled the moral victory of certain gentlemen who are determined to bury our organisation... Everything is endangered by this activity and it must be put right. To that end we propose:
>
> That all those with official responsibilities should withdraw from them and return to the unions.
>
> That in order to confront the repression, the FAI should put itself at the head of the struggle, forgetting for a moment that fascism is in Aragón.[71]

Following this intervention, which was enthusiastically seconded by the affinity group Los Mismos, the Plenum broke to attend the unveiling of a plaque honouring Durruti.[72] This unveiling took place before an enormous crowd gathered in front of the Casa CNT-FAI, with speakers addressing the multitude from a raised platform adjacent to the building. When the Plenum reconvened, several newly arrived delegates presented their credentials. Given the turn that the Plenum was to eventually take, it is probable that the break in proceedings had been taken advantage of in order to alert senior figures of the libertarian movement to what was taking place in the meeting room of the Casa CNT-FAI, and that the arrival of the new delegates reflected concern on their part. Campos, who had attended the early sessions of the Plenum, along with José Xena, Federica Montseny and García Oliver, who would each make interventions at it subsequently, all spoke at the unveiling of the plaque, as reported in *Solidaridad Obrera* on 2 July 1937. The same edition, appearing on the second day of the Plenum, bore on its front page the headline "The CNT will collaborate with the Government to win the war."[73] Given that this was not accompanied by any new development or public agreement on the part of the CNT, we may speculate that it was published solely as a deliberate attempt to influence the ongoing debate at the Plenum. Voices defending the position of the *comités superiores* had been scarce in its early sessions. The intervention of the group Z, to which Fidel Miró belonged, urged that the committees "be given a margin of trust so they might act with the rapidity that the present moment demands," but this was responded to by

---

71   "Acta del pleno regional de grupos anarquistas de Cataluña."
72   Members of *Los Mismos* included José García Perpina of the *Agrupación Faros* and José Pascual San José, of the Transport Workers' Union.
73   *Solidaridad Obrera*, 2 July 1937.

An enormous crowd gathers in front of the Casa CNT-FAI for the unveiling of a plaque dedicated to Durruti. The speakers are stood on a raised platform in front of the building, to the right of the entrance. The people gathered on the first-floor balcony doubtless include attendees at the Regional Plenum of the FAI. Pérez de Rozas, Arxiu Fotogràfic de Barcelona.

Members of the *comités superiores* preside over the unveiling alongside the chief of police Ricardo Burillo, then spearheading operations against revolutionaries in Barcelona. I believe Burillo is the bald man with a moustache. Next to him (l-r): Aurelio Fernández, Juan García Oliver, Ricardo Sanz, unknown man in glasses, Dionisio Eroles. Pérez de Rozas, Arxiu Fotogràfic de Barcelona.

a point of order stating that the Local Federation did not recognise this affinity group.[74]

After the Peninsular Committee called for unity of action, affirming that "the FAI must formulate a minimum programme to be obeyed by all," the delegate for the group Humanidad observed that there were two currents present in the hall: that represented by the delegates and that represented by the Peninsular Committee. A working group was formed to elaborate a position paper synthesising the mood of the Plenum that would be discussed at a later session. Thus, after a further, fourth, session in which the discussion was again dominated by oppositional voices urging a settling of accounts with the enemies in the rear and a vanguard role for the FAI in the libertarian movement, the Plenum reconvened to hear and discuss the manifesto presented by the working group. It had been drawn up by seven delegates, of whom three had already made radical interventions – Tapia Colman, Merino and Viladomiu – while the presence of another oppositional anarchist, José Peirats, on behalf of the group Irreductibles, ensured a majority against the line of the Peninsular Committee. This combination also suggested an alliance between the combative voluntarism of Merino and the purist scruples of Peirats. It is likely, given the content of the manifesto presented, that José María Lunazzi provided the lone voice in opposition to the radical measures proposed.[75] It began with a "purist" affirmation reminiscent of Peirats's intervention at the National Congress of the CNT in May 1936: "The Iberian Anarchist Federation reaffirms its fundamental principles and affirms that it is not a class organisation but one of a widely libertarian and iconoclastic spirit."[76] It went on to suggest, "in keeping with the spirit of the Plenum," the following concrete proposals: withdrawal from all official positions, a public declaration that the "counterrevolutionary repression" must cease immediately or the FAI would take the lead in combatting it "regardless of the situation of the war (which we, more than anyone, desire to win)," "integral collectivisation," socialisation "of all those activities that the workers deem appropriate," and the creation of Confederal warehouses to oversee exchanges with the collectives in order to put an end to speculation.[77] In essence, then, this manifesto was a restatement of the radical programme that had developed prior to May and a reaffirmation, despite the assurance that the anarchists "more than

74   The reason why the affinity group Z did not officially belong to the Local Federation in Barcelona is not provided in the minutes. It is interesting to note, however, that the Local Federation was not above using bureaucratic methods to silence its critics.

75   The other members of the group were F. Alberola, of the Asturias group, and Pedro Serra Tubau, of the Agrupación A, from Gerona.

76   For Peirats's intervention at the National Congress in Zaragoza, see Chapter One.

77   "Acta del pleno regional de grupos anarquistas de Cataluña."

anyone" desired victory in the war, of the will to fight "the counterrevolution" regardless of such considerations.

Although the manifesto was a faithful reflection of the mood of the
Plenum up to that point, it was subjected to further discussion. No sooner
had it been read out than one delegate, representing the anarchist grouping of Vilafranca, insisted that it not be made publicly available. Further
delegates opposed the withdrawal of comrades from official positions for a
variety of reasons, not least because of the implication that this would have
for the production of arms, a source of particular pride to the libertarian
movement in Barcelona, given the notable role of anarchists in creating a
viable war industry in the city.[78] Since "official positions" potentially ranged
from ministries of government and municipal councillors to commissions of
industry or workplace-based positions of authority, it was possible for delegates to agree with the withdrawal of some comrades and not others, and
this was reflected in the discussion. There was further disquiet with regard
to the fact that most members of the FAI who held official positions did so
in the name of the CNT, in accordance with the agreements of the latter
organisation; there was unease at the possibility that accepting this proposal
would mean breaking the famous *trabazón* between the libertarian organisations as well as provoking a mass exodus of anarchists from positions of
responsibility at all levels. The potential implications of the manifesto may
have influenced the apparent volte-face on the part of the delegate of the
group Los Mismos, who warned that "we must be very clear about what this
Plenum agrees to, or we will have cause to regret it very soon."[79]

If the opening remarks with regard to the manifesto suggest a change
in the mood of the Plenum, this was to be reinforced by the intervention of
García Oliver who, given that this is the first time he appears in the minutes,
must surely not have been present prior to this session. While previous delegates had been censured by the chair when straying from the point or making overly long contributions, the same rule did not apply to the man who
had until recently been, in the name of the CNT, the Spanish Republic's
Minister of Justice, and was now Secretary of the CAP in Cataluña.[80] His
speech to the Plenum took in references to the Russian and French revo-
lutions, the economic situation in Spain and various recollections relating
to the early days of the struggle, causing the secretary responsible for the

78   See Javier de Madariaga, "Les Indústries de Guerra. La fabricació, distribució, ad-
      quisició, control i experimentació de material bèl·lica," in *Breu Història de la Guerra
      Civil a Catalunya*, ed. by Josep M. Solé Sabaté and Joan Villarroya (Barcelona: Edicions
      62, 2005), 317–28.
79   "Acta del pleno regional de grupos anarquistas de Cataluña."
80   On the role of García Oliver in the CAP, see the recollections contained in Paz, *Viaje al
      pasado*, 196–8, and Peirats, *De mi paso*, 349–51.

minutes to admit defeat and stop recording his intervention. While lacking an engagement with the issues as they had been expressed hitherto, it is possible that his words had an effect on wavering delegates, particularly when declaring that the anarchists "must not and cannot abandon any position but on the contrary must take more every day."[81]

As the debate dragged on into a sixth session, further important figures of the anarchist movement made an appearance, defending the record of state collaboration and urging the need for libertarian unity. Among the speakers were an unnamed representative of the National Committee of the CNT, Federica Montseny, Francisco Isgleas and José Xena, the majority of whom were speaking not as delegates of affinity groups but as observers with an "informative" role. Montseny had in fact been sent by the National Committee of the CNT on an explicit mission to intervene in the Plenums of the Catalan libertarian movement.[82]

José Peirats made an impassioned defence of the oppositional position in response to García Oliver, declaring that it would be preferable to have "honour without ships than ships without honour" and: "If it is necessary to use violence let us use it, between the violence of our enemies and that of ourselves the latter is preferable, and if it is necessary to reinforce our positions by unleashing another 19 July then so be it."[83] This call for anarchist violence was somewhat uncharacteristic on the part of Peirats and a further example of the contemporary confluence of purist and voluntarist perspectives among radicals. Peirats also asked that if the manifesto presented by the working group was rejected, it be "recorded in the minutes, so that it may be archived and recognised as a historical document of the current revolutionary movement." However, this tone of defiance was itself indicative of the direction that the debate was taking. The Plenum finally approved the counter-proposals of the affinity group Germen to reject the manifesto, "accept the proposals and orientations agreed to at the Plenum of the CNT with regard to collaboration," and grant to the *comités superiores* "authority to work in accordance with the circumstances of the moment."[84]

A Plenum that had threatened to expose the divisions in the libertarian movement through the adoption of proposals that would have marked a complete rupture with the policy of the *comités superiores* thus resulted

81 Ibid.
82 Montseny was accompanied by Manuel Amil Barcia. See "Reunión del Comité Nacional del 30 de Junio de 1937," CNT (España) Archives (IISG) 68 C. On Amil Barcia, see the biography in Iñiguez, *Esbozo de una enciclopedia*, 40.
83 "Acta del pleno regional de grupos anarquistas de Cataluña." Peirats was alluding to the phrase "Spain prefers honour without ships to ships without honour," attributed to the nineteenth-century Spanish naval officer Casto Méndez Núñez.
84 Ibid.

in what was in effect the only alternative outcome: a timid renunciation of the autonomy of the Catalan anarchist affinity groups and a voluntary ceding of decision-making responsibility to the movement's leadership. Nevertheless, it should be borne in mind that this was consequent upon the flooding of the Plenum by non-delegate libertarian grandees. Although not wishing to claim that the radical anarchists formed an absolute majority within the Catalan FAI, the abrupt change in the direction of the Plenum evinced by the minutes suggests that the radicals and the positions they defended were sufficiently persuasive as to dictate the tenor of assemblies, but only up until the point at which they were trumped by the appearance of the *comités superiores*.

The *comités superiores* had thus shown themselves capable of blocking the Local Federation of the Barcelona FAI from winning the Regional organisation to its positions. Further opportunities to radicalise the wider libertarian movement through its traditional mechanisms would be thin on the ground. Many radical anarchists would soon leave the rearguard to participate in an anti-fascist war whose purpose they were now beginning to question. For the *comités superiores*, meanwhile, the Plenum of July 1937 had provided the fig leaf of democratic approval for their continued exercise of executive decision-making power. However, the extent to which this power could truly be brought to bear in making the libertarian movement a homogeneous organisation was limited and would be tenaciously contested by the same anarchists that had attempted to elaborate an alternative to state collaboration.

Neo-anarchism and the FAI

Following the voting down of radical anarchist proposals to withdraw from state collaboration, the Peninsular Committee of the FAI sought to advance the "legalisation" of the anarchist organisation – that is to say, its formal constitution as a political organisation. This was intended to facilitate its participation in state bodies and thereby increase the libertarian presence in organs of collaboration. As the Peninsular Committee reported, "In many town halls, provincial councils and other organisations, the participation of our specific organisation on equal terms with the Communists and Socialists has been prevented, owing to the allegation that it is not a normally constituted organisation."[85] It had been worrying for the *comités superiores* that Manuel Irujo, the Basque Nationalist Minister of Justice under Negrín, had

85   See "Comité Regional de GG/AA/ de Andalucía. Circular Urgentísima," CDMH, PS Barcelona, 11/10.

used the FAI's continued "illegality" as an excuse to eject the organisation's delegates from representation in the running of the judiciary. Furthermore, legalisation would provide the Peninsular Committee with an opportunity to alter the internal organisation of the FAI along lines that had been discussed as far back as December 1936 and which implied, as far as many radical anarchists could see, the adoption of a party political structure. The principal measure of this restructuring was the proposed replacement of the affinity groups, the "*grupos*," by larger "*agrupaciones*," based on geographical locality and open to all self-declared anarchists, as the basic unit of the organisation.

The twin measures of legalisation and restructuring had been brought forward by the Peninsular Committee for discussion as a last-minute addition to the agenda of the Regional Plenum of the Catalan FAI in July. This was eventually rejected after a long and bitter debate, during which some radical anarchists lamented that "we are wasting our time, when neo-anarchism has won the battle over true anarchism."[86] Thus, when a delegation of the Catalan FAI made its way to Valencia the following day to participate in the Peninsular Plenum of the organisation, it was without a mandate to approve legalisation and the concomitant restructuring of the FAI. The Aragonese affinity groups had likewise viewed the Peninsular Committee's proposal with scepticism. In Valencia, their delegate averred that "the political situation has not yet been resolved in such a way as to suggest the abandonment of tactics appropriate for underground activity" and that, furthermore, "if the FAI is turned into an organisation of the masses it will lose its specific content."[87]

Remarkably, despite faithfully relaying the arguments of its affinity groups, the Aragonese delegation put its signature to the position paper elaborated at the Peninsular Plenum in which the new structure was detailed. That it did so may have been in response to pressure exerted by the Catalan delegation, which also reneged on the mandate with which it had been entrusted. This latter delegation, which included Juan Manuel Molina, nominated by García Oliver, and Simón Tapia Colman, of the Hispania group, read a statement explaining their actions that the Aragonese delegation also adhered to:

The Catalan delegation, in view of the unanimity of the Plenum, accepts its part of the working group and signs the position paper, explaining

86   "Acta del pleno regional de grupos anarquistas de Cataluña." This intervention was made by the delegate of the affinity group *Pompeyo Gener*, which included Mariano Viñuales.

87   *Memoria del Pleno Peninsular de Regionales*, 15–17.

its vote by reference to the fact that certain of the organisational procedures that form the new structure are already practised in the region. Its
vote is nevertheless conditional upon the final resolutions of the region
that it represents.[88]

The unanimity referred to here was entirely illusory as the Plenum was
in fact divided, with three regions, Levante, Andalucía and the Centre,
mandated to favour restructuring and two, Cataluña and Aragón, to oppose it, representing a total of 615 affinity groups and 775 affinity groups,
respectively.

The determination of the *comités superiores* to press ahead with the
restructuring of the FAI resulted in an impasse. The continued hostility
of the Catalan affinity groups meant that no delegation was sent from the
region to attend the Peninsular Plenum of the FAI in August. There, the
Catalan region's proposal that a National Congress be held to determine the
structure of the FAI was read out. While it was agreed that such a Congress
should be held "when circumstances permit," it was nevertheless considered
opportune to immediately press ahead with the restructuring given that it
was agreed to "unanimously by all the regions represented in the Plenum."[89]
The illusion of unanimity once again served to grant legitimacy to a process designed to silence oppositional voices by removing the mechanisms
by which libertarian organisations had formerly ensured federalist practices.
If radicals could not be silenced by the regional organisations, then those
regions would simply be ignored by the national body.

On 17 October, an assembly was called in Barcelona that was open "to
all anarchists… whether affiliated to the FAI or not," in order to constitute
the Agrupación Anarquista de Barcelona (Barcelona Anarchist Grouping
– AAB), in accordance with the new structure of the FAI, in spite of the
fact that this was opposed by a majority of affinity groups in the city.[90] As
a consequence, "a good number of anarchist affinity groups and individuals" were present at the Casa CNT-FAI, with several speakers commenting
on the impressive number of attendees. Merino had by this point resigned
as Secretary of the Local Federation, owing to the divisions in the FAI.[91]
The assembly had been called by his replacement, Alejandro Gilabert,
who hoped that a "harmonious conclusion" could be arrived at with the

88   Ibid., 44.
89   See "Actas del Pleno Peninsular de Regionales," Federación Anarquista Ibérica Archive
       (IISG) 49 A.
90   *Solidaridad Obrera*, 17 October 1937.
91   See "Primera sesión del pleno anarquista, celebrado el día 17 de octubre de 1937, para
       tratar de la nueva estructuración de la FAI," CDMH, PS Barcelona, 1335/08.

recalcitrant affinity groups. He was to be swiftly disabused of this notion, however.[92]

Many attendees defended the traditional structure of the FAI based on affinity groups, with the delegate from the *Sagitario* group judging the AAB to be "doomed to failure," while Grau declared that "there has been an attempt made to destroy the affinity groups, but in spite of everything these groups remain the nerve centre of our movement."[93] One Martínez averred that "perhaps it will soon be the affinity groups who must re-conquer our freedoms on the street." Iglesias, who also raised the question of insurrectionary activity, declared that "Gilabert and other comrades have said that those who accept the new structure do so with the intention of saving our movement," but he believed that it would have the opposite effect, and that

> the only means by which the situation might be saved is through an insurrection of workers and soldiers… anarchists cannot collaborate with any Government or political party, as with them we cannot make the revolution nor win the war, and if we want to save the revolution it is necessary to return to the principles that we have abandoned.[94]

Similar sentiments were expressed by Julián Merino, whose resignation and short-lived withdrawal from the FAI did not prevent him from dominating the assembly's first session. As far as he was concerned, the new structure was a manoeuvre of reformists, which had "the 'virtue' of breaking up [the] movement."

Had the supporters of the new structure hoped that an opening up of the FAI to new members might drown out oppositional voices, the minutes of this assembly, which testify to radical interventions from people apparently attending in an individual capacity, suggest that it had the opposite effect. The newly constituted AAB did not, in fact, generate much enthusiasm, and was founded with an initial number of only thirty-seven

92   Ibid. By this point, the post of Regional Secretary vacated by Severino Campos had also been filled, by the teacher José de Tapia, who defended the restructuring of the FAI at this assembly. Alejandro Gilabert, who also defended the restructuring of the FAI, was a veteran of the libertarian movement and the founder of the satirical anti-Communist review *Criticón*.

93   "Primera sesión del pleno anarquista." The individual Grau may have been Generoso Grau of the Food Supplies Union, who would become a prominent member of the CNT during the Franco dictatorship: see Iñiguez, *Esbozo de una enciclopedia*, 285; or may have been Antonio Grau Alminana of the affinity group Acción and the Transport Workers' Union.

94   "Primera sesión del pleno anarquista." As with the intervention above of Martínez, the popularity of the name Iglesias makes it difficult to establish who this activist may have been.

members, including several of the most prominent figures of Catalan anarchism.[95] In the meantime, the absence of its members from Plenums of the Local Federation meant that there were effectively two FAIs in Barcelona during this period, the AAB and the Local Federation of affinity groups, in which latter organisation Merino promptly resumed his post as Secretary. The outcome of this situation was that, at the same time as the Peninsular Committee of the FAI reaffirmed its commitment to government collaboration in December 1937, the organisation of affinity groups in Barcelona unanimously passed a motion that declared its intention to take to the unions the "suggestion that the FAI, in accordance with its agreements, withdraw from all political lines and from all the collaborationist organisations, nor intervene in any anti-fascist committee while anti-fascists are persecuted, jailed and massacred."[96] It further affirmed its autonomy relative to the national organisation by constituting its own, extra-legal, *Comité Pro Presos*," "constituted as they used to be before 19 July," in opposition to the newly restructured *Comisión Jurídica*.[97] The Plenum ended with Merino once again urging his comrades to return to their unions and ensure the influence of the FAI in the workplace. Merino certainly did his best to lead by example in this regard. Within days of this Plenum he was to be found at a Plenum of unions proposing the formation of a *Comité Pro Presos* alongside the delegate of the Food Supplies Union.[98]

The deadlock continued into 1938. In March, partisans of the new structure returned to a meeting of Barcelona affinity groups on a fruitless mission to persuade the Local Federation that it should be the AAB rather than the affinity groups that were to represent the region at a forthcoming Peninsular Plenum.[99] In opposition to this, the delegate for the affinity group Afinidades declared that

---

95   Initial members of the AAB included Montseny, Toryho, Miró, Escorza, Santillán, Grunfeld, Sánchez Saornil and Maguid. See "Copia del Acta de constitución de la Agrupación Anarquista de Barcelona," CDMH, PS Barcelona, 1437/15.

96   "Acta del pleno de la Federación Local de Grupos de Barcelona, que se celebra el día 4/12/37," CDMH, PS Barcelona, 1307/7. The position of the Peninsular Committee of the FAI was outlined on 13 December in a communiqué that ferociously denounced the repression and sectarian activities of the Communist Party, albeit without naming it once. It nevertheless reaffirmed its commitment to anti-fascist collaboration. See "Frente al maniobro bajo, La FAI ratifica sus propósitos de colaboración y entendimiento con todos los sectores antifascistas," CNT (España) Archives (IISG) 49 A.

97   "Acta del pleno de la Federación Local de Grupos de Barcelona."

98   See "Acta del Pleno de Sindicatos celebrado el día 8 de diciembre," CDMH, PS Barcelona, 1307/5. This meeting also agreed that only activists that had joined the unions prior to 19 July should be entitled to hold positions of primary responsibility.

99   "Acta de la reunión de delegados de GGAA de Barcelona celebrada el día nueve de marzo de 1938 en el salon de actos de la Casa CNT-FAI," CDMH, PS Barcelona, 1437/15.

the reason for the current situation is the behaviour of the CNT and the FAI, who have been distracted from their real mission. We must make every effort to defend our last remaining bastion and preserve its vitality... The Confederal organisation is headed for humiliation and defeat and this is what we are struggling against, against the morbidity that surrounds us and which they are trying to introduce into anarchism.[100]

In a tacit acknowledgement of their declining influence over their constituents, the *comités superiores* eventually admitted defeat with regard to the FAI, and all of the individuals who had participated in founding the AAB resigned on 3 September 1938. On 15 September, the then Regional Secretary of the FAI, José Xena, wrote to the Local Federation of Affinity Groups to inform it that "we have received a letter from the AAB in which they have let us know that the groups that constitute the mentioned grouping have either withdrawn or been dissolved."[101] By this point, however, the organisation had served its purpose of officially marginalising the Local Federation and preventing it from advocating its positions at a national level. Unable to reprise the successful radicalisation of the libertarian movement that had been effected during the early years of the Republic, the radical affinity groups were forced to contemplate the defence of the revolution and its partisans from a position of increasing isolation.

The revolution in retreat

In order to defend the integrity of their movement, radical anarchists in Spain had to defend the spaces in which they operated. The organisational space afforded by the libertarian movement's federalism, which had guaranteed the autonomy of the affinity group and the Catalan JJLL, was defended against the centralising tendencies within the libertarian organisations. Also under permanent threat of closure were the physical spaces in which anarchist activity had developed in the Republican rearguard since July 1936: the neighbourhood premises of the defence committees, the MMLL, the JJLL and educational centres. In the case of the last of these, libertarian concern was not devoted solely to the threat of eviction but towards constructing a space which could not be encroached upon by the militarised ideology of the Republican state. Even the least strategically minded of purist radical anarchists were therefore forced to consider the practical

100   Ibid.
101   See CDMH, PS Barcelona, 1335/11.

question of how to preserve the revolution against a creeping statist and capitalistic restoration.

Following the abandonment of the barricades in May, radical anarchists had hoped that a showdown with the counterrevolution could yet be won, and the revolutionary spirit of 19 July recovered. In June 1937, *Frente y Retaguardia* had mocked the "order" that had been imposed on Cataluña and Aragón, echoing Rosa Luxemburg's famous "Order Prevails in Berlin" in ironically reporting certain declarations of Joan Comorera, "the shoe-shine boy of the Catalan bourgeoisie," to the effect that victory had been obtained over the "fascists and provocateurs" within the ranks of Spanish anarchism.[102] A further article affirmed that Barcelona remained "a battle ground," and that the struggle had not yet been given up.[103] To prevent any insurrectionary resurgence, throughout the summer and autumn of 1937 the security forces dismantled the networks of centres and neighbourhood defence committees that had facilitated the uprising in May.

In June, the occupation and closure of the headquarters of the revolutionary committee of Les Corts, housed in a former convent, took place at the hands of a squadron of Assault Guards.[104] The social centre run by the Agrupación Los de Ayer y Los de Hoy was raided and the entire contents of its library removed. The Agrupación wryly commented that the quality of its enemies' publications would surely improve as a consequence.[105] In August, the arts centre run by the Fine Arts and Liberal Professions union of the CNT was also raided and its contents confiscated.[106] Several of these operations were consented to by the Catalan Regional Committee of the CNT in a spirit of bureaucratic fatalism. So it was that in July 1937 the Committee rubberstamped the abandonment of the headquarters of the defence committee of Sants in the Plaça Espanya, which it understood was soon to be the target of an assault by the forces of the Generalitat.[107]

This attitude was mirrored at a national level by the *comités superiores*, who refused to countenance an armed defence of the collectives and of the Regional Defence Council of Aragón in August. According to César M. Lorenzo:

102   *Frente y Retaguardia*, 26 June 1937. "Order Prevails in Berlin," the last known piece of writing by Rosa Luxemburg, may be found at https://www.marxists.org/archive/luxemburg/1919/01/14.htm [accessed 4 December 2017].

103   *Frente y Retaguardia*, 26 June 1937.

104   See Berenguer, *Entre el sol*, 95–8.

105   See the *Boletín de la Agrupación Anarquista Los de Ayer y Los de Hoy*, July 1937.

106   See María Eugenia Prece, "Barcelona y Guerra Civil," http://ccpe.org.ar/textos.pdf [accessed 3 December 2017], part of a series of works related to Gustavo Cochet held at the Museo Gustavo Cochet.

107   See "Reunión del Comité Regional celebrada el día 8 de julio de 1937," CNT (España) Archives (IISG) 39 A.

their passive attitude can be explained by their lack of concern for an organisation that had been constituted without their authorisation and by flouting internal discipline; it can also be explained by their desire to collaborate with Negrín, and consequently to avoid provoking any serious conflict that would poison relations.[108]

In this context, those activists who considered that the hegemony previously enjoyed by the libertarian movement in Cataluña and Aragón could yet be recovered by force realised that, sooner or later, the ongoing operations of the security forces would make any such strategy untenable.

Such was the reasoning of activists in the CNT-affiliated Transport Workers' Union of Barcelona, whose Secretary was Julián Merino, when in August 1937 they prevented police from carrying out a register of their union headquarters. The union was summoned to defend its actions at a meeting of the Regional Committee of the CNT on 10 August, at which García Oliver, Xena and Dionisio Eroles were all in attendance, where the potential scale of this defensive operation became apparent. Merino, speaking on behalf of the Union Council, declared that the union was responding to the provocations of its enemies: "We are losing our conquests piece by piece. We have lost almost all of the centres of production that we gained in the heat of the revolution."[109] The union, he said, had already handed over garages, cars and tanks to the police, with the result that its functions had been disrupted and its members had gone unpaid:

These and many other abuses have so disheartened the activists, who suspect that everything is gradually being lost, and, fearing the moment when defending ourselves will have become impossible, they have risen in anger and agreed to the self-defence for which we are being so criticised. All that the council has done is to take on board the agreements arrived at by the majority of the members.[110]

This little-recorded event provides a fascinating example of how individual CNT unions were able to arrive at the kind of bold resolutions that the intervention of the *comités superiores* had obstructed over the summer at

---

108   Lorenzo, *Los anarquistas españoles*, 249.

109   "Reunión extraordinaria celebrada el día 10 de Agosto de 1937; por el Comité Regional de Cataluña; estando presentes los delegados siguientes, Artes Gráficas, Alimentación, Productos Químicos, Transporte, Secretario, Más, Luz y Fuerza, Eroles, Isgleas, García Oliver, Siderometalurgia, y la Junta del Sindicato de Transporte," CNT (España) Archives (IISG) 39 A.

110   "Reunión extraordinaria celebrada el día 10 de Agosto."

the Plenums of the FAI.[111] But it was precisely this isolation from the rest of the libertarian movement that was invoked by José Juan Domènech, former Councillor of Supplies in the Generalitat and then Regional Secretary of the CNT, when he demanded that the union abandon its stance:

> Only two options remain: either the attitude of the Transport Workers' Union will be supported by the other unions of the Organisation, and then the Organisation as a whole; or the Union, after this act of violence, will find itself isolated and abandoned by its comrades and therefore outside of the Organisation.

It seems clear that only the second option was conceivable to the Regional Secretary, and the possibility of an armed movement of the whole of the CNT against the counterrevolution arising from the bottom up can only have been disingenuously entertained given the role of the *comités superiores* when faced by such a movement the previous May. In fact, the *comités superiores* dreaded a repetition of the May events, and suspected that the security forces in Barcelona were intent on provoking an altercation.[112] The intervention of José Xena at this meeting suggests that this fear was far from groundless:

> Yesterday the Union was prepared, with arms in hand, to prevent the Civil Guard from carrying out a register [of the headquarters], and the affinity groups and neighbourhood committees were aware of this attitude, and were also prepared to come out in support of this grand movement, something that should have been made known to the Liaison Committee, which is [the organ that] must control all such movements when they are necessary.[113]

More remarkable than the wilful self-deception implied by Xena's suggestion that the Liaison Committee could head up rather than quash any such initiative is his admission that the libertarian networks that had mobilised in May had maintained their channels of communication and capacity for autonomous action in spite of the heavy repression they had undergone. Merino, clearly, was a key point of continuity in this respect. García Oliver, whose memoirs accord Merino a pivotal role in the mobilisation of May,

---

111   The proceedings of this meeting have recently been referred to in Guillamón, *La represión contra la CNT*, 318–20.

112   On the intentions and activity of the security forces in this period, see Godicheau, *No callaron*, 83–4.

113   "Reunión extraordinaria celebrada el día 10 de Agosto."

intervened at length at the meeting in August in a tone of extraordinary ferocity:

> At the front much greater events are occurring than here, and any comrade that steps out of line is tried and shot… the Transport Workers' Union was not unconnected to the propaganda carried out against government collaboration… and these tactics are inappropriate and deceive the people. Whosoever inspires these movements is a TRAITOR and if there are ten who are behind them there are ten TRAITORS. The people do not show as much support for us as we would like. If we take to the streets and lose then our loss would be THE GREATEST BETRAYAL OF ALL TIME… you present us as reformists, but we are no less revolutionary than anyone else… If the situation is as Xena has described, Popular Tribunals will certainly be necessary TO PUNISH THE INSTIGATORS.[114]

This remarkable speech demonstrates, perhaps as much as any other single document, the transformation that the experience of state collaboration and the anti-fascist war had imposed upon the anarcho-syndicalist movement in Spain and the divisions this had given rise to. García Oliver had once been the chief theoretician and practitioner of that impetuous anarchist voluntarism that he now considered an act of treachery worthy of the harshest punishments. The Secretary of the CAP concluded that

> everything that is going on is influenced by our enemies who want to break the alliance or pact between the CNT and the UGT and there is therefore no alternative but to create a Revolutionary Tribunal, and that whosoever deserves it, let [justice] be meted out to him WITHOUT QUALMS.[115]

In spite of the threats of García Oliver, who in his capacity as Secretary of the CAP would also make vague but equally ominous insinuations to the oppositionists Santana Calero and Peirats, the minutes record that the delegates of the Transport Workers' Union demanded proof of what had been alleged against them and "remained unconvinced of the need to change their attitude."[116] The meeting ended with the representatives of the *comités superiores* expressing the wish that an assembly of the various Barcelona unions due

---

114   Ibid. Capitalisation of words as they appear in the minutes.
115   Ibid.
116   Ibid. On García Oliver threatening Peirats and Santana Calero, see Ealham, *Living Anarchism*, 112.

to take place that afternoon would succeed in convincing the representatives of the Transport Workers' Union to drop their combative stance.

It is likely that this meeting also ended in stalemate, as the state of tension was to continue into the following month, with police raids on JJLL headquarters and anarchist centres culminating in the assault on the building known as "Los Escolapios" on 20 September. This former religious school was the headquarters of the cultural grouping Agrupación Faros, the Food Supplies Union and the city centre defence committee. The activists present in the building in the early hours of the morning refused to open its doors to a detachment of Assault Guards, who returned with artillery and tanks. The CAP was charged with mediating between those inside the building and the police, and was informed that the building would be subject to aerial bombardment if it was not abandoned within ten minutes.[117] Nevertheless, those inside submitted to the demands of the CAP that they abide by "the agreements taken in previous Plenums" rather than the threats of the police.[118] While some of those already wanted by the authorities for their involvement in the May days were able to escape from the building, those who handed themselves in were to have their fate decided by the newly formed Tribunales Especiales de Espionaje y Alta Traición (Special Tribunals of Espionage and High Treason).[119]

The meeting of anarchist affinity groups that took place in the wake of these events saw similar sentiments expressed to those aired at the Regional Plenum of Anarchist Affinity Groups in July and the extraordinary meeting of the Regional Committee of the Catalan CNT on 10 August, discussed above. The delegate of the group Dinamita Cerebral (possibly Teodoro García of the Metalworkers' Union) denounced the CNT leadership for allowing "all the conquered positions to be snatched from us bit by bit... Another 19 July is coming and we must prepare ourselves if we do not want to lose."[120] However, there was an increasing sense of desperation in the interventions of delegates and an acknowledgement of a certain amount of impotence and isolation. The delegate of the affinity group Convicción y Firmeza noted bitterly that "we have lost one of the most important strategic points of the city, but it does not matter, because we are a political party." He had seen, he claimed, "battle-hardened comrades in tears," but this "cannot be taken into account because it is the organisation itself that

117   See "Acta del Pleno de GGAA, celebrado en Barcelona el día 21 de Septiembre de 1937," CDMH, PS Barcelona, 1307/7; also Godicheau, *No callaron*, 83–4, and Guillamón, *La represión contra la CNT*, 402–12.

118   See "Acta del Pleno de GGAA."

119   See Godicheau, *No callaron*, 85–9. The prisoners were eventually released in the early part of 1938.

120   See "Acta del Pleno de GGAA."

is authorising everything that is happening."[121] Censure of the Regional Committee of the CNT was universal, and there were calls for its removal, with the delegate of the Móvil group declaring that it was "high time that we begin to expel the irresponsible elements," while other delegates questioned the role of García Oliver, Secretary of the CAP. The delegate of the group Afinidad, in reference to García Oliver and José Juan Domènech, wondered whether "we are communists" and that, if not, "then we must not allow a certain number of individuals to determine what goes on."[122] In the absence of a leadership that would stand up for the persecuted anarchists of the rank and file, the delegate of the affinity group Humanidad found it "perfectly natural that a defence committee has rebelled and acted of its own account." Noting that the Local Federation of unions had come to an agreement with Ricardo Burillo, Director General of Security in Cataluña, which allowed the police to carry out registers of union buildings, the delegate went on to observe that "either the Organisation has been bought off or else it is happy to take on all the responsibility for what is happening."[123]

In the context of organisational isolation, delegates questioned what kind of role the FAI could have. If it was to be the vanguard of the libertarian movement, how could the affinity groups of Barcelona remain beholden to regional and national leaderships that quashed any autonomous initiative? The delegate of the Sagitario group, protesting "the conduct of the Organisation," declared that it was time for "the FAI to act of its own accord and not merely tail the CNT."[124] This, however, led to a debate, as delegates defended the FAI's traditional *trabazón* with the unions. The delegate of the Rebeldes group located the weakness of the FAI in the fact that its activists had:

> situated themselves outside of the unions, either due to negligence or because the majority of comrades occupy positions in other places. This cannot continue. We must go directly to the unions and take on responsible posts so that we can, in this way, guide the unions according to the perspectives of the FAI.[125]

This was also the position expressed by Merino in his capacity as Secretary of the Local Federation, a line he consistently enunciated, perhaps unsurprisingly, given his additional position as Secretary of the Transport

---

121   Ibid.
122   Ibid.
123   Ibid.
124   The Sagitario group included Martín Gibel, Vicente Serna and Miguel Garrofe (their FAI membership cards can be found in CDMH, PS Barcelona, 1793/1).
125   "Acta del Pleno de GGAA."

Workers' Union. However, the delegate of the Sagitario group explained that there were difficulties in influencing the unions owing to the "continuous offensive that comes from the arrivistes," saying that he had been elected president of his union but that he was "boycotted shamelessly by other elements from the same union."[126]

In reality, these arguments were not contradictory: the influence of the FAI as a specifically anarchist voice within the Spanish labour movement had been diluted on the one hand by the official duties "in other places" of many of its members and on the other by the influx of new recruits to the CNT after 19 July 1936. Consequently, the libertarian movement had been, as one anarchist put it, "invaded" by "a moderate spirit."[127] Yet organisational neglect and the ideological underdevelopment of new recruits was of less importance than the political defeat that the movement's old hands had been able to inflict on the radicals of the Local Federation. The May days had provided, after all, an eloquent refutation of the "moderate spirit" thesis. Then the Local Federation had been able to assume its vanguard role by placing itself at the intersection of a radical alliance that had gestated in the front and in the rear, in the workplace and in the street.

The positions and strategies that the Local Federation defended over the summer of 1937, in the pages of *Anarquía* and in the Plenums of the FAI, were a continuation and consolidation of the radical programme worked out in the first third of the year and, in their clear prioritisation of the revolution over the immediate requirements of the war, in fact represented a radicalisation of that programme. Two opportunities had presented themselves for this programme to be carried forward through a reprise of the May days, in the defence of the Transport Workers' Union and the "Escolapios" buildings, in August and September. However, leaving aside the important question of the relative increase in the violent resources of the state in Barcelona, two crucial contextual differences prevented this from taking place. First, since May the *comités superiores* had unambiguously set themselves in opposition to the radical mid-level and grassroots activists of the movement. One outcome of this was that the intervention of these committees at the Regional Plenum in July deprived the defence committees and affinity groups of the mandate that the FAI had been able to grant them in April. It further meant that the committees could rely on activists specifically tasked with quashing autonomous activities when they arose. Second, the radical alliance that had been fundamental to the May days had begun to fracture, due to internal and external pressures. These latter two phenomena will be discussed in more detail in the chapter that follows.

126   "Acta del Pleno del GGAA."
127   Ibid.

Conclusions

In spite of being ejected from the Ministries and Councils of government in Valencia and Cataluña, the libertarian movement in Spain remained important to the administrative functioning of the Republican state, and its most prominent representatives remained committed to the Republican war effort, accepting the nationalist and militarist corollaries of state collaboration during wartime. In opposition to them, those currents representing the conscience of the Spanish revolution attempted to advance a different policy in the aftermath of the May events, demonstrating in the process the continued confluence of perspectives among voluntarist and purist radicals. While several voluntarists and purists of the pre-war period had become ardent supporters of collaboration, among the oppositionists we also find many veterans of the struggle against *treintismo*, who shared a vision of the FAI as the radicalising agent or anarchist vanguard of the CNT. This shared vision enabled voluntarists and purists, including several members of the JJLL, to advance a unified perspective at the Regional Plenum of Anarchist Affinity Groups in July 1937. This anti-collaborationist tendency was therefore made up of the same "categories" of Spanish anarchism that had successfully allied to unseat the moderates from their positions of responsibility during the Second Republic and, as before, was composed chiefly of mid-level CNT activists and union delegates who also belonged to the FAI.

As for the category of *"treintismo,"* it persisted insofar as it continued to be used as a derogatory term for those anarchists who appealed to exceptional circumstances to justify collaborating with Republican politicians.[128] During the civil war, this category was swollen by militants who were neither ideologically nor temperamentally "moderate," but who nevertheless had become convinced of the need to prioritise anti-fascism over the social revolution. Their positions in governmental bodies or even in the *comités superiores* gave this prioritisation a professional imperative, while the course of the war gave it a moral urgency that brooked no disagreement. Consequently, those influential anarchists who had become convinced that the importance and grandeur of the Spanish libertarian movement was such that its intervention in the direction of the anti-fascist state was both necessary and potentially decisive would spend much of 1937–1938 engaged in a tireless propaganda campaign whose chief objective was to persuade their former comrades to no longer behave like anarchists. For this they were labelled *"treintistas"* regardless of their activity prior to 19 July. In October 1937, Merino recalled the "struggles that the reformists of those days waged

128   See the denunciation of the Regional Committee of the Catalan CNT in *El Amigo del Pueblo*, 19 May 1937.

against the FAI in 1931," noting that "it is precisely today, in the midst of a revolutionary period when it would seem that those reformist intentions have been achieved."[129]

In this chapter I have set out how the radical anarchists of Barcelona responded to this challenge. The problem of the relationship to the state would be dealt with by withdrawal from official positions, that of the anti-fascist war by a readjustment of priorities that would see the counterrevolution met in armed confrontation in the rearguard, and that of the moderation of the CNT by a renovation of the *comités superiores* and a reaffirmation of the vanguard role of the FAI. Evidently, this would have supposed a complete break with the trajectory undertaken by the *comités superiores* up to this point. In opposing such proposals, the *comités superiores* employed bureaucratic measures to shut down oppositional voices at National Plenums and to censor the anarchist press. They also, however, did their utmost to persuade wavering activists, to defend their activity and to win votes at fractious Local and Regional Plenums.

Certainly, the *comités superiores* in Barcelona were aided by the fact that the nerve-centre of activity for the insubordinate middle-ranks of the movement was rarely further than a corridor or a staircase away, in the enormous Casa CNT-FAI. As Germinal Gracia, an activist in the JJLL, later recalled:

> During the revolution, the old house of Francisco Cambó played host to a constant coming and going of people, all up to their ears in work and looking for solutions that were not always possible… The three upper floors… of the requisitioned building were occupied by the three Regional Committees of the CNT, the JJLL and the FAI, in that order. The Local Federation of Affinity Groups, Co-ordination, the Office of CNT-FAI Propaganda, and other departments, including an enormous meeting hall on the first floor, took up the rest.[130]

The physical proximity of the opposing wings of the movement in Barcelona had proven an obstacle to radical initiative during the May days and ensured that non-delegate grandees were able to intervene at the Regional Plenum of Anarchist Affinity Groups of Cataluña in July. That their presence appears to have been decisive may indicate, to an extent, their ongoing prestige within the movement and the limits of the radicals' appeal. We might also cite the experience of defeat in May and the ongoing repression of the libertarian movement, as well as the losses at the front, as being conducive to

129   "Primera sesión del pleno anarquista."
130   Víctor García, "José Xena Torrent: Aporte para una biografía necesaria," *Orto*, 54 (1989): 32. I am grateful to Nereida Xena for providing me with a copy of this article.

fatalism, a tendency, discussed in the following chapter, that can be seen in the choice of some radicals to enlist in the army. Anarchist activity was immeasurably complicated in this period by the absorption of much of the libertarian movement into mechanisms of state control, through participation in the army and security forces, in nationalised or semi-nationalised industries and directly in administrative or governmental bodies. This accelerated the bureaucratisation of the CNT-FAI, characterised by a proliferation of committees tasked with preventing precisely the varieties of oppositional anarchism dealt with in this book. Thus, as we have seen in this chapter, the state closure of libertarian spaces was mediated by the libertarian movement itself, through bodies such as the CAP, whose representatives gave their tacit consent to the abandonment of defence committee headquarters and had oppositional newspapers shut down, refusing to countenance that such spaces could exist even beyond the borders of Spain.

So it was that Julián Merino found himself confronted by Xena and García Oliver in August 1937, the latter insinuating that he should be shot, after undertaking one more in a series of audacious revolutionary measures. While he was neither cowed nor inactive, Merino admitted to his disillusion at a Plenum two months later:

> I have read a letter addressed to the comrades from the Secretary [Alejandro Gilabert] who regrets that anarchism has become isolated, and I too am bitter that there isn't a comrade to be found with the necessary perception and courage to defend the ideas.[131]

For Merino, the limits to revolutionary transformation in July remained a source of frustration: "had we wanted to, we could have instituted our ideals on 19 July. Lamentably, we did not."[132] We have seen, however, how after the "missed opportunity" of July, radical anarchists had nevertheless found a way to push the revolution forward, had forged new alliances and, ultimately, revealed the fragility of the project of state reconstruction through a mass uprising in Barcelona. It was in the period following this second failure to "institute anarchist ideals" that the radicals increasingly found themselves backed into a corner.

131   "Primera sesión del pleno anarquista."
132   Ibid.

AQUI NO HA PASADO NADA

4/50

The return to bourgeois normality is depicted in an engraving by an engraving by Gustavo Cochet, photographed by Mario Gómez Casas, reproduced by permission of the Museo Gustavo Cochet and the Ministerio de Innovación y Cultura de Santa Fe. The caption reads: "Nothing happened here."

CHAPTER SIX

The Experience of Defeat, 1937–1939

It could be objected, and the realities that we are experiencing in this period of war confirm it, that we are moving with giant steps towards state capitalism, which for the proletariat will take the form of a new system of dependence; that the worker will only be valued as the stuff of the workshop or factory, and his personal liberty will be completely cut off... It is dangerously fatalist to accustom oneself to the state of things as they are in the belief that they cannot be changed, or to simply hide behind the played-out and imported cliché of the "circumstances." Let us reject that fatalism and return to our previous, so regrettably forgotten line of conduct. Let us be worthy of Anarchy.[1]

The above passage is taken from an article signed by Tomás Cabot that appeared in *Esfuerzo*, a publication resuscitated as an organ of the Catalan JJLL in the autumn of 1937.[2] It is immediately notable for the sophistication of its critique, particularly in the identification of "state capitalism" as the emerging dominant tendency in the economy of the Spanish Republic. This phrase was chiefly associated with "ultra-left" and anarchist analyses of the decline of the Russian Revolution, and was used within a year of the Soviet takeover by the group around the short-lived newspaper *Kommunist*. This publication expressed similar concerns to those of Cabot, warning that the Soviet Republic was threatened by an "evolution towards state capitalism': "The introduction of labour discipline in connection with the restoration of capitalist management of industry... will diminish the class initiative, activity and organisation of the proletariat. It threatens to enslave the working class."[3] In August 1918, the First All-Russian Conference of the

1   *Esfuerzo*, 7 October 1937.
2   The title had formerly appeared, prior to June 1937, as a flysheet, edited by Juan Santana Calero. See Chapters Three and Four. Santana Calero was also heavily involved in the later publication, although its official editor was Ramón Liarte. I have not been able to find any information regarding Tomás Cabot aside from his contributions to *Esfuerzo*.
3   Taken from the first issue of *Kommunist*, published in April 1918 by the "Left Communist" St Petersburg Committee and the St Petersburg Area Committee of the Russian Social Democratic Labour Party (the Bolsheviks), cited by Lenin in N. Lenin, "'Left-

185

Anarcho-Syndicalists pledged to struggle "for emancipation from state capitalism."[4] Oppositional anarchists in Spain recognised the parallels with what had unfolded in Russia. Amador Franco wrote in *Esfuerzo*:

> If we analyse what happened in that [Russian] movement, walking in the footsteps of the epic struggle of the Kronstadt sailors and in the struggles of the peasants in Ukraine, the stages undergone by that people, in its fight against global capitalism and the armies of its interior, seem to us to be the same as in our struggle, save for differences of time and characteristics... Furthermore, the partisans of true communism had to confront those who, in the name of the proletariat, in fact operated behind its back.[5]

The parallels are instructive; both in Russia in 1918 and Spain in 1937, revolutionary changes in daily working life had been truncated, and dissident currents confronted revolutionary leaderships, Bolshevik and anarcho-syndicalist, who considered their participation in the state to be irreversible, and the increasing state control of industry to be inevitable, and presented both phenomena as steps on the path to victory.[6]

The two related concerns revealed in the above citation from Tomás Cabot, that the Spanish revolution had not led to a lasting emancipation of the working class, and that it was the duty of anarchists to resist a fatalist acceptance of this state of affairs, were now unambiguous dividing lines between radical anarchists and the *comités superiores* of the CNT-FAI, who were wedded to both the increasing centralisation of workplaces under state control and to a fatalist, or "tragic," reading of the Spanish revolution. Through recourse to such a reading, the CNT representatives attempted to make their positions immune to criticism by presenting them as inevitable adaptations to the drama of the civil war. At an Extraordinary Congress of the IWMA in Paris in December, the CNT delegation declared: "No-one must be allowed to speculate over our tragedy. It is a question of justice and

---

Wing' Childishness," a series of articles published in *Pravda* in May 1918, available at https://www.marxists.org/archive/lenin/works/1918/may/09.htm [accessed 5 December 2017].

4   See "Three Resolutions' in *The Anarchists in the Russian Revolution*, ed. by Paul Avrich (London: Thames and Hudson, 1973), 117.

5   *Esfuerzo*, 24 October 1937.

6   Lenin declared that "state capitalism would be a *step forward* as compared with the present state of affairs in our Soviet Republic. If in approximately six months' time state capitalism became established in our Republic, this would be a great success and a sure guarantee that within a year socialism will have gained a permanently firm hold and will have become invincible in our country": Lenin, "'Left-Wing' Childishness."

morality."[7] As the above citation from *Esfuerzo* shows, however, such enjoinders rang hollow when directed at CNT members in Spain who were, after all, actors in the same drama. Consequently, the internal opposition, the existence of which the CNT's *comités superiores* denied to the world, voiced its rejection not only of "state capitalism" but also of the denial of its agency, its revolutionary will.

Despite the defiant appeals to revolutionary will and continued anarchist strength, the defeat of May had brought fissures in the alliances effected by radical anarchists. As we will see in this chapter, a rejection of fatalism was often accompanied by signs of a retreat into ideology and introspection. This was owing on the one hand to strategic shortcomings and ideological blind spots, but on the other to a fear that the radicals' defeat on the streets and in the meeting halls would lead to a lasting defeat for anarchist ideals. In an article entitled "Permanent Effects of a Temporary Position" published in *Frente y Retaguardia*, José Peirats made the connection between the CNT's state collaboration and a perceived ideological decomposition in the libertarian ranks:

> Many of the youth already think like perfect Communists or republicans, although they do so in the name of the CNT. Therein lies the danger. That of taking seriously a purely theatrical and transitory role. These are the permanent effects of a temporary position.[8]

In the previous chapter, I showed how the leadership stratum of the libertarian movement successfully asserted its power and authority over the radical activists who had tried to force a change in policy. By autumn 1937, radicals lamented that "neo-anarchism" had "won the battle over true anarchism."[9] The focus of this chapter will therefore shift from the battle between these currents to their independent activity, through which one sought to use its increasing centralisation and concessions to its allies to influence state policy, and the other to reaffirm its traditions, preserve its autonomous activities and prevent the collaborationist policy of the *comités superiores* from contaminating the grassroots. The attempts of the former current to increase its influence were in vain, while the increasingly impotent calls to action of the latter lacked the strategic viability that they had acquired prior to May 1937. This was in part due to a weakening of the solidarities – with radical women, foreigners and the POUM – that had helped to animate that mobilisation. Isolated, radicals were left with little option but to, as Cabot put it, "return to their previous [pre-war] line of conduct,"

7   "Actas del Congreso de la AIT celebrado en París."
8   *Frente y Retaguardia*, 26 June 1937.
9   "Acta del pleno regional de grupos anarquistas de Cataluña."

of propaganda, prisoner support and rational education. With the war's end, the defeats of both statist anarchism and its radical alternative were subsumed under the enormous human catastrophe that engulfed Spain. All that was left for those who survived was to attempt to draw conclusions from the experience.

The apex of statist anarchism

Following the May days, the divide between the leading cadres of the CNT and its remaining activists in the rearguard was such that the organisation has been described as being effectively, if not formally, split.[10] However, the first National Plenum of the organisation that followed these events did not reflect the division existent in the libertarian movement, its moment of controversy limited to the Andalusian delegates' censure of a National Committee communiqué regarding Francisco Maroto.[11] This document, signed by the National Secretary Mariano Rodríguez Vázquez on 3 May 1937, was issued in response to a letter sent by Maroto, whose imprisonment had become a *cause célèbre* for the radical wing of the libertarian movement throughout the Republican zone.[12] The communiqué implied that, contrary to widespread belief among libertarians, Maroto – a veteran CNT member described variously in the communiqué as "a kid" and "a puppet" – did indeed have a case to answer.[13] Nevertheless, it was also clear that his true crime, as far as the National Committee was concerned, was to have publicly criticised the *comités superiores*. There was no sign at the Plenum of what the National Committee referred to in its communiqué as the "notorious irresponsible elements that abound in our ranks."[14] The expulsion of the AAD was ratified unanimously, and it was decided that Liaison Committees be set up in the regions to further cohere the different branches of the libertarian movement.[15]

This latter measure had been proposed by the Catalan delegation to end "the lack of unity among the three branches of our movement."

10   See François Godicheau, *La Guerre d'Espagne*, 330–5.
11   See "Comité Nacional Circular N° 7," CNT (España) Archives (IISG), 46 B.
12   See Chapter Four.
13   At a Peninsular Plenum of the FAI in July, Maroto averred that this assertion could have been used against him by the authorities. The response of the Peninsular Committee of the FAI was to repeat the line of the National Committee of the CNT, that Maroto's temperament had led him into a trap set by his political enemies. See *Memoria del Pleno Peninsular de Regionales celebrado en Valencia los días 4, 5, 6 y 7 de Julio 1937* (Valencia: FAI, 1937), 25–31.
14   "Comité Nacional Circular N° 7."
15   See "Acuerdos del Pleno Nacional de Regionales."

These Committees were to focus on propaganda, defence and investigation, although both the delegation for the Central region and the National Committee also raised the possibility of creating an "organ of political direction" within the movement.[16] In the aftermath of the May events, the *comités superiores* were thus sketching out an institutional framework by which the three branches of the libertarian movement could be transformed into a single, top-down entity.[17] Attempts to take up the challenge issued by the JJLL of Gràcia during that mobilisation, to replace those *comités superiores* "sealed off" from the rest of the movement, therefore faced an uphill battle as the bureaucratisation of the CNT continued apace despite the organisation's exit from central government, an event echoed at the regional level when the reorganisation of the Generalitat led to the ejection of the CNT at the end of June. The CNT objected to the reduced influence that it would have in the reshuffled cabinet Companys had presented to the organisation. "No longer strong enough to impose conditions," the CNT was simply excluded.[18]

It is possible that the departure from these governmental bodies in fact accelerated the process of bureaucratisation in the libertarian movement, as most former Ministers and Councillors were subsequently ushered into existing or newly established *comités superiores*. In his memoirs, Horacio M. Prieto alleges that the National Committee under the jurisdiction of Rodríguez Vázquez was "converted into a monstrous bureaucratic apparatus full of draft-dodgers and people who did little other than 'hang around' and waste time."[19] In Cataluña, as discussed in the previous chapter, García Oliver was named Secretary of the newly created Political Advisory Commission, the CAP. It was viewed with some suspicion by Catalan anarchists, not least because its stated function of coordination was supposedly already being carried out by the aforementioned regional Liaison Committee. At a meeting of the Regional Committee of the Catalan CNT on 2 July 1937, Pujol, the delegate for the Metalworkers' Union, commented on the acronym meaning "head" in Catalan, and on the apparent desire of its members to place themselves above the norms of the libertarian organisations.[20] As we have seen in the previous chapter, the principal role of the CAP was to enforce radical anarchist submission to the *comités superiores* and state authorities. On 12 July, complaints were again made at a Regional Committee meeting about the multiplicity of committees,

16   See "Actas del Pleno Nacional de Regionales."
17   This observation is also made in Peirats, *The CNT, Vol. 2*, 184.
18   Pagès i Blanch, *La Guerra Civil espanyola a Catalunya*, 120. See also Lorenzo, *Los anarquistas españoles*, 223–5, and Peirats, *The CNT, Vol. 2*, 198–202.
19   Prieto, *Secretario General de la CNT de España en 1936, Tomo II*, 184.
20   "Reunión del Comité Regional y demás comités responsables celebrada el viernes día 2 por la tarde del mes de julio de 1937," CNT (España) Archives (IISG) 39 A.

accompanied by the suggestion that "many comrades want to quit work in order to pretend that they are looking after the organisation."[21]

In *Ideas*, "Fontaura," the pseudonym of the veteran purist Vicente Galindo Cortés, wrote:

> The bureaucracy is taking on terrifying proportions. Certain individuals are living in the best of worlds. They are "emancipated" from labour – because spending three or four hours chatting in an office cannot be called work – and they receive salaries such as they had never dreamed possible.[22]

By the autumn of 1937, Severino Campos, having resigned from his position as secretary of the Regional Committee of the Catalan FAI, made no attempt to hide his scorn for those in positions of responsibility in the libertarian organisations:

> Where there were ideas these ideas remain. Those who say that they sacrificed them never had them... They spend their days on a slippery slope. From the centre of the political whirlwind they breathe putrefied air that withers and numbs them... individuals that puff themselves up, believing themselves to be great men that influence "the realities of the moment"... are nothing but ambitious and conceited pygmies.[23]

Prieto, whose commitment to anti-fascist priorities had led to a revision of principles that would shortly see him openly advocate the formation of a libertarian political party, took a contrary approach. At the Congress of the IWMA in December 1937, he chided German representatives from the DAS: "if the German comrades had understood something of principles and of the necessity of sometimes altering them, fascism wouldn't have succeeded [there]... Sacrosanct principles, in the midst of the current struggle, should pass onto a secondary plane."[24] Prieto went on to emphasise the need for organisational discipline with brutal frankness:

> Every idea requires an organisation in order to conquer the world, not based on a sentimental whim, but forged in a single bloc and maintained by implacable sanctions on indiscipline. Down with the principles and

21   "Reunión del Comité Regional de Cataluña celebrada el día 12 de julio de 1937 estando presentes casi todos los miembros del mismo," CNT (España) Archives (IISG) 39 A.
22   *Ideas*, 20 May 1937.
23   *Faro*, 12 November 1937.
24   "Actas del Congreso de la AIT celebrado en París."

theories that have failed and which lead us to new disasters! New procedures for new times! Regular army, collaboration with the government, renovation of all principles of economic harmony that we considered intangible, it is necessary to know how to discipline oneself, to satisfy the comrades of the UGT, the petite-bourgeoisie etc.[25]

This final allusion to satisfying the UGT and the petite-bourgeoisie hinted at the *comités superiores'* plans for the CNT's Economic Plenum to be held the following month, in January 1938. There, the CNT National Committee set the agenda, in which it advocated a centralised economy in which industries under its control would be run by an Economic Council, and made concessions to the UGT on the long-standing, contentious issue of wage differentials.[26] At the Congress of the IWMA, Alexander Schapiro, described by Prieto as "the greatest enemy of the CNT," characterised the economic conceptions put forward by the CNT as representing "a retreat to the well-known ideas of corporative or reformist unionism."[27] The "new system of dependence" envisaged by Cabot in the citation from *Esfuerzo* at the beginning of this chapter, in which the worker "will only be valued as the stuff of the workshop or factory," seemed to be given credence by the declarations at this Congress of Rodríguez Vázquez, who indicated that workers' control of industry and assembly-based workplace democracy, even among CNT members, were now anathema to official CNT policy:

The times in which we live do not permit either abundance or equality. They demand from everyone an elevated contribution of sacrifice that is hard to agree to, and which is even harder to demand of those who have joined the organisation more out of self-interest than idealism. That is why we must compromise with reality. We cannot allow workers to determine for themselves the mode of their salary; we cannot give a blank cheque to everyone, especially not the arrivistes... in such a situation it is highly natural that the complicated problems of the libertarian movement be reserved for the old guard, of absolute solidity.[28]

With "the old guard" in charge and a "dependent" workforce robbed of any decision-making power, workplace relations were thus established

25   Ibid.
26   See Peirats, *The CNT, Vol. 3*, 1–17. On wage differentials, see Mintz, *Anarchism and Workers' Self-Management*, 108–9, and Castells Duran, *El proceso estatizador*, 18–19.
27   "Actas del Congreso de la AIT celebrado en París." For this description of Schapiro, see Prieto, *Secretario General de la CNT de España en 1936, Tomo II*, 148.
28   Ibid.

along traditional lines, a shift that had been reinforced after May 1937 by an increase in injunctions from the CNT hierarchy to the Spanish workforce to increase productivity and leave questions of living standards until after the war.[29] For Schapiro, such arguments rested on the "sophistry of capitalism that has always been employed to oppose the demands of the proletariat."[30] In other words, the CNT leadership had positioned itself as an opponent of proletarian demands, and was prepared to buttress itself with capitalist ideology in order to do so. This explained why it now faced its own members from a position of power and authority, a process that Schapiro did not hesitate to describe as "bolshevisation."

The attempt to forge the libertarian movement into a "single bloc" was doomed to failure, but nevertheless took a step forward through the formation, on the initiative of García Oliver, of the Executive Committee of the Libertarian Movement in Cataluña, confirmed at a Plenum at the beginning of April 1938. Diego Camacho, who was in attendance, recalled that there were

> many [delegates] there whom I did not recognise… alongside other very well-known activists who before July 1936 had been the most ardent extremists of the FAI, but who by this time… were showing themselves to be much more reformist than the so-called "*treintistas*" had been.[31]

Listening to the speech of García Oliver, Camacho had the impression that the Executive Committee was being presented to the movement as a fait accompli, and that it would face only minority opposition from "young libertarians and certain affinity groups from Barcelona. And so it was."[32]

The Executive Committee was composed of five delegates from the CNT, three from the FAI and two from the JJLL. Fidel Miró, one of its members, recalled: "This organisation, unprecedented in the anarchist movement – which always employed federalist structures – would have in its hands the single command of the Confederal and libertarian masses."[33] The body was intended to facilitate rapid decision-making "without the need for multiple consultations between the committees and the grassroots of the organisation," but in reality operated as a kind of tribunal judging hapless CNT members accused of desertion and theft in a context of accelerating

29   See Monjo and Vega, *Els treballadors i la guerra civil*, 164–8; Mintz, *Anarchism and Workers' Self-Management*, 116–24, and Seidman, *Workers Against Work*, 132–42.
30   "Actas del Congreso de la AIT celebrado en París."
31   Paz, *Viaje al pasado*, 251.
32   Ibid. 251.
33   Miró, *Vida intensa*, 234–5.

military catastrophe at the front and increasing hardship in the rear.[34] The Executive Committee arrogated to itself the power to expel individuals, groups, unions and committees, and committed itself to the application of militarisation and to fighting against desertion and breaches of public order. Furthermore, it pledged to extend prisoner solidarity only to those activists whose incarceration could be put down to "error or misunderstanding" on the part of the authorities, and committed the CNT and the FAI to collaboration in regional and national governments.[35] The outline of the Committee's duties was signed on 4 April, and the re-entrance of the CNT into national government was confirmed two days later by the appointment to Negrín's cabinet of the veteran Asturian activist Segundo Blanco as Minister of Education.

At this point, in an episode that was to demonstrate the difficulty of press-ganging the ranks of the libertarian movement into a command structure, the Executive Committee began a lengthy back-and-forth with the local and regional committees of the JJLL, whose delegates to the Committee resigned, left for the front or were withdrawn with almost farcical frequency over the following months until, on 2 July 1938, a Plenum of neighbourhood activists of the JJLL stated its intention that the Local Federation of the JJLL should no longer be represented on the Executive Committee, declaring "that it would never submit to a body that in essence negated both the confederal structure of the CNT and the anarchism of the FAI."[36] Summoned to a meeting on 16 July, the delegates of the JJLL were invited by García Oliver "to consider the seriousness of creating a split in the movement," but this injunction met with short shrift from representatives determined to honour the agreements of their Plenum.[37] The following month, the Executive Committee announced the suspension of the Local Federation of the JJLL for breaches of discipline, calling a local Plenum to elect a new committee, but this was successfully boycotted by the libertarian youth. The Executive Committee itself ceased to exist shortly afterwards, although, as its founder remembered, "barely anyone noticed."[38]

Over the course of 1938, the *comités superiores* of the libertarian movement had taken several steps intended to shore up discipline in its ranks and commit to economic policies that would appeal to the dominant forces of

34   Ibid. 235–7.
35   "Informe del comité ejecutivo del movimiento libertario sobre la actitud de la federación local de JJLL de Barcelona y de su comité y sobre su posición con relación al movimiento libertario de Cataluña," CDMH, PS Barcelona, 514/08.
36   Paz, *Viaje al pasado*, 251.
37   "Informe del comité ejecutivo del movimiento libertario."
38   García Oliver, *El eco de los pasos*, 503.

Spanish anti-fascism. They were rewarded in March by a pact with the UGT, in which their erstwhile ally Largo Caballero no longer had any influence, and in April by representation in Negrín's "counterrevolutionary government," but even so could find no way of influencing state policy. Beginning the year advocating the creation of an Economic Council through which the organisation would centrally administer the CNT-controlled industries, from March the *comités superiores* merely requested union representation alongside the UGT in a governmental Higher Economic Council, which the CNT was still hoping to establish "as a matter of urgency" as late as October.[39] Early in 1938, the organisation acquiesced to the Generalitat's takeover of Barcelona's socialised public entertainments industry.[40] In May, the National Committee sent a communiqué to the Regional Committees with the news that the electricity sector, for which Joan Peiró was responsible in the Republican government, was to be "militarised," under the terms of which workers' control would cease and foreign ownership would return. Unsurprisingly, the National Committee stressed that it would not be prudent to circulate this information among the wider membership.[41] By the end of the year, the Catalan war industries, a great source of pride to the CNT, had also been nationalised.[42] Nor did the organisation's concessions appear to have any impact on the battlefield, where the year began and ended with demoralising defeats at Teruel and the Ebro.

In the spring, Bujaraloz, Caspe and Lleida, towns whose names are richly evocative of the high points of the Spanish revolution, fell to the Nationalist army during its Aragón offensive. Amidst increasing suspicion, disillusionment and defeatism, the libertarian movement called a National Plenum for mid-October, while the Republican army, including thousands of teenaged members of the Libertarian Youth called up as a part of the famous *quinta del biberón*, played its final card at the Ebro. At this Plenum, the balance sheet of collaboration was discussed, revealing a tendency among certain grandees of Spanish anarchism, expressed by the Peninsular Committee of the FAI, to reposition themselves as defenders of anarchist orthodoxy. Meanwhile, Prieto made the case for the FAI to formally convert itself into a political party, and Rodríguez Vázquez defended Negrín and his policy of resistance. Although the Plenum ended with a commitment to continued collaboration with the government, the National Committee was losing support for its adherence to Negrín's administration among

39   Peirats, *The CNT, Vol. 3*, 37 and 203.
40   See *La Vanguardia*, 22 January 1938. Rank-and-file resistance to this measure is discussed in Richards, *Lessons of the Spanish Revolution*, 188.
41   National Committee communiqué, 10 May 1938, CDMH, PS Barcelona, 523/17.
42   Peirats, *The CNT, Vol. 3*, 115–35.

the movement's notable personalities, with Germinal de Sousa and Pedro Herrera (both of the FAI Peninsular Committee) and Federica Montseny all denouncing Negrín and expressing scepticism as to his commitment to continued resistance.[43]

Following the fall of Barcelona in January 1939, the CNT in the remaining, Central and Southern, Republican zone collaborated with the ill-fated National Defence Council in what became known as the Casado coup. The National Defence Council, headed by Colonel Segismundo Casado and the moderate Socialist Julián Besteiro, declared itself the sole authority in the territory at midnight on 5/6 March 1939, deposing Negrín and excluding the PCE from Republican power. Previously, CNT delegates from the Republican zone had travelled to France to make contact with the exiled National Committees of the CNT and the FAI and returned to report that the leadership of the libertarian movement was already "defeated" and had given up the war as a lost cause.[44] With the defeat and exile of its National Committee, the CNT's collaboration in Negrín's government and commitment to its policy of resistance was over.

Since Negrín had assumed office, thousands of libertarian activists had been jailed and their revolutionary achievements dismantled. All this had been carried out with great energy and violence, to no discernible reward either in the corridors of power or on the battlefield, where Communist ascendancy had resulted in there being, according to a report of the FAI Peninsular Committee in October 1938, "thousands upon thousands of comrades who admit to being more afraid of being murdered by the competitor by their side than of perishing in the fighting with the enemy opposite."[45] That same month, soldiers arrested anarchist activists distributing *Ruta*, the mouthpiece of the JJLL, whose members had mobilised in huge numbers prior to the Battle of the Ebro. In November, a communiqué was issued by the command of the Eastern Army that "rapid and energetic" action should be taken against those reading or distributing it.[46] On the eve of defeat, CNT activists in the Republican zone considered the displacement of Negrín and a reckoning with the Communists to be necessary for a variety of reasons:

43   Ibid. 195–7.
44   Frank Mintz and Graham Kelsey, "El Consejo Nacional de Defensa y el movimiento libertario," in *Cuadernos de la Guerra Civil. Consejo Nacional de Defensa* (Madrid: Fundación Salvador Seguí Ediciones, 1989), 9.
45   Cited in Peirats, *The CNT, Vol. 3*, 159.
46   See, respectively "Informe que presenta el delegado de la IV zona de JJLL, acerca de la detención de los compañeros Manuel Barcelon Vernet y Salvador Saladie Ros de la localidad de Vandellos," and the communiqué sent by the Secretary of the CNT in Reus to the organisation's Defence Section in Barcelona, dated 26 November 1938, in Archivos de la Confederación Regional del Trabajo de Cataluña, Fundación Anselmo Lorenzo, 39D.

to continue military resistance, prevent the PCE from securing a privileged evacuation for its own activists at the cost of the libertarians, avoid a PCE takeover of the armed forces, or else a combination of the above.[47]

One of those relied upon to quash Communist resistance to the National Defence Council was the anarchist commander Máximo Franco, an early opponent of militarisation who had participated in the fighting during the May days and had collaborated in *Frente y Retaguardia*. Following the collapse of the Aragón front, where his division had gained a reputation as a haven for anarchists fearful that the hostility of Communist commanders would see them used as cannon fodder or shot from behind, he narrowly escaped a court-martial at the hands of the Communist colonel, Juan Modesto. However, while anarchist involvement in the fighting that took place in and around Madrid and Ciudad Real may have relied upon libertarian and Communist enmity, it was far from a settling of accounts, still less a sequel to the May days. Then, anarchists like Máximo Franco had fought for the revolution and against the state. During the squalid episode that brought the war to an end, they fought in the interests of delusional politicians whose efforts to secure honourable conditions of surrender from the enemy were predictably fruitless. Those politicians who wished to then escaped from Republican Spain. Meanwhile, Máximo Franco found himself caught in a rat trap with tens of thousands of his comrades at the port of Alicante, between the Nationalist forces and the sea, and took his own life.

Undoubtedly, the increased emphasis on organisational hierarchy within the libertarian movement had not led to greater dynamism but, on the contrary, merely aggravated resentment and rivalries among the *comités superiores* while stymying autonomous initiative. Frequently, activists were faced with a brick wall. When, for example, the Local Federation of the JJLL in Barcelona was summarily informed of the expulsion from the CNT of one of its members, it was unable to ascertain the causes of the expulsion in over a fortnight of correspondence with the Local Federation of Unions.[48] Likewise, when Julián Merino – himself a founder member of the Executive Committee of the Libertarian Movement – wrote to the same Local Federation calling for an expanded meeting of all committees and activist groups to discuss their response to the urgent situation Barcelona had found itself in, he was met with the bureaucratic response: "in reality, even allowing for the delicate situation of the Catalan fronts, there is a Regional Liaison Committee of the Libertarian Movement that we would

---

47   See Mintz and Kelsey, "El Consejo Nacional de Defensa", 9. Also Paul Preston, *The Last Days of the Spanish Republic* (London: William Collins, 2016), 164.

48   See various letters, from 15 December 1938 to 5 January 1939, CDMH, PS Barcelona, 842/1.

consider the more appropriate recipient of this request."[49] This was on 7 January 1939, less than three weeks before the entrance of the Francoist troops into Barcelona.

It would seem likely that Merino had joined the Executive Committee of the Libertarian Movement precisely to take the initiative in organising resistance to the Francoist advance. It is also conceivable that García Oliver had been able to persuade him of the plausibility of a scenario that he would later outline in his memoirs, of the Executive Committee taking on a vanguard role in Cataluña in the event of a popular reaction against Negrín.[50] In all other respects, the Executive Committee could be described without hyperbole as the culmination of everything that Merino had fought against for over a year previously. Days before the fall of Barcelona, he was charged (or more likely tasked himself) with organising remaining anarchists or anarchist sympathisers into defence battalions in the name of the FAI.[51] In the event, however, a suicidal, last-ditch defence of the city was not attempted, and he crossed the border into France with thousands of his fellow defeated comrades. As Merino must have understood better than most, the possibility of such "Numantian" resistance, regardless of the wing of the Republican state that advocated it, depended on the mobilising potential of the revolutionary energies and alliances that all wings of the state had collaborated in extinguishing and dismantling over the course of the war. However, while state repression was the principal cause of the breakdown of these revolutionary alliances, they had also been weakened by contradictions internal to the revolutionary movement.

The fracturing of revolutionary solidarities

In the previous chapter we have seen how the combination of alliances that had formed the revolutionary vanguard of spring 1937 was targeted by armed police actions that closed neighbourhood centres and kept order at the bread queues. While the sources analysed in the final subsection of that chapter show that the projected mobilisation in defence of the headquarters of the Barcelona Transport Workers' Union in August was able to rely on the same core activists' network as in May, it is possible that any such mobilisation would already have lacked the wider support that the previous uprising had generated. This was due primarily to objective factors, chiefly the increased repression the libertarians had to face. It was also the case,

---

49   Ibid.
50   García Oliver, *El eco de los pasos*, 503.
51   See *La Vanguardia*, 20 January 1939.

however, that, as the extent of the defeat of May became apparent, revolutionary solidarities began to wane. As had become clear before May, the new revolutionary impulse generated by the socialisation campaign was entirely dependent on the continued hegemony of armed worker activists. With these activists increasingly subject to arrest and imprisonment, a limiting of the radical anarchist imagination and vision became apparent. The alliance of spring 1937, made up of revolutionary refugees, deserters from the front, activists in the defence committees and affinity groups, the MMLL, the JJLL and activists in the POUM, began to fracture.

The post-May repression had led to a particularly precarious situation for foreign revolutionaries. Italian anarchists who had left the front in opposition to militarisation had participated in the May mobilisation, while the German members of the DAS had also played an important role in the build-up to and during the May days. Within days of those events, the building that housed the International Committee of Anti-fascist Emigrés in Barcelona was occupied, apparently by agents of the Soviet Union, who proceeded to arrest those inside and anyone who entered.[52] After the murder of Berneri and Barbieri, and with many of their number named in the letter Largo Caballero sent to Joan Peiró as "suspicious elements" with "FAI-issue passports," most Italian anarchists in Barcelona opted to enlist in anarchist divisions and return to the front.[53] By the end of June 1937, most of the members of the DAS were either in jail or had been forced to leave Spain.[54]

For revolutionary activists from fascist countries, jail brought with it the terrifying prospect of deportation. The first *Comisión Jurídica* set up by the Catalan CNT reported in June that it had been able to prevent this from being carried out with immediate effect.[55] Nevertheless, the danger lingered, as attested to by a letter sent by José Grunfeld to the *comités superiores* in August on behalf of three German refugees who had fought in an anarchist division.[56] The matter was brought up by the delegates of the CNT's sister organisations at the Extraordinary Congress of the IWMA in December 1937. There, the CNT's National Secretary, Rodríguez Vázquez,

52   See Kirschey, "A las barricadas," 175–6.

53   Aguzzi, "Un anarquista italiano," 162. On the Largo Caballero letter, see Chapter Three.

54   Nelles et al., *Antifascistas alemanes en Barcelona*, 371–6.

55   "Informe que presenta la comisión jurídica de la organización confederal de Cataluña a los comités regionals y locales de las organizaciones confederal y específica," CDMH, PS Barcelona 842/4.

56   See letter from José Grunfeld to the Comité de Enlace, 3 August 1937, CDMH, PS Barcelona 512/8 and biographical details of the men in question, Karl Brauner, Ernst Galanty and Paul Helburg, in Nelles et al., *Antifascistas alemanes en Barcelona*, 407–14. Brauner and Galanty had left the Durruti Column in April 1937 in protest at the form taken by militarisation; see Chapter Three.

dismissed the matter, commenting: "After all, the foreign comrades have come of their own account; they have come to a country in revolution, and if a little, of everything should occur we cannot be held responsible for it."[57] There is no doubt that, for activists on the ground, the *comités superiores'* flippancy towards the fate of their foreign comrades was as much a source of outrage as their perceived inactivity on behalf of Spanish anarchist prisoners. Nevertheless, the more radical sectors of the libertarian movement frequently appealed to a similar kind of Spanish exceptionalism to that which informed the approach of the *comités superiores*.

The editorial that *Solidaridad Obrera* published in May 1937 under the headline "Our revolution must be Spanish!," discussed in the previous chapter, was criticised harshly by Alexander Schapiro but found an unlikely defence in the pages of *Ruta*, the mouthpiece of the JJLL, the following month, in an article titled "Our internationalism" signed by D. Díaz y Díaz.[58] The author took offence at the accusation of nationalism, affirming that anarchism "makes common cause with all the exploited and oppressed people in the world," but did not consider this incompatible with exceptionalism or essentialism. The anarchist insistence on autonomy could thus be interpreted in a nationalist sense, and Díaz y Díaz averred that:

> Without ceasing to be anarchists and internationalists, we struggle for an eminently Iberian revolution… This is why we defend the purity and independence of our revolution. We consider foreign meddling in our affairs to be pernicious and we condemn the attempts of some people to establish rules of conduct and procedure on our behalf.[59]

While "foreign meddling" was used as a blanket pejorative aimed principally at the interests of the "great powers" in Spain, in this context it is hard not to see an implicit disregard for the foreign anarchists who had fought in the anarchist militia and played an active part in the May days alongside the JJLL. As Schapiro had put it in his counterblast to the original offending editorial:

> This is a barely disguised attack on the anarchists and syndicalists who came from almost every country to support the burgeoning Spanish revolution… which they believed would be the first act of a revolution that would soon spread beyond the borders of Spain… For them it was not a question of race or of civilization.[60]

57   "Actas del Congreso de la AIT celebrado en París."
58   I have been unable to discover any information about this author.
59   *Ruta*, 3 June 1937.
60   "Informe sobre las actividades de las organizaciones y de algunos anarquistas franceses."

At an anarchist meeting in Barcelona in October 1937, Julián Merino appealed to such critiques emanating from France in support of his rejection of the FAI's new structure. Nevertheless, he also denounced the "importation of comrades from abroad who, when they come to Spain, know nothing of our Confederal or Specific organisation but, wanting to intervene and to occupy posts as soon as they arrive, have wrecked the CNT and the FAI."[61] Here, Merino used language reminiscent of the *comités superiores* in their denunciations of foreign critics of CNT policy. Given that he was at the forefront of attempts to arrest the retreat of the revolution through extra-legal measures, it is unsurprising that Merino laid the blame for what was happening on "those elements that ensure that nothing practical can be done," among whom he numbered the Argentinians who had arrived in Barcelona under the patronage of Diego Abad de Santillán and who were supportive of the centralising tendencies within the FAI.[62] However, it was inconsistent and unprincipled to draw attention to their geographical origins, particularly when there was no shortage of either foreign-born radicals in Spain or home-grown impediments to the methods favoured by the oppositionists.

Such native impediments to revolution were likewise conveniently forgotten by anarchist purists when they appealed to the supposedly innately anarchistic characteristics of the Spanish people.[63] A contributor to the revived JJLL review *Esfuerzo* asserted in the autumn of 1937 that "a profoundly libertarian and individualist spirituality" was "characteristic of the Spanish people."[64] The appearance of essentialist tropes regarding the supposed character of the Spanish people within the oppositional anarchist press indicates something of a blind spot among radical anarchists to the role that such myth-making played in the reconstruction of the Republican state, a process which had left these revolutionaries marginalised and vulnerable to police raids, harassment and murder. They also provided a form of ideological cover for the *comités superiores*, who used precisely such appeals to justify the silencing of oppositional voices. At the aforementioned Congress of the IWMA, the delegation of the CNT declared:

As Spaniards we have a different mentality and we are participating in a struggle of a racial character that concerns ourselves alone… What is

61   "Primera sesión del pleno anarquista."

62   These include José Maria Lunazzi, José Grunfeld, Jacobo Prince and Jacobo Maguid.

63   On the partial acceptance among anarchists of the idea that anarchism formed an essential part of a specifically Spanish character, see Álvarez Junco, *La ideología política del anarquismo español*, 254, and Smith, "Izquierdas y nacionalismos," 147.

64   *Esfuerzo*, 7 October 1937.

at stake is the destiny of a revolution, and not personal opinions or the small-minded moaning of refugees grouped in ghost sections.[65]

Moreover, the radical anarchists' inconsistencies in this regard revealed an absence of serious reflection on the characteristics of the alliance that had formed in the Catalan rearguard in the first half of 1937. As well as contributing to the radicalisation of the Local Federation of the FAI, foreign anarchists had been an integral and highly active component of the revolutionary mobilisation in May. By failing to appreciate the value of the solidarities generated in this period, radicals were partly culpable for the weakening of revolutionary forces.

This phenomenon was also in evidence in the JJLL's relations with the POUM in the aftermath of the May events. Santana Calero's call in *Esfuerzo*, in the second week of May, for "fraternisation and alliance among all young revolutionaries" encountered an immediate obstacle in the outcome of the Regional Congress of the JJLL at the end of the month. Confusingly, Santana Calero was likely a co-signatory of a proposal discussed at the Congress and published beforehand in *Ruta*.[66] The signatories of this proposal urged that relations with all "political elements" be broken off, stating that "Our contact with the so-called Youth Front should be suspended."[67] Even after fighting on the same side of the barricades as the POUM, the purist current of the JJLL refused to make distinctions as to the efficacy of alliances with "Marxists," and had been strengthened in their conviction that such "political" tactics represented an "abandonment of principle."[68] The rationale of this approach was explained at the Congress by the delegate for the socialised public entertainments industry, who wondered: "how are we going to unify with young Marxists when they are fighting among themselves?"[69] The nuanced understanding of the leadership of the JSU as something other than "Marxist," which had allowed Santana Calero among others to appeal to that organisation's membership on the basis of a shared, authentically revolutionary, socialism, had clearly failed to convince all libertarian activists. Nevertheless, the FJR was defended on such terms by

65   "Actas del Congreso de la AIT celebrado en París."
66   *Ruta*, 14 May 1937. The signatories were the JJLL sections of the anarchist stronghold of La Torrasa in L'Hospitalet de Llobregat, Seo de Urgel, one of the border regions then experiencing heavy police repression, the Malatesta Batallion, the Barcelona health workers and the town of Mollerusa in the province of Lleida. Amorós names the corresponding delegates as, respectively, Peirats, Liarte, Amador Franco, Santana Calero and Vicente Rodríguez: Amorós, *Los Incontrolados*, 186.
67   *Ruta*, 14 May 1937.
68   Ibid.
69   "Actas del Congreso Regional de las JJLL celebrado en Barcelona los días 15 de mayo y siguientes," CDMH, PS Barcelona, 239/03.

several delegates at the Congress. The delegate of the distribution sector affirmed that the FJR was a vehicle through which to attack the JSU, while the delegate of Premià de Mar went as far as to declare that the participation of the local JJLL in the FJR would continue regardless of the decision of the Congress.[70] However, the fact that the delegate from Gràcia could support the purists' proposal, even after the formation in that neighbourhood of a committee composed of anarchists and POUM members during the May days and the promulgation by the neighbourhood JJLL of a manifesto that explicitly recognised the POUM as "authentic revolutionaries," is demonstrative of the level of opposition to the FJR at the Congress. In spite of evident division, a majority eventually agreed to completely separate the JJLL from "political" activity. The nineteen-year-old Ramón Liarte was named the new Regional Secretary, in place of Fidel Miró.

Miró's absence from the Congress may have inclined the balance towards the purist position. Detained during the May events, the outgoing Regional Secretary's involvement was limited to a letter favouring the continuation of revolutionary unity. Also absent was Alfredo Martínez, the Secretary of the FJR and its most prominent promoter within the JJLL, who was missing, presumed murdered. Aside from these absences and the traditional purist antipathy to "politics," however, it should also be borne in mind that this Congress took place with a national governmental crisis as its backdrop. The crisis had been provoked by Communist determination to accuse the POUM of responsibility for the May events and to have the party declared illegal as a consequence. For the *comités superiores*, also happy for the POUM to take the blame, any association with the party was now toxic. Wilebaldo Solano, Secretary of the POUM's youth section, the JCI, was therefore correct to perceive a confluence of interests among the *comités superiores* and the purist tendency of the JJLL at this Congress.[71] There was an "extensive" intervention by the Regional Committee of the FAI, which made reference to the ongoing ministerial crisis in Valencia, and bluntly stated that the JJLL lacked a Regional Committee "appropriate for the times."[72] Given that the Secretary of the JJLL was in prison and two other Committee members, Martínez and the Uruguayan Juan Rúa, had disappeared in suspicious circumstances, this intervention is illustrative of the kind of cynical opportunism Solano identified.[73]

70   Ibid.
71   Wilebaldo Solano file, Col·lecció Ronald Fraser, AHCB, 87.
72   "Actas del Congreso Regional de las JJLL celebrado en Barcelona los días 15 de mayo y siguientes," CDMH, PS Barcelona, 239/03.
73   Juan Rúa was the Regional Committee delegate for liaison with JJLL combatants in Aragon. He was detained at a control point en route to the front and was never seen again. See Paz, *Viaje al pasado*, 178.

Although the avowed apoliticism of the purists clashed with the policy of the *comités superiores* and would provoke further divisions in the libertarian movement in the months to come, the intention of the former to return the JJLL to a role strictly limited to propaganda and education would have been preferable from the point of view of the *comités superiores* to an ongoing commitment to revolutionary unity with the POUM, with all the complications that might imply for the CNT on a governmental level. In their rejection of "politics," therefore, the purists were, consciously or not, performing a political role. As Solano put it: "At that point, they [the *comités superiores*] did not have a replacement team within the JJLL that would carry out their policy and they turned to the most extreme *faistas* with whom they were in disagreement in order to change it."[74] The voluntarist position of alliances among "authentic revolutionaries," advocated in the flysheet *Esfuerzo* and in the May manifesto of the JJLL of Gràcia, could thus be sidelined. Miró, meanwhile, would find himself persona non grata at the headquarters of the regional JJLL on his release from prison, and would be coaxed into the national structure of the FIJL as a defender of collaborationist orthodoxy by Pedro Herrera, who was a fellow member of the affinity group Nervio, and Rodríguez Vázquez.[75] The attentions of the *comités superiores* would then turn again, as we saw in the first subsection, to disciplining the purists, a contested process that would endure for the remainder of the war.

Following this break with the solidarity of the barricades effected with the POUM, the purists of the JJLL also indirectly distanced themselves from the radical voluntarists in the FAI during the struggle to prevent the restructuring of that organisation. At a Regional Plenum of Catalan Anarchist Affinity Groups in August, several purists of the JJLL left the hall midway through proceedings, crying out: "Long live anarchy!" A meeting hastily arranged in Valencia in an attempt to avoid a split took place soon after, with Xena acting as mediator between Peirats, a representative of this faction, and Montseny, of the Peninsular Committee, but came to nought.[76] Even in the absence of the purists of the JJLL, the attempted conversion of the FAI in Cataluña into a "legal" political organisation would be bitterly contested by Merino and other radicals through the Local Federation. After the walkout, however, the JJLL purists did not attend the Plenums of the latter body, leaving the voluntarist rather than the purist current to take up the cudgels against the "neo-anarchists" in the Catalan FAI. The alliance of purists and voluntarists within this organisation, which had been so effective in previous struggles, was now effectively defunct.

74   Wilebaldo Solano file, Col·lecció Ronald Fraser, AHCB, 87.
75   See Miró, *Vida intensa*, 206 and 209–10.
76   See the recollections of Peirats, *De mi paso*, 346–8.

The final element of the radical alliance had been revolutionary women. In the aftermath of the May events, maintaining the solidarities that had seen members of the *Patrullas de Control* distributing food to the bread queues and women's demonstrations and riots in the first half of 1937 was made immeasurably more difficult by a heavy police presence responsible for disarming revolutionaries and keeping order at the queues. In other respects, however, the alliance was undermined by anarchists themselves, particularly with regard to the anarchist women's organisation, Mujeres Libres (MMLL). In 1937–1938, the extension of the draft in the rearguard led to vacancies in administrative roles in the libertarian organisations and in socialised industries that were frequently occupied by women. Joaquina Dorado Pita became president of Barcelona's Economic Council of the Socialised Woodwork Industry, Sánchez Saornil became secretary of Solidaridad Internacional Antifascista (International Antifascist Solidarity, an organisation set up by the CNT to raise funds abroad, to compete with the Communist-dominated International Red Help and to avoid relying on the IWMA), while the incorporation of women into the committees of the FIJL became crucial to sustaining the organisation in this period.[77]

This did not lead to a place at the table of the libertarian movement for the MMLL, which had constituted itself as a national federation in August 1937. Its autonomous agenda was viewed, particularly by the FIJL, as competing for support among the same constituencies. In October 1938, the recently created Women's Secretariat of the FIJL complained that the MMLL continued to recruit younger women to its organisation in spite of the decision of the former that the women's organisation should restrict itself to the recruitment of "adults."[78] Even in Barcelona, where the JJLL affirmed and defended its own right to autonomy, and where no women's secretariat had been set up, young women activists were not encouraged to join the MMLL and were given the false impression that this was an organisation for women aged thirty and over. The fact that many women were members of both the MMLL and the JJLL but did not openly talk about the former at meetings of the latter suggests that the opposition of the youth organisations had in fact succeeded in preventing the MMLL from actively recruiting from the ranks of the youth organisation.[79]

77   Santamaría, "Juventudes Libertarias y Guerra Civil," 220; Fontanillas, "De lo aprendido," 11–2; Garangou, *Les Joventuts Llibertàries*, 297–301.

78   "Exposición del problema de las relaciones de las secretarias femeninas de la FIJL con 'Mujeres Libres' Que presenta a studio de las regionals la secretaria femenina peninsular," CDMH, PS Barcelona 140/4.

79   See Fontanillas, "De lo aprendido," 12; Vega, *Pioneras y revolucionarias*, 216–20.

The JJLL in Cataluña thus lost a further opportunity to formalise the solidarities established in the run-up to and during the May events by distancing itself from the MMLL. Nor did the latter organisation seek to cement its oppositional stance in this period, in spite of the fact that its combativeness, autonomy and strategic outlook were all at variance with the direction in which the principal libertarian organisations were headed. Sánchez Saornil was a founding signatory to the restructured Barcelona Anarchist Grouping (AAB), while the MMLL itself sought official recognition as a branch of the Spanish libertarian movement. In October 1938, the MMLL, uninvited, sent a delegation to the National Plenum of the Spanish Libertarian Movement where, despite the great risks that some delegates had taken to reach Barcelona, they were forced to sit out the first sessions, only entering the Plenum when the matter of "auxiliary organisations" was discussed.[80] The proposal of the MMLL, that the Federation should be granted official status as a branch of the Libertarian Movement, was not voted upon, and the question was set aside for a future that, in the event, did not arrive.

Given that, as Martha Ackelsberg has concluded, the likely "sticking point" for the other branches of the movement was the MMLL's "demand for autonomy in setting its goals and priorities," we might wonder why the potential for increased solidarity between the organisation and the Catalan JJLL, whose fate it shared, seems to have been squandered in this period.[81] A partial explanation can be found in the fact that the MMLL always affirmed its proximity to the CNT and, in need of the organisational support and resources that its official recognition by the libertarian movement would bring, it was unlikely to adopt an oppositional position wholesale as had the JJLL. We might also consider, however, that the need for an independent women's organisation to combat sexism, both in wider society and within the libertarian movement, represented a stumbling block for many oppositional anarchists, and not only the *comités superiores*. An article in the first number of *El Quijote*, the publication of the Los Quijotes del Ideal affinity group, was illustrative of male anarchist insecurity and condescension in this regard. Lamenting the "loneliness" of adolescent girls desperate to find a young "hero" but encountering only the "brutality of the male," the author wondered

> What will become of her? Will she find a companion to guide her and defend her from the dangers to which she is exposed? Will she find a friend who understands her and can look after her as a mother does a

80   See Ackelsberg, *Free Women*, 191–7.
81   Ibid. 196.

wayward child? Or will she meet a hysterical woman who drags her into the depths of sapphism? Who knows?[82]

In a similar, albeit less overwrought, vein, *Faro*, a radical publication edited by Santana Calero and discussed in more detail in the following subsection, carried a note on the front page of its edition of 26 November 1937 which insisted that the MMLL must not behave like a "rabidly feminist organisation." The explanation that it offered for the "lack of fraternal relations" between the JJLL and the women's organisation was that certain comrades of the MMLL "combined a lack of responsibility with a counterproductive and feverish exclusivism."[83]

We have seen how the *Mujeres Libres* publication drew attention to the aggressive chauvinism of one male "comrade" at a women's demonstration; it might also be worth paying attention to the gendered terms in which anarchists considered their activism. In the oppositional press and at meetings, radicals frequently enjoined their audience to "be men," and lamented the absence of "virile gestures" on the part of their comrades and the "castrating" effects of anarchism's antitheses, religion and the state.[84] Such terminology was, of course, extremely common in 1930s Spain, and is unlikely to have been as off-putting then as it is now, but it nevertheless indicates a gendered ideal of activism that women would have continually had to confront when they participated in the movement.

The rise of the MMLL during the Spanish civil war is an indication of the extraordinary vitality of the anarchist movement in that country, and of the deeply transformative qualities of the revolution. The radical French publication *L'Espagne Nouvelle*, edited by André Prudhommeaux, asserted: "Even if the revolution is crushed in Spain, it will not have failed in moral terms, and its resurrection will be assured, because it has enabled the formation of the Mujeres Libres Federation and allowed its voice to be heard."[85] The period of the Spanish revolution provides historians with the all too rare opportunity to consider the multiple recorded interventions of women activists who developed their own platforms and activities. The rise of the MMLL further shows, however, that the existence of an autonomous women's organisation corresponded to a need brought about by sexism internal to the anarchist movement. In fact, following the initial days of exaltation in the summer of 1936, it was rare for the prominence of women in the

82   *El Quijote*, 11 September 1937.
83   *Faro*, 26 November 1937.
84   For the injunction to "be men," see *Ruta*, 3 June 1937. For castration as a metaphor, see *Evolución*, September 1937. On the virile gesture, see the following subsection.
85   Quoted in *Mujeres Libres*, 13, autumn 1938.

revolution to be reflected on by male anarchist writers. Tomás Cabot, writing in the revived *Esfuerzo*, provided one exception:

> Of the many decisive factors that have been thrown up by this war against the fascist hordes, there is one that stands out with a shining light of its own, as a value unknown before now and which promises to be a decisive and fundamental force for the future, that of women... Their rapid adjustment to the revolutionary and constructive days of July has been enormously influential and demands the particular interest of libertarians.[86]

Although Cabot did not mention the MMLL in the article, his insistence on women's "self-sufficiency," and the appearance of an advertisement for a new MMLL publication on the same page, would have likely been welcomed by the Federation as a gesture of solidarity from within the ranks of the JJLL.

The articles of Tomás Cabot in *Esfuerzo* indicated a willingness to reflect on the experience of the revolution. During this period, the effort to draw conclusions from this experience became increasingly visible in the pages of publications associated with the JJLL. If the JJLL had been unable to draw entirely coherent political and strategic conclusions from its participation in the revolutionary alliance that had animated the mobilisation of May, it was not alone in this failure, and nor was this failure absolute. The purpose of this subsection is not to provide a retrospective moral judgement on the ideological imperfections of anarchist activists, but rather to show how the recession of revolutionary horizons brought with it a turning inwards of revolutionary forces and a fracturing of the solidarities generated by the revolution's expansive phase. Nevertheless, it is possible to see this turning inwards in a more generous light. For example, the frustration that activists in the libertarian youth organisations expressed towards the MMLL was at least in part due to their desire to see a healthy gender balance in the JJLL. Antonia Fontanillas, who remembered being given the false impression that the MMLL was an organisation for older activists, also recalled the encouragement that better-known male activists gave her to take on positions of responsibility in the youth organisations.[87] Moreover, while the defeat of the revolution constricted the spaces in which radical activists could operate in this period, their attempt to return to the fundamental principles of anarchism enabled them to persist in the cultural, educational and reflective labour that had characterised the movement prior to the civil war.

86   *Esfuerzo*, 24 October 1937.
87   Fontanillas, "De lo aprendido," 12.

Anarchists in isolation

As we have seen, the initial reactions of several radical anarchists to the defeat of May were marked by continued faith in the fighting capacity of the revolutionaries and a voluntarist approach to the task of changing the course of the libertarian organisations. By the autumn of 1937, this optimism had been all but extinguished. The attention that radicals paid in the following period to "salvaging the prestige" of anarchism has led historians to consider purist anarchism in this period to have had a merely "testimonial" character.[88] It is certainly the case that this impulse to defend the integrity of Spanish anarchism was consequent upon the defeat of practical proposals intended to reorient the strategy of the libertarian organisations, and that, in the face of the increasing centralisation of the same, there were signs of a withdrawal into introspection and ideology. Nevertheless, this period also saw a return to the tactics of the pre-war period, which involved propagating and defending libertarian practices in the fields of education and culture, in opposition to Republican Spain's post-revolutionary dominant ideology and police force. The "testimonial" role of radical anarchists also led to some critique and reflection on the nature of the defeat they had suffered.

On 9 July 1937, the Catalan JJLL, by now estranged from the rest of the FIJL, produced a manifesto that justified its decision to prioritise fidelity to anarchist ideas over the demands of the war and organisational unity. It contrasted the permanence of the "purely anarchist tendency" of the JJLL to the transitory "circumstantialism" of the CNT and the FAI. While it was reasonable to suppose that the latter organisations would "return to these [purely anarchist] principles, tactics and objectives in the more or less near future," this could only be assured by "maintaining in the sector most susceptible to reformist contamination the anarchistic spirit that has always informed our libertarian activities."[89] Over the summer, while the question of how to accommodate the Catalan section within the FIJL rumbled on, three new publications appeared from within its ranks, all dedicated, as the manifesto put it, to "what is fundamental and permanent about anarchist ideas and not with what is politically convenient."

El Quijote was a weekly produced under the auspices of the affinity group Los Quijotes del Ideal in Clot. Purist in tone, its first issue declared its intention to be "somewhat removed from the terrible 'today' in which

88   Santamaría, "Juventudes Libertarias y Guerra Civil," 219.

89   See "Exposición ampliada del punto de vista del movimiento juvenil libertario de la regional catalana según la ponencia aprobada en su último congreso de juventudes libertarias celebrado en Mayo," CDMH, PS Barcelona, 238/5.

we live."[90] *Evolución*, the mouthpiece of the FECL, was a monthly edited by Ada Martí, who wrote a critique of democracy in its first issue that would have been anathema to the "neo-anarchists." Declaring revolution and democracy to be mutually exclusive concepts, Martí reflected that the previous six years "should have been sufficient to show us the painful truth of this affirmation."[91] Diego Camacho, a member of Los Quijotes del Ideal, recalls being shown the first issue by Martí, who told him that it had a print run of four thousand editions:

> It's not much… but it is important to say what we are saying. It is painful to read the official press of our movement. What is worse: with the commonplace of the circumstances they are justifying anti-anarchism. With our voice and that of others we intend to unmask the falsifiers.[92]

In that spirit the new publication's editorial railed against the "circumstantialists" of the *comités superiores*:

> They shun the struggle, they fear the atmosphere of the street. Comfort has turned them into amnesiacs and the ranks of the sell-outs are full to bursting. They talk of sacrifices and compromise; they point to the ignorance of the masses to justify their wavering because they lack a fighting temperament. They are mere harlequins dressed up as martyrs, who with a herd-like mentality… want to become mayors, parliamentarians and ministers, that infamous triptych of privilege and slavery.[93]

The other new publication to emerge was the revived *Esfuerzo*. Submitted to, and duly decimated by, the state censor, the editorial line of *Esfuerzo* stressed the need for unity among the libertarian youth, a unity that it considered possible only through adherence to anarchist ideas and the rejection of external alliances. Although they occasionally published articles that were optimistic or voluntarist in their interpretation of the moment, these new publications indicated the growing level of alienation of the Catalan JJLL from the rest of the Spanish libertarian movement. There was an identifiable tendency among purists in the organisation to close ranks and to concentrate on countering what Peirats had termed the "permanent effects" of circumstantial collaboration. As a contemporary article in the similarly purist *Frente y Retaguardia* put it: "Let us set our own house in

90   *El Quijote*, 11 September 1937.
91   *Evolución*, September 1937.
92   Paz, *Viaje al pasado*, 218–9.
93   *Evolución*, September 1937.

order, learn those ideas that we extol… let us stand guard over the purity of our movement."[94]

In *El Quijote*, Vicente Rodríguez, an influential member of the JJLL, indicated a preparedness to break entirely from the libertarian organisations:

> The organisation as such is worthy of our efforts depending on the quantity of ideas that we perceive in it or are able to inject into it. Organisation for the sake of organisation is no different to violence for the sake of violence… What is more, if our continued presence in a given organisation must imply the renunciation of our own methods in terms of the diffusion or practice of the ideas that sustain us, then we can never justifiably remain in it. The only work that could be carried out in such circumstances would be that of disintegration and discord, a work that is acceptable as long as disintegration and discord is applied to the traditional enemy: authoritarianism. And all those who, having lost faith in the constructive capacity of the masses, use their supposed superiority to justify becoming a leading elite, are authoritarians.[95]

Given that radical anarchists were normally at pains to state that they did not want a split in the movement, this article is remarkable for outlining how such a split could be justified. Rodríguez stopped short of openly advocating sabotage of the libertarian organisations, resorting to the commonplace trope that the Spanish masses, infused with an anarchistic spirit, would oblige them to return to their true path. Whether or not such optimism was truly felt by the author, the article concluded in far less sanguine terms:

> backed into a corner whereby either the organisation or the ideas must perish, we would always prefer the disappearance of the former over the latter, as ideas give rise to organisation while an organisation without an ideological base cannot give rise to ideas.[96]

This prioritisation of principles over organisation was frequently expressed at this time and was a clear response to the attempted homogenisation of the movement according to the criteria of the *comités superiores*. It would be expressed at the Congress of the IWMA in December 1937, and was also at the root of a row between the Catalan School of Activists, set up under the auspices of the CNT veteran Manuel Buenacasa as a training

94   *Frente y Retaguardia*, 1 September 1937.
95   *El Quijote*, 11 September 1937.
96   Ibid.

centre for libertarian activism, and José Peirats. Peirats, a close friend and comrade of Vicente Rodríguez, had refused to deliver a talk at the School on the subject of how to organise a Congress, objecting that he would only be prepared to talk about "ideas."[97] Prior to its suppression, *Frente y Retaguardia* had also come into conflict with the School, after featuring an article in which it urged it "not to become a political institution, preparing the new deputies of the FAI." In response, it was announced that the School would report the purists' aspersions to the Regional Committees of the CNT and the FAI, "so that they might make the appropriate decisions."[98]

The most dramatic consequence of the purists' ambivalence towards the libertarian organisations came at the Regional Congress of the JJLL beginning on 10 October 1937, where it was decided to sever the organisational link that had previously existed between the JJLL and the Catalan FAI. This was due to the restructuring of the latter organisation, "which provides evidence of a fundamental alteration of anarchist principles."[99] According to the Confederal press, the sticking point was the freedom of the oppositional affinity groups to remain outside of the restructuring process and therefore not be grouped into larger *agrupaciones* according to locality.[100] According to Peirats, however, the problem was rather the new declaration of principles that accompanied the restructuring, which implied that the FAI was no longer committed to a struggle against all states, but only against the establishment of "a dictatorship of caste or party."[101] That this was the crux of the issue for purist anarchists was reaffirmed in an article in *Frente y Retaguardia*:

> There cannot remain the least doubt that, on declaring themselves enemies of the "totalitarian state," the "neo-anarchists" also know how to distinguish, as has always been the skill of Marxists and republicans, between the democratic state and the state *per se*… What remains of the classic anarchist criterion that attributes totalitarian properties to every state, considering its supposed moderation to be a temporary affair dependent on the degree of resistance or conformity of its subjects?[102]

November 1937 saw the appearance of a new publication of the JJLL, *Faro*, edited by the tireless Juan Santana Calero. Like *Esfuerzo*, its editorial line defended the position of the Catalan JJLL and, as with his previous

97 *Amanecer. Órgano de la Escuela de Militantes de Cataluña*, November 1937.
98 *Amanecer. Órgano de la Escuela de Militantes de Cataluña*, December 1937.
99 See Fernández Soria, *Cultura y libertad*, 38, and *Esfuerzo*, 14 October 1937.
100 *Solidaridad Obrera*, 12 October 1937.
101 Peirats, *De mi paso*, 348. See also "Estatutos generales de la Federación Anarquista Ibérica," Federación Anarquista Ibérica Archive (IISG) 49 A.
102 *Frente y Retaguardia*, 1 September 1937.

endeavours, through *Faro* Santana Calero attempted to bring together purist and voluntarist criticisms of the official libertarian movement. What is also striking about this publication, however, is the self-conscious way in which it situated itself within the *international* anarchist movement. Its first number, in a heavily censored editorial, affirmed that:

> In the face of perverted adulterations of anarchism, situated in a tendency that is yet to be convincingly refuted, we stand by... the robust ideological content affirmed in the position paper approved at the Extraordinary Congress in May... The JJLL of Cataluña are not determinists. They believe in the efficacy of the will... In a time of confusion and ideological decay... the JJLL must show themselves to be compact and strong, motivated by a single ambition: to offer their responsibility and rootedness in the ideas to international anarchism.[103]

In spite of its appeal to "will," itself typical of Santana Calero, *Faro* did not indicate in its pages how acts of will might renew the Spanish revolution or recover for the libertarian movement its former spirit. Instead, its focus was on preserving the integrity of anarchist ideals, a task that, as the above passage indicates, was of international scope. This commitment to internationalism was further demonstrated by the publication's hosting of articles by Alexander Schapiro and the French anarchist teacher Lucien Barbedette.

While *Faro* focused on the endurance of anarchist principles, to highlight this propagandistic and "idealistic" labour is not to suggest that members of the JJLL withdrew from practical activity. Their continued endeavours in the field of education and in struggling to resist the militarisation of popular culture and children's activities are also abundantly attested to in the pages of their press. The university was one such battleground. *Evolución* lamented that "we have been forced to acknowledge that as far as pedagogy is concerned, the proletarian achievement of July has not made the least impact."[104] In the early days of the war, the FECL and the JJLL had held an assembly in Barcelona to discuss the possibility of creating a "People's University."[105] The initial involvement of the celebrated anarchist doctor, Félix Martí Ibáñez, in the initiative ceased on his taking on a governmental role in the Department of Health as a delegate of the CNT, and the project was rendered inoperable by the absence of any wider organisational support. By the late summer of 1937, while anarchist students wrote articles

103   *Faro*, 12 November 1937.
104   *Evolución*, September 1937.
105   *Solidaridad Obrera*, 27 August 1936.

denouncing the increasing tuition fees imposed by the universities, the veteran anarchist journalist Felipe Alaiz initiated an intemperate exchange with Martí Ibáñez on the subject of the "People's University." Alaiz linked the project's failure to the moral and ideological failure of those anarchists who had accepted collaboration with the state.[106]

As it was, anarchist educational projects were undertaken in the remaining centres and "free schools" of the JJLL, the MMLL and in cultural groupings such as the Agrupación Los de Ayer y Los de Hoy. However, these were carried out in spite of the principal libertarian organisations and against the prevailing current of the times. As an article in *Faro* lamented:

> The free education that children were promised has become a slave of the state… Children are given the same educational materials as before the war. While it is true that they are now proffered material of a coarsely anti-fascist hue it is nothing more than this: anti-fascist… And, in greater numbers, people with neither scruples nor the most elementary of pedagogical sentiment cultivate, with publications of the worst kind, a war-like spirit in the young.[107]

In this sense, the anarchists of the JJLL and the affiliated students' organisation, the FECL, had "returned" to their "previous line of conduct" as they had been urged to by Tomás Cabot in the pages of *Esfuerzo*; fostering an oppositional, parallel culture to that of the Republican state in much the same way as they had done before the war began. In so doing, they were also defending the autonomy of the spaces they had conquered in the summer of 1936, maintaining the spirit of rational education against the encroachments of the dominant ideology of statist anti-fascism.

Hugo García considers the anti-fascist activities that children were encouraged to engage in at school to be among the strongest evidence of the "emergence of an antifascist collective identity in Republican Spain" during the civil war, an identity that "superimposed itself on the radical culture that middle-class republicans and revolutionary workers had shared since the 'democratic revolution of 1868' and the short-lived First Republic of 1873."[108] The anarchist relationship to this emerging culture of anti-fascism was at first ambiguous. At the beginning of the war, anarchists on

106   See *Ruta*, 12 and 26 August, and 2 September 1937.
107   *Faro*, 26 November 1937.
108   Hugo García, "Was there an Antifascist Culture in Spain during the 1930s?," in *Rethinking Antifascism: History, Memory and Politics, 1922 to the Present*, ed. by Hugo García, Mercedes Yusta, Xavier Tabet and Cristina Clímaco (New York: Berghahn, 2016), 92–113.

the one hand wished to stress their pre-eminent role in the anti-fascist struggle and on the other to dissociate that struggle from the fight to save or restore the Second Republic. Nevertheless, by the end of 1937, the *comités superiores* of the libertarian movement were happy to consider themselves component parts of an anti-fascism understood in the historical sense of an enlightened and progressive tradition, as set out by García above. At the December Congress of the IWMA, José Xena defended the anti-fascist alliance because of "what the fascist danger constitutes! It is not only a threat to the CNT-FAI! It has set out on the destruction of liberalism, of Marxism, of the workers' movement in general and of all the democratic and republican traditions of the bourgeoisie!"[109] Meanwhile, radical anarchist dissension from this position was informed not only by alienation from this broader progressive tradition but also by the perception of a retreat from this tradition on the part of statist anti-fascism. This could be detected in the militarist betrayal of rationalist pedagogy denounced in the pages of *Faro* and, even more strikingly, in the campaign in defence of religious freedoms.

Anti-fascism was the ideological glue that had replaced anti-clericalism as the most important unifying factor among Spain's otherwise fractious progressives in 1936, but only after the beginning of the war had brought with it a wave of popular anti-clerical violence in which all sectors of this progressive alliance took part.[110] After this subsided, the respective rise of anti-fascism and fall of anti-clericalism was so rapid that, by the end of 1937, anti-clericalism in Spain was the almost exclusive preserve of radical anarchists. As discussed in Chapter Three, the possibility of an anti-fascist alliance of the youth including both the JJLL and the JSU had initially foundered on the insistence of the latter that Catholic organisations should be invited to join. From May 1937, the Republican Government officially pursued a policy of "religious normalisation" that was fiercely denounced in the pages of the radical anarchist press, while the PCE characterised such anti-religious sentiment as "false revolutionism."[111] For anarchists, the Catholic Church represented one of "the rotten elements of society that had brought about the brutal situation in which we now live," and the failure of the revolution "in its violent moments" to uproot it completely had been a fatal error: "Due to this benevolence the enemy has been able to undermine

---

109   "Actas del Congreso de la AIT celebrado en París."

110   See Maria Thomas, *The Faith and the Fury: Popular Anticlerical Violence and Iconoclasm in Spain, 1931–1936* (Brighton: Sussex Academic Press, 2013), 74–99.

111   *Ruta*, 3 June 1937. On the government's change in religious policy, see Hilari Raguer, *La pólvora y el incienso. La iglesia y la Guerra civil Española (1936–1939)* (Barcelona: Ediciones Península, 2001), 326–7.

LA LUS SE HISO EN EL INTERIOR DEL TEMPLO
ASI SE HAGA EN NUESTRO ENTENDIMIETO

3/50

An engraving by Gustavo Cochet, completed after a visit to the partially demolished church of his neighbourhood, where he was impressed by the appearance of light and sky seen through the still standing main door. Photographed by
Mario Gómez Casas, reproduced by permission of the Museo Gustavo Cochet
and the Ministerio de Innovación y Cultura de Santa Fe. The caption reads: "Let the
light that illuminates the interior of the temple light up our understanding."

the [revolutionary] organisations."[112] The "anti-religious spirit of young Spaniards" that anarchists affirmed was often born of the experience of a harsh and truncated educational experience at the hands of the country's religious orders.[113] Unsurprisingly, the press of the JJLL was united in opposing the governmental campaign, the mouthpiece of the FECL urging its readers to "react energetically against this unspeakable plague, which is attempting to re-emerge dressed in the spellbinding garb of anti-fascism."[114]

The analyses contained in the publications of the Catalan JJLL in this period, and the fact that they provided a platform to both disaffected militants of the Spanish libertarian movement and veteran anarchist exiles abroad, are indicative of the strength of the libertarian culture in Cataluña, which was capable of renewing itself and whose militants applied their principles to a critique of the movement to which they belonged. In an atmosphere of increasing fatalism brought about by the disastrous course of the war, the commonplace response of radical anarchists was to affirm that "anarchism is not fatalist. It is the antithesis of Marxism."[115] In this context, in an article for *Le Combat Syndicaliste* reproduced in *Faro* and addressed "to the circumstantialists," the anarchist Lucien Barbedette echoed García Oliver at the Madrid Congress of 1931 by raising the spectre of Lenin in order to criticise the "false security" that the Marxist belief in a "fatal process" gave the workers:

> Lenin threw himself into the fray with passion when the Russian debacle began; he demonstrated practically that the energy of a man plays a highly important role. Socialists and communists propagated their convictions without being passive spectators, intervening in the most important events of the epoch.[116]

This period also saw more considered positions emerge that hinted at how the experience of defeat could be used to draw programmatic conclusions. For Amador Franco, writing in *Esfuerzo* at the end of October 1937, the problems of the Spanish revolution could not be solved by a Spanish Lenin, "the clichéd requirement of a man of iron will to direct the revolution," still less a "revolutionary government." The essence of the revolution was defined as "a struggle between authority and liberty. Between politics

---

112   *Hombres Libres*, 4 June 1937.
113   *Ruta*, 3 June 1937. On the educational experiences of the editor of *Ruta*, José Peirats, see Ealham, *Living Anarchism*, 16–21.
114   *Evolución*, September 1937.
115   *Faro*, 12 November 1937.
116   *Faro*, 19 November 1937.

and the people. Between the organisations of labour and those of the State." If the revolution were to be anarchistic, it would imply "not a transfer of powers, but a total change in the way of life." Franco conceived of the revolutionary process in the following terms:

> The expropriation of the bourgeoisie, the disappearance of commerce from our country and its replacement by free exchange, and the mutual understanding of the regions that make up the country through regional councils or other organs not subject to the law, but structured in grand Congresses of the producers through mutual agreement, the annulment of the State… Such are the tasks to fulfil in the revolutionary period.[117]

This evocation of grand workers' congresses as the fora through which social life could be organised echoed the programme put forward in 1934 by Valeriano Orobón Fernández, but was nonetheless highly innovative in the context of late 1937 and in its recognition that a chief inadequacy of the Spanish revolution at that point was precisely the absence of any such organisation outside of the unions through which workers could fraternise and advance an independent agenda.[118] While the "Junta" advocated by the Friends of Durruti (AAD) might also have been intended to be read in this light, it is unlikely that radicals such as Franco subscribed to such a reading, given the distrust that the "authoritarianism" of the AAD had prompted among purists.[119] Instead, we might see his vision of revolutionary change as an extension of the maximalist interpretations of the socialisation campaign, discussed in Chapter Three. Having spent the greater part of the war on the Aragón front, Franco would have been aware of the Regional Federation of collectives agreed to at the congress in Caspe, while his close friend and collaborator Peirats would likely have related to him his experience of organising a mass assembly in Lleida during the socialisation campaign. Franco's analysis of the revolution's limitations provides further evidence that critical reflection on the revolutionary experience was not limited to the AAD in

117   *Esfuerzo*, 24 October 1937.

118   Orobón Fernández had proposed a minimum programme as a basis for revolutionary unity between the CNT and the UGT at the beginning of 1934. The programmatic basis of his proposal was "revolutionary proletarian democracy": the socialisation of the means of production, union control over the economy, and the executive power, in all non-economic questions, of delegates elected and subject to recall by the people. He used as a historical precedent for this the Bavarian Soviet Republic of April 1919, in which left socialists, communists and anarchists had participated. See Gutiérrez Molina, *Valeriano Orobón Fernández*, 268–77.

119   See Chapter Four and Guillamón, *Los Amigos de Durruti*, 64–5.

1937. While his analysis was innovative, however, his proposals for a change of course within the libertarian movement would have been familiar to both the voluntarists and purists of that year:

> Only one option remains open to us: the reaffirmation of anarchism; that is, if we still have time. To carry this out we need the unanimous will of everyone and the abandonment of ministerial scheming and "circumstantialist" tactics... We must take on all the responsibility of marching forward to new conceptions. We must be worthy of history and of our ideas.[120]

Alongside the new publications that emerged under the banner of the JJLL in autumn 1937, *Alerta...!* appeared in Barcelona, produced by the city's defence committees and issued without prior submission to the censor. It also affirmed its steadfast adherence to anarchist principles, its editorial declaring itself "tired of paradoxes. Anarchist ministers... anarchist governors... anarchist mayors and councillors... Anarchist police... anarchist jailors... Climb the ladder if that is your ambition... but do not call yourselves anarchists."[121] It provided sombre, if defiant, reading for partisans of the Spanish revolution. Under the headline "The proletariat has gained nothing," the editorial of its first issue drew up a critical balance sheet of the revolution's trajectory:

> We have lost thousands and thousands of comrades, the flower of our activist base... Of the Revolution barely anything remains, and what little that does is not consolidated. We will have to go back, to find the spirit of 19 July, to raise it up again and keep it strong, without trusting in anybody, without paying attention to any commonplace slogans.[122]

By the time that this editorial was published, nearly six months had passed since the May days, when the defence committees, alongside their allies in the Catalan JJLL, anarchist affinity groups and various unions of the CNT, had mobilised their forces in an attempt to recover on the streets of Barcelona the "spirit of 19 July." Since May, two further opportunities had presented themselves, in August and September, to begin where they had left off, but on both occasions their initiatives were nipped in the bud by the libertarian hierarchies.

---

120   *Esfuerzo*, 24 October 1937.
121   *Alerta...!*, 23 October 1937. On *Alerta...!*, see Godicheau, "Los periódicos clandestinos," 190–4.
122   *Alerta...!*, 23 October 1937.

By 1938 the defence committees had changed their name to *comités de coordinación* (coordination committees) in a bid to minimise police attention. As the course of the war sapped the radical anarchists of morale and numbers, and the ongoing process of state reconstruction robbed them of their resources, the *comités superiores* were the targets of pent-up frustration. In August 1938, the neighbourhood coordination committee was the chief signatory of a letter of protest written in the name of the Libertarian Movement of Armonía de Palomar (the name given to the Barcelona suburb of Sant Andreu during the war), which read:

> While it seems that those who are considered the foremost figures of our movement are treated with a certain consideration by the official elements of other parties and organisations, this is not the case for the immense majority of our activists who are persecuted, jailed and even murdered, as in the worst times of counterrevolutionary repression. Nevertheless we are yet to witness a single virile gesture on the part of our Committees or our most representative men to prevent such abuses.[123]

The final "virile gesture" that libertarian Barcelona bore witness to would in fact come not from its "most representative men" but from the Mujeres Libres. On the second anniversary of the outbreak of the war, Sánchez Saornil had avoided drawing up the kind of brutal "balance sheet" that *Alerta...!* had published, considering it too "painful" a task. Nevertheless, she maintained, as did the publication of the defence committees, an ongoing fidelity to the "spirit of 19 July":

> Since that glorious day a thousand circumstances beyond our control have altered the course of events: our civil war has been converted into a war of independence, our social war into a vulgar defensive war; our intentions have been twisted and our boldest initiatives smashed against the closed cycle of 1936–1938; but nobody can say that our will is broken...
>
> Circumstances have trapped us in an iron cage; they have forced us into a retreat that we have accepted only because we know that 19 July continues to burn within us, lighting up the darkness of our torture as our only hope... the only truth and the only way out.[124]

In fact, precisely because its organisation was unrecognised on an official level and operated for the most part outside the state, the MMLL

123   CDMH, PS Barcelona, 842/17.
124   *Mujeres Libres*, autumn 1938.

had retreated less distance than most. In Cataluña it had initially cooperated when, in July 1937, the Generalitat created the Institut d'Adaptació Profesional de la Dona (Institute for the Professional Training of Women), which had been founded as an institutional continuation of the MMLL's work in training unemployed women and helping them into apprenticeships via the CNT and MMLL-run School for the Professional Training of Women.[125] By the end of the year, however, the MMLL had withdrawn from the Institute, claiming that its "completely statist" working methods had created "a mere employment exchange scheme" with no educational content whatsoever.[126] The MMLL not only protected its autonomy against the encroachment of the state but also in resistance to the political pressures to join the Communist-led Agrupación de Mujeres Antifascistas (Antifascist Women's Grouping). In August 1938, Sánchez Saornil wrote an open response to one such injunction from Dolores Ibárruri, the famous secretary of that organisation:

> Our Federation… is a revolutionary organisation with its own perspective on the war and a clear concept of its mission that goes beyond a limited anti-fascism… Rather than allow Mujeres Libres to be absorbed we would prefer to continue on the road taken… if necessary without the official support that others enjoy, but maintaining the integrity of our specific character.[127]

The MMLL continued with its educational programme through the Casal de la Dona Treballadora (Working Women's House), founded in Barcelona at the end of 1936, where by 1938 up to 800 women attended a wide variety of classes every day. The success of the project led to the CNT's Food Supplies Union to provide the Casal with larger premises, and the final mobilisation of anarchist Barcelona came at the end of 1938 in defence of this building. A standoff had developed when the Bank of Spain, on whose board the CNT had a delegate representative, attempted to have the MMLL evicted from the premises by the Finance Ministry in order to instal its own offices.[128] The MMLL had initially agreed to accede to the authorities' demands, on the understanding that suitable replacement accommodation would be found to enable the activities of the Casal to continue. Before

125   Ackelsberg, *Free Women*, 152–3.
126   "Delimitación de las funciones que desempeñan 'Mujeres Libres' y el instituto de adaptación al trabajo de la Generalidad," CDMH, PS Barcelona, 1412/1.
127   *Solidaridad Obrera*, 14 August 1938.
128   See "Informe sobre los incidentes surgidos con motivo de la imposición del Ministerio de Hacienda para que cediéramos el edificio del 'Casal de la dona treballadora' al Banco de España," CDMH, PS Barcelona, 1049/22, and Ackelsberg, *Free Women of Spain*, 196.

such premises could be located, however, the Casal was twice threatened with forced eviction by armed police, causing the MMLL to call on the support of the *comités superiores* of the libertarian movement and the CNT's Minister of Education in the Republican government, Segundo Blanco. On the morning of 14 December 1938, a detachment of armed police was met by the passive resistance of the Casal's inhabitants. Unable to find a suitable replacement building, the Subsecretary of the Finance Ministry was invited by Federica Montseny and Sánchez Saornil to visit the Casal, where the standoff continued. There he was greeted by a demonstration of 500 women alongside other supporters of the MMLL and, on being shown the premises, made assurances that the eviction would be called off until a suitable replacement could be found. The withdrawal of the police and the confirmation of this promise by the Finance Minister eventually came later in the day. A matter of weeks before the fall of Barcelona, the MMLL had shown the continued capacity of practical libertarian projects to generate community support in spite of and against the state. Long after the defeat of the revolution had been confirmed, the Casal de la Dona Treballadora provided persistent testimony to its achievements, and the ability of its partisans to defend its traces even on the eve of their violent erasure.

Conclusions

Because 1939 represented a defeat for both Spanish anarchism as a whole and the anti-fascist forces more generally, its experience was of a different scale to that suffered by radical anarchists after May 1937. It brought with it new imperatives, new hardships, new depths of suffering, and forced new and disparate fates upon the activists foregrounded in this book. These ranged from execution at the hands of the victors, either in the immediate aftermath of the war or following capture as part of the underground resistance, and exile (for the most part in France and Central and South America) to semi-clandestine existence in Spain, where being recognised as a former anarchist activist could mean imprisonment or death. This makes the period between May 1937 and the end of the civil war of crucial historical importance for excavating the reflections and activity of the war's "first losers": the partisans of revolution and social war.

We have seen how, in this period, radical anarchists fought a rearguard action to slow the retreat of the Spanish revolution, on the streets, in the meeting halls and in the pages of their press. Although they exhibited ideological and strategic shortcomings, the regenerative culture of Spanish anarchism, particularly in the strongholds of Cataluña and Aragón, was such that these may yet have been overcome had time not run out. By the end of the war, there were already clear signs of a backlash within the JJLL against the patriotic language and sentiment the movement was susceptible to. In the JJLL publication *Faro*, which published contributions from the international anarchist movement, Antonio Morales Guzmán, former secretary of the Local Federation of the CNT in Granada, provided one of the more coherent statements of anarchist internationalism to appear in this period, stressing that anarchists had to combat:

> all borders, all dividing lines and every division of race, class or sect. The young libertarians know well enough that beyond those borders our brothers and sisters live in hunger, poverty and exploitation. Our war, the war of all peoples who struggle to free themselves from the yoke of tyranny, is not Spanish, and still less nationalist.[129]

Likewise in the pages of *Ruta*, where the departure from the editorial board of José Peirats had not led to any diminution of the publication's radicalism, the imminent catastrophe of the war's end did not prevent contributors from focusing on questions of principle, with a vigorous rejection of nationalism to the fore. Federico Ruffinelli, Secretary of Propaganda in the JJLL, who was remembered by Antonia Fontanillas for encouraging her to take on positions of responsibility in the organisation, wrote in October 1938:

> We anarchists have no fatherland... All wars are fought in the name of the fatherland and in the interests of the capitalists, who are the only patriots... The time has come for our organisation to say it loud and clear: either we are patriots, or we are anarchists.[130]

The same edition contained a critique of the concept of national independence, asserting that anarchists "struggle against all those who threaten the freedom of the people, whether they are Spanish, German or English... We cannot limit ourselves to acting only in the spheres marked out by the nations... We are internationalists and citizens of wherever we find ourselves."[131]

Such considerations were curtailed before they could result in any analysis of why anarchists remained susceptible to nationalism and how this had been a factor in their participation in the Republican state. In fact, the

129   *Faro*, 19 November 1937.
130   *Ruta*, 8 October 1938.
131   Ibid.

insistence on reaffirming the permanence of anarchist principles in this period may have militated against any such reflections taking place. The articles in the radical press offered comforting reading in this sense. In spite of the disaster unfolding around them, anarchists reassured themselves that there was no need to "rectify" their ideals. As Vicente Rodríguez had put it, "have the ideas failed? No! Men have." This account failed to understand state collaboration as a multilayered phenomenon involving thousands of CNT and FAI members, which had amplified and instrumentalised existing contradictions within the movement, contradictions which had to do not only with ambiguous attitudes to government and formal politics (these the purists could perceive), but also with questions of gender and patriotism. Instead, state collaboration was seen as a failing of individuals, whose ambition, lack of fervour or simple miscalculation had led them into a cul-de-sac, while the "idea" remained unblemished and resplendent, guarded by true believers and ready to be taken up once more when circumstances allowed. This left the radical currents in the movement susceptible to being disoriented and outflanked by a return to orthodoxy on the part of a section of the *comités superiores*.

In the last article he wrote before his death, the purist Vicente Rodríguez considered the proposal of Horacio M. Prieto that the FAI convert itself into a libertarian political party:

> There is no need to make a song and dance about it. It is pointless to get upset when a line of action reaches the end of its road. Excusing errors by appealing to circumstances carries with it the danger of considering those circumstances to be permanent... In the revision of principles and "innovations" proposed by the comrade, we only perceive the desire to further entrench what we were told was only circumstantially to be tolerated.[132]

Prieto's proposal had garnered little support among the *comités superiores*, and Rodríguez likely had libertarian grandees in mind when he pointed out the absurdity of their considering heretical what was merely the logical outcome of their collective trajectory during the war. To accept their reversion to orthodoxy as genuine would mean that "by magic, the circumstances have changed abruptly and without a transitional period."[133]

This was in fact the argument that notable members of the libertarian movement would make in exile. Although they lacked credibility, there was

132   Originally published in *Tiempos Nuevos*, October–November 1938, quoted in Peirats, *Figuras del movimiento*, 281–5.
133   Ibid.

little that purists could do beyond pointing out the absurdity of the newly rediscovered orthodoxy of Montseny, Herrera, Xena and others. After the Second World War, José Peirats, living in Venezuela, was called upon to support the "orthodox" current of the CNT against those who, basing themselves on the perspectives of the clandestine National Committee in Spain, favoured participation in the post-war Republican government in exile. Peirats confronted his interlocutor, José Xena: "The argument they are making now is the same that you made before: 'we are dictated to by the circumstances, the war goes on.'" "Very well," replied Xena, "but we have shown ourselves capable of rectifying our conduct." Peirats was contemptuous: "It was when you were wearing epaulettes that you had to rectify your conduct, not now."[134] Nevertheless, Peirats did not abandon the fold, and in a sense the self-conception that the purist current had cultivated after the May days, of holding the fort while the statist experiment was played out, left him little alternative. Hostages to their own integrity, anarchist purists remained the loyal servants of organisations that, regardless of their official ideology, had not rid themselves of the underhand politicking and bureaucratic high-handedness that had come to dominate the movement's upper echelons during the war.

134   Peirats, *De mi paso*, 516.

Conclusion

In this book, radical anarchist opposition to the reconstruction of the Republican state has been shown to be more coherent, more consistent and broader than has been understood hitherto.[1] What has become clear over the course of this work is the scale of the challenge that this opposition faced. This was primarily because of the depth and complexity of the process of state reconstruction that the libertarian movement had become implicated in. Governmental participation was only one aspect of a process that absorbed hundreds of activists into administrative tasks, while thousands more worked in industries under state control throughout the Republican territories. The phenomena arising from the revolutionary interregnum of summer 1936, from the militia columns to the prominence of women, from the union takeover of industry to the Republic as a haven for anti-fascist refugess, all came under threat as the state consolidated itself, with the libertarian organisations playing an important, if ambiguous, role in the process.

State collaboration began through a series of ad hoc responses to urgent situations, starting with the agreement of the Catalan CNT to participate in the CCMA. During this process, the democratic decision-making procedures of the libertarian movement were often bypassed, in part because of the exigencies of the circumstances. This fact alone should give us pause when we consider the oft-repeated claim that the majority of the CNT's membership agreed with the policy of state collaboration. The fact that radical opponents of this policy were able to enact a mass, armed mobilisation in Barcelona in May 1937, backed up by a universally observed general strike, provides further grounds for scepticism. While this book has not established that oppositional anarchists had majority support among the wider membership of the CNT, it has made a case for the continuing popular legitimacy of the radicals' anti-state project in the face of state reconstruction. If, with hindsight, this project seems to have been doomed, it can be readily appreciated why this did not appear to be the case for contemporaries, given the extensive working-class sympathy for radical positions and the ongoing mobilising capacity of oppositional anarchists.

---

1   The final reflections in this Conclusion owe much to conversations with Liz Stainforth.

In myriad ways, radical anarchists had attempted to meet the challenge of state reconstruction over the course of the war, considering the process to be reversible and inconsistent with their vision of anti-fascism as necessarily internationalist, anti-sexist and anti-capitalist. In the first half of 1937, the socialisation campaign granted the radicals the opportunity to enact projects that went beyond the mere assertion of union power and control, while calling for the extension of socialisation to the sphere of consumption helped to foster important connections between the defence committees, the MMLL and the bread queues in Barcelona in the period preceding the May days. However, the campaign also revealed vulnerabilities in the radical agenda. By making appeals to the UGT, it demonstrated the continued division of the organised workers and the absence of the kind of extra-union body later envisaged by Amador Franco that could enact socialisation on the basis of a working-class democracy capable of superseding union discipline.

The socialisation campaign had proven that an upturn in revolutionary activity could take place in spite of the libertarian movement's collaboration with the state, but in doing so had also obscured the extent to which the CNT as an organisation had been impacted by state collaboration. In May 1937, Julián Merino helped coordinate an anti-state mobilisation from inside the movement's headquarters in Barcelona, under the noses of the *comités superiores*. Because this insurrection was not enacted in defiance of libertarian organisational norms, but rather according to the mandate that a Local Plenum of the FAI had granted in April, it had a claim to legitimacy and therefore to the resources of the movement headquarters. Nevertheless, this proximity of the mobilisation's coordinators to the *comités superiores* left them vulnerable to bullying and manipulation. There were no channels outside the libertarian movement through which such a revolt could have been brought about, but by May the libertarian movement was so compromised by state collaboration that even a newly mandated revolutionary committee could be brought to heel through bureaucratic manoeuvre.

After this point, the radical alliances forged during the socialisation campaign began to fracture. In the revolution's expansive phase, radicals had been occupied by the question of how to advance towards specific goals and to defend concrete achievements. Common interests were easier to perceive in this period. When the defeat that the May events represented became apparent, activists dismayed by their outcome no longer focused on how to bring about libertarian communism, but on what it meant to be an anarchist. This led to a return to educational projects, to prisoner solidarity work and to new journals and reviews, but also to a narrowing of ambitions and a retreat from the solidarity of the barricades. So it was the largest component of the alliance in May, the JJLL, abandoned its pact with the youth section of the POUM, left the Local Federation of the FAI and became involved in a quarrel with the MMLL. Nor did this turning inwards of the radicals produce a convincing explanation for the failure of the revolution beyond a failure of "men" to uphold their anti-statist principles. This reduced the question of collaboration to a moment of decision and neglected the pre-existing contradictions within the movement, which not only helped to explain why state collaboration had taken place, but also militated against the radicals' effectiveness. These contradictions included the elevation of *notables* to positions of prominence in spite of the organisations' egalitarian functioning, and the persistence of nationalist and sexist attitudes and tropes.

There was also the question of the residual republican influence in the anarchist movement. This could be seen in both a narrowly Spanish sense, as anarchists and republicans had shared in both the vicissitudes of exile and the debates and discussions of the *ateneos*, and also in the sense of a broader European Enlightenment tradition stretching back to the French revolution. This informed a progressive outlook that justified the defence of "democratic civilisation" advocated by Montseny and echoed by Xena at the Paris Congress. Their emphasis on the anti-civilisational nature of fascism was reminiscent of the characterisation in the infamous "Manifesto of the Sixteen" of Germany's action during the First World War as "a threat not only against our hopes of emancipation, but against all human evolution."[2]

Neutrality in the First World War had helped create the conditions for the initial growth of the CNT, and also shielded the movement from the more traumatic associations that split revolutionary syndicalism in France and elsewhere, leaving organised anarchism abroad much smaller, but also more inured to the appeals of "democratic" militarism. When these depleted currents of international anarchism met the representatives of the *comités superiores* in Paris in December 1937, they could not even find a common ground on which to debate the questions of the day. Rodríguez Vázquez informed them that the presence of foreign anarchists in Spain was not required unless they "come with disciplined troops; that is to say, with military discipline, with a military conception and military commanders, because we do not need anything else."[3] However, while opposition to the military discipline advocated by the *comités superiores* at the front and in

---

2   The "Manifesto of the Sixteen" was issued in 1916 and signed by fifteen prominent anarchists, including Peter Kropotkin, declaring support for the Allied war effort. See Christiaan Cornelissen et al., "The Manifesto of the Sixteen" (1916), trans. by Shawn P. Wilbur (2011) <http:libertarian-labyrinth.blogspot.co.uk/2011/05/manifesto-of-sixteen-1916.html> [accessed 6 December 2017].

3   "Actas del Congreso de la AIT celebrado en Paris."

the rear was common to Spanish radicals and their international comrades, oppositionists also had to contend with widespread unease among activists that any disruption to the war effort leading to a fascist advance would be blamed upon the anarchist movement. How, then, could the movement and the war be combined?

For Alexander Schapiro, the question rested on a false premise:

> In reality, the idea of a "revolutionary war" is a disastrous mistake, the same that led Kropotkin and his friends to the Sacred Union in 1914. There is no such thing as a revolutionary war. What is legitimate is the armed and combatant revolution, which has as its indispensable, essential base the economic transformation of society.[4]

The "armed and combatant revolution" envisaged by Schapiro provides an accurate description of the July days of 1936 and the early advances of the militia columns prior to the commencement of trench warfare. Whether or not the war had become conventional, it would certainly have drained the libertarian movement of energy and resources, but once the "armed and combatant revolution" had surrendered to conventional military discipline, the connection between the fighting and the social and economic transformation in the rearguard became harder to sustain. The refusal to countenance independence for Spanish colonies made this even clearer: a conventional war appeared to demand a conventional state. Whether or not the radical alternative, of infiltration or enemy-held cities, guerrilla tactics when in retreat, autonomy for Spanish Morocco and moving, as Camillo Berneri put it, from a "war of position to a war of movement," would have been successful is moot, as these initiatives were impeded at every turn by the acceptance of conventional military logic by the *comités superiores* of the libertarian movement.[5]

As had occured in the case of the Russian revolution, the reconstitution of the state in Spain proved incompatible with the consolidation and extension of revolutionary phenomena, while civil war, and the urgent assessment of priorities that it entailed, was the means by which the revolutionary organisations became, to a greater or lesser extent, agents of state reconstruction. The assumption of official responsibilities and the experience

---

4   Ibid.

5   Berneri, *Entre la Revolución y las trincheras*, p. 9. That such tactics would not have been entirely fanciful is indicated by the military historian Antony Beevor, who has written that, by 1937, the Republic's "only hope lay in continuing regular defence combined with unconventional guerrilla attacks in the enemy rear and rapid raids at as many points as possible on weakly held parts of the front": Beevor, *The Battle for Spain*, 349.

of wielding authority allowed pre-existing ideological inconsistencies and embryonic bureaucratisation to be accepted as necessary, while the war gave their justification moral urgency. These processes meant that the organisational life of the CNT was entirely transformed. It became an important supplier of administrative and governmental personnel, and of directors of the wartime economy. As in the Russian case, the absorption of activists into administrative roles exacerbated the growing divorce between those members with official roles and the wider membership, from the "mid-level" union and defence committee delegates down.[6] The CNT was converted into a hierarchical body, its *comités superiores* effectively remaining state functionaries even after their ejection from government, as they carried out the essential task of imposing discipline on recalcitrant elements of their membership.

In this period, the libertarian movement faced the stark alternative of pushing the revolution forward – "going for everything" – or collaborating in the maintenance of the status quo as a lesser evil. In different contexts and with different stakes, this essential question recurs as a perennial problem of the left to this day, albeit with less dramatic consequences. In Spain in 2011, the Arab Spring-inspired movement of the *indignados* appeared to have provoked a crisis of legitimacy for the democratic state that emerged from the post-Franco Transition. Although its desire for "real democracy" lacked the depth, historical support and transformational programme of libertarian communism, the movement carried a utopian impulse that, as a common refrain of the time put it, could not be contained by ballot boxes. Indeed, in what was a strikingly heterogeneous and incoherent movement, one of the few points of consensus was a rejection of representative democracy. Nevertheless, the development of this assembly-based phenomenon into a structural challenge to capital and state, itself by no means guaranteed, was foreshortened by the emergence of the political party Podemos. In the excitement of immediate change that parliamentary democracy promises, the intractable problems posed by the form of the modern state itself are put to one side.

Does the anarchist experience in the Spanish civil war speak to this dilemma? When the *notables* of the movement elected to defer confronting such problems in July 1936, they simultaneously over- and underestimated the capacities of the movement. On the one hand, they considered the strength of their organisations to be such that they could compromise with a project of state reconstruction without vastly diminishing their autonomy

---

6   On this phenomenon in Russia, see Alexander Rabinowitch, *The Bolsheviks in Power: The First Year of Soviet Rule in Petrograd* (Bloomington: Indiana University Press, 2008), 393–3.

and authority. On the other, they underestimated the creative potential of the organisations' activists and sympathisers. It was this creative capacity that enabled radical anarchists to elaborate a programmatic alternative to the project of state reconstruction. If it is hard to imagine how this programme might have been successful, we should also be alert to how our imaginations are constrained by past defeats. Today as yesterday, those who desire a radical change in the trajectory of human history face enormous obstacles. However, when we consider the incapacity of modern states to offer solutions to the urgent global problems of war, climate change and forced displacement, and the limited ambitions of existing projects to reform them, a continued inclination to underestimate our capacities condemns us to a permanent experience of defeat.

For the radicals studied in this book, anarchism was the "anti-state," which implied reorganising society in such a way that its inhabitants might be more than the stuff of the factory, prison or barracks.[7] It also meant that one's claim to a share in this society or a voice in how it is run would not depend on one's wealth, gender or place of birth. In education and social care, anarchists attempted to apply this world-view in spite of the encroachments of a nationalist and militarist dominant ideology. The struggle in these spheres has only been lightly touched on in this book, but further research would likely prove as illuminating for the study of both radical anarchism and the process of state reconstruction as has the more broadly political focus of the present work. Likewise, further comparative work would be necessary to establish the extent to which the argument presented here – of state reconstruction as the essential dynamic by which revolutionary energies are coopted and revolutionary phenomena shut down – is more broadly applicable.

The breadth and complexity of radical anarchism in the Spanish revolution corresponded to the multifaceted nature of state reconstruction. Through opposition to every aspect of that process, from militarisation and the disarmament of the defence committees to the domestication of the revolutionary organisations and the imposition of nationalist and patriarchal norms, the radical anarchists were able to affirm the broad parameters of the international anarchist tradition and demonstrate its capacity for renewal. This latter capacity remains a source of hope for those who see the struggles of the past as related to the tasks of the present, and as a foreshadowing of a possible future.

7   *Frente y Retaguardia*, 1 September 1937.

Recurring Personages

José Alberola
A rationalist schoolteacher and member of the FAI, Alberola was a prominent critic of moderation in the CNT in the early years of the Second Republic. During the war he opposed government collaboration and resigned from his post on the Regional Defence Council of Aragón when it was reorganised in December 1936. He later worked as a teacher in Mexico, and was murdered in obscure circumstances in Mexico City in 1967.

Jaime Balius
A member of the editorial board of *Solidaridad Obrera* at the outset of the war, Balius would become increasingly critical of the process of state reconstruction over the course of 1936. A contributor to *Ideas*, the mouthpiece of the libertarian movement in Baix Llobregat, he would help found the AAD in March 1937. Following the May days he was subject to the rumour-mongering of the *comités superiores* and the harassment of the authorities. After the war he contributed to the anarchist press in France and sought to defend the legacy of the AAD.

Camillo Berneri
Berneri was an Italian anarchist and anti-fascist exile who was living in Barcelona at the outbreak of the civil war. Highly sensitive to the danger of the Spanish libertarian movement being "bolshevised," he expressed this fear both before and during the war. Berneri fought at the front in the summer of 1936 but was forced to return to Barcelona on medical grounds. There, he published critiques of state collaboration and the persecution of the POUM. He was murdered by Stalinists during the May days of 1937.

Diego Camacho
A young anarchist active in the JJLL of Clot and in his local defence committee, during the war Camacho was a founder member of the Los Quijotes del Ideal affinity group, which criticised the policy of state collaboration from a purist perspective and produced the *El Quijote* review. Under the

pseudonym of Abel Paz, he would later become an important historian of Spanish anarchism.

Gustavo Cochet

Cochet was an Argentinian artist who had lived in Europe since 1915. A member of the CNT and the FAI, during the war he was a leading member of the Fine Arts section of the former and contributor to the anarchist press. His Goya-inspired engravings bear witness to the revolution and its defeat. He died in Argentina in 1979.

Joaquina Dorado Pita

Dorado Pita was a member of the CNT-affiliated Woodworkers' Union in Barcelona at the outbreak of the war. As an active defence committee and JJLL member, Dorado Pita participated in the street fighting in July 1936 and May 1937. Delegate of the affinity group *Luz y Cultura*, it is likely that she formed part of the working group at the Barcelona Plenum of affinity groups in April 1937 that played an important role in preparing the ground for the latter rising. By the following year she had become president of Barcelona's Economic Council of the Socialised Woodwork Industry. A lifelong anarchist activist, Dorado Pita would suffer torture and imprisonment due to her activities in the libertarian underground after the war. She died in 2017.

Buenaventura Durruti

Durruti won fame as a "man of action" alongside García Oliver, Francisco Ascaso and others in the years prior to the Second Republic. In the years that followed he supported the insurrectionary essays undertaken in the name of libertarian communism. During the war he led the Durruti Column and opposed the militarisation of the militia. He was killed in mysterious circumstances at the Madrid front in November 1936.

Antonia Fontanillas

From an anarchist family, Fontanillas was an active member of the JJLL during the civil war and worked in the offices of *Solidaridad Obrera*. Following the war, she was an activist both in the clandestine movement in Spain and later in exile in France. Until her death in 2014 she remained dedicated to honouring the memory of her generation of comrades, and the present author was a beneficiary of her generosity in sharing materials and memories.

Diego Franco Cazorla

Better known by the pseudonym Amador Franco. Only sixteen when the war began, Franco fought on the Aragón front and provided some of the more lucid and trenchant critiques of state collaboration. A member of the JJLL and the libertarian student organisation, the FECL, Franco was a regular contributor to the oppositional press. Following the war he remained active in the libertarian movement, frequently crossing from France into Spain on clandestine missions. In July 1946, on one such mission, he was arrested and executed.

Sinesio Baudilio García Fernández

Better known by the pseudonym Diego Abad de Santillán, García Fernández was a leading member of the FAI in the years immediately prior to the civil war and a representative of the organisation in the CCMA from July 1936. He was the leading member of the Nervio affinity group, associated both prior to and during the war with the attempts to introduce greater centralisation and discipline into the libertarian movement.

Juan García Oliver

During the Second Republic, García Oliver was instrumental in the organisation of the Barcelona defence committees and a proponent of "revolutionary gymnastics." From July 1936 he represented the CNT in the CCMA, and from November he was Minister of Justice in the Republican government. Following the ejection of the CNT from central government, García Oliver became Secretary of the CAP and sought to enforce internal discipline in the Catalan libertarian movement.

José Manzana

A former military officer, Manzana would eventually replace Durruti at the head of the Durruti Column and oversee the militarisation of the same. A member of the enlarged Regional Defence Committee that ordered the demobilisation that brought the May days to an end, Manzana was a controversial figure who has remained the subject of rumours regarding the death of Durruti.

Ada Martí

A journalist and student during the civil war, Martí was an important activist in the FECL, a member of the MMLL and a possible member of the Friends of Durruti, who participated in the libertarian mobilisation in Barcelona in May 1937. An assiduous contributor to the anti-collaborationist anarchist press, Martí edited *Evolución* and its successor, *Fuego*. Although vouched for by respected anarchist comrades, Martí was denied membership of the CNT in its post-war French exile in unclear circumstances. She died in 1960.

Julián Merino

By the beginning of the war Merino was a veteran organiser and leading member of the Maritime Transport Workers' Union. At the front he was involved in setting up the Regional Defence Council of Aragón and on returning to Barcelona he became Secretary of the Local Federation of Anarchist Affinity Groups. Instrumental in the libertarian mobilisation of the May days, he would continue to oppose government collaboration throughout 1937.

Fidel Miró

Regional Secretary of the JJLL until May 1937, Miró was a member of the Nervio affinity group before the war and a close associate of Santillán. Together with Alfredo Martínez, Miró defended revolutionary unity with the JCI. This brought him into conflict with purists in the JJLL, a conflict that would continue following his removal as Secretary, when he was elected General Secretary of the FIJL.

Federica Montseny

A member of the famous Urales family that produced the anarchist review *La Revista Blanca*, in the years prior to the war Montseny was a fierce critic of *treintismo*. From November 1936 to May 1937 she was Minister of Health in the central government, and following the ejection of the CNT became a prominent figure in the Peninsular Committee of the FAI. A defender of collaboration during the war, in exile she returned to orthodox anarchist positions and, alongside her partner Germinal Esgleas, played a controversial role in the splits and recriminations that benighted the Spanish libertarian movement.

José Peirats

A seasoned activist and union organiser by the beginning of the war, Peirats would become one of the most prominent critics of government collaboration, first as editor of *Acracia* in Lleida, and after May 1937 as a leading member of the Catalan JJLL. A committed anarchist throughout his life, Peirats would go on to become the most important anarchist historian of the CNT.

Joan Peiró

A prominent gradualist on the National Committee of the CNT at the outset of the Spanish Republic, Peiró would serve as Minister of Industry in the government of Largo Caballero from November 1936. Following the German invasion of France, Peiró was extradited at the request of the

Spanish government in 1941. He was executed in 1942, having rejected overtures from the Francoists to cooperate with the regime's vertical unions.

Eduardo Pons Prades

Only fifteen at the outbreak of the civil war, Pons Prades joined the CNT in 1937 and participated in the socialisation of the woodwork industry in Barcelona. As a soldier in the Republican army, he fought at Guadarrama, Brunete and the Ebro, and assisted in the evacuation of the wounded to France after the fall of Barcelona. An active member of the French resistance during the Second World War, Pons Prades would later become a prolific journalist and historian.

Horacio M. Prieto

National Secretary of the CNT during the autumn of 1936 when the decision was taken to join the government of Largo Caballero, Prieto was forced out of this post during the scandal that was caused by the removal of the government from Madrid to Valencia. An intransigent defender of collaboration, in 1938 Prieto advocated the formation of a libertarian political party and continued to propagate his variety of libertarian "possibilism" after the war.

Rodolfo Prina

Better known by the pseudonym of Lucio Ruano, Prina was a member of the anarchist action group that murdered the Catalan nationalist Badia brothers in April 1936. A member of the Durruti Column, following the death of its founder Prina briefly took over his command. Accused of arbitrary murder and pillage, he was killed in an operation authorised by the CNT in July 1937. He appears to have formed a part of the committee that had directed the anarchist mobilisation in Barcelona two months earlier.

Joan "Remi'

The anonymous interviewee of Joan Casanovas Codina whose testimony is contained in the Fonts Orals department of the AHCB. A member of his local defence committee and of the *Patrullas de Control* in the Barcelona suburb of Sants.

Vicente Rodríguez

The editor of *Acracia* alongside José Peirats, Rodríguez was a founder member of the Catalan JJLL and the libertarian student body, the FECL. A perceptive and coherent proponent of the purist critique of government collaboration and an assiduous contributor to the oppositional press, often under the pseudonym "Viroga," Rodríguez died of tuberculosis in France in 1941.

Mariano Rodríguez Vázquez

Rodríguez Vázquez was an autodidact and organiser in the Construction Workers' Union of the CNT. Regional Secretary of the Catalan CNT at the outbreak of the war, he would become National Secretary following the removal of Prieto. A defender of collaboration and internal discipline, Rodríguez Vázquez died in France in June 1939, drowned in the Marne River. The circumstances of his death are considered suspicious because he was known to be a strong swimmer.

Lucía Sánchez Saornil

One of the founders of the Mujeres Libres grouping, Sánchez Saornil made a significant contribution to the development of anarchist theory in Spain. Her writings in the *Mujeres Libres* review also include some of the more trenchant critiques of collaboration and capitalist democracy to appear in the wartime anarchist press prior to the May days. Sánchez Saornil later became Secretary of the CNT's international aid organisation, Solidaridad Internacional Antifascista, and appears to have become removed from the more radical wing of the organisation, joining the AAB in October 1937. Nevertheless, she continued to insist on the independence and anarchist character of the MMLL throughout the war, in spite of increasing pressure for it to merge with the Communist-led Antifascist Women's Association.

Juan Santana Calero

A founder member of the FIJL in Málaga, Santana Calero was a tireless writer and editor. After his arrival in Barcelona early in 1937, he contributed to *Ideas*, *Esfuerzo* (in both its incarnations) and *Faro*, among others. A member of the AAD as well as the Catalan JJLL, he was the subject of malicious rumours of cowardice, which, it has been suggested, were the cause of his remaining in Spain after the war, where he died in a gun battle in 1939.

Alexander Schapiro

Schapiro was a veteran anarcho-syndicalist who had participated in the Russian revolution. Exiled from that country in 1922, Schapiro became active in the IWMA and, as its General Secretary, wrote a critical report on the CNT during the Second Republic. As a member of the CGT-SR in France, Schapiro became one of the more vocal critics of CNT policy over the course of 1937, both in the French anarchist press and at Plenums of the IWMA.

José Xena

A rationalist teacher and member of the FAI, Xena provided the only vote against collaboration in the CCMA at the Catalan Regional Plenum of July 1936, as a delegate of the Baix Llobregat region. A contributor to *Ideas*, the mouthpiece of the libertarian movement in that region, Xena's attitude to state collaboration appears to have been somewhat ambiguous prior to May 1937. On the one hand, he was involved in attempts to socialise the economy of L'Hospitalet; on the other, he briefly occupied the post of Mayor of the town. After the May days he became a defender of the policy of the *comités superiores* and insistent on the need for internal discipline. His activism continued in exile in Venezuela, where he founded a libertarian cultural centre and edited *AIT*, the mouthpiece of the Federación Obrera Regional Venezolana (Venezuelan Regional Workers' Federation).

Bibliography

Archives

AHCB – Arxiu Històric de la Ciutat de Barcelona (Barcelona)
BPA – Biblioteca Pública Arús (Barcelona)
ANC – Arxiu Nacional de Catalunya (Barcelona)
CDMH – Centro Documental de la Memoria Histórica (Salamanca)
Fundación Anselmo Lorenzo (Madrid)
IISG – Internationaal Instituut voor Sociale Geschiedenis (Amsterdam)
Modern Records Centre, University of Warwick
PDLR – Biblioteca del Pavelló de la República de la Universitat de Barcelona (Barcelona)

Primary Sources

Memoirs, eyewitness reports and contemporary articles and correspondence
Andrade, Juan, *La revolución española día a día* (Barcelona: Nueva Era, 1979)
Andrade, Juan, "La revolución española y el POUM," in *Juan Andrade (1897–1981). Vida y voz de un revolucionario*, ed. by Pelai Pagès, Jaime Pastor and Miguel Romero (Madrid: La Oveja Roja, 2008), 69–101
Ascaso, Joaquín, *Memorias (1936–1938) hacia un nuevo Aragón* (Zaragoza: Prensas Universitarias de Zaragoza, 2006)
Azaretto, Manuel, *Las pendientes resbaladizas (los anarquistas en España)* (Montevideo: Germinal, 1939)
Bakunin, M., *The Political Philosophy of Bakunin: Scientific Anarchism*, ed. by G. P. Maximoff (London: The Free Press of Glencoe, 1964)
Berenguer, Sara, *Entre el sol y la tormenta* (Barcelona: Seuba Ediciones, 1988)
Berneri, Camillo, "En defensa del POUM" (1937), http://2014.kaosenlared .net/component/k2/item/19975-en-defensa-del-poum.html [accessed 12 December 2017]
Berneri, Camillo, *Entre la Revolución y las trincheras* ([Paris?]: Ediciones

239

Tierra y Libertad, 1946)

Berneri, Camillo, "Moscú y Berlin," in *Orto (1932–1934) revista de documentación social*, ed. by Javier Paniagua (Valencia: Biblioteca Historia Social, 2001), 989–993

Bueso, Adolfo, *Recuerdos de un cenetista II. De la Segunda República al final de la guerra civil* (Barcelona: Ariel, 1978)

"Correspondencia entre Diego Camacho ('Abel Paz') y Juan García Oliver," *Balance. Cuaderno de historia, 38* (2014)

Cochet, Gustavo, *Caprichos: Estampas 1936–1938* (Santa Fe: Espacio Santafesino Ediciones, 2014)

Cruells, Manuel, *Mayo Sangriento. Barcelona 1937* (Barcelona: Editorial Juventud, 1970)

Fontanillas, Antonia, "De lo aprendido y vivido," unpublished memoir (Dreux, 1996)

García, C., H. Piotrowski and S. Rosés, eds, *Barcelona, mayo 1937. Testimonios desde las barricadas* (Barcelona: Alikornio ediciones, 2006)

García, Miguel, *Miguel García's Story* (London: Miguel García Memorial Committee, 1982)

García Oliver, Juan, *El eco de los pasos. El anarcosindicalismo…en la calle…en el Comité de Milicias…en el gobierno…en el exilio* (Paris: Ruedo Ibérico, 1978)

Goldman, Emma, *Vision on Fire: Emma Goldman on the Spanish Revolution*, ed. by David Porter (Oakland: AK Press, 2006)

Horn, Gerd-Rainer, ed., *Letters From Barcelona: An American Woman in Revolution and Civil War* (London: Palgrave Macmillan, 2009)

Iglesias, Ignacio, *Experiencias de la Revolución. El POUM, Trotski y la intervención soviética* (Barcelona: Laertes, 2003)

Kropotkin, P. A., "The State: Its Historic Role," in P. A. Kropotkin, *Selected Writings on Anarchism and Revolution*, ed. by Martin A. Miller (London: The MIT Press, 1970), 210–264

Langdon-Davies, John, *Behind the Spanish Barricades: Reports from the Spanish Civil War* (London: Reportage Press, 2007)

Lenin, N., "'Left-Wing' Childishness," a series of articles published in *Pravda* in May 1918, https://www.marxists.org/archive/lenin/works/1918/may/09.htm [accessed 5 December 2017]

Leval, Gaston, *Collectives in the Spanish Revolution* (London: Freedom Press, 1975)

Liarte, Ramón, *Entre la Revolución y la Guerra* (Barcelona: Picazo, 1986)

Lister, Enrique, *Nuestra Guerra. Aportaciones para una Historia de la Guerra Nacional Revolucionaria del Pueblo Español 1936–1939* (Paris: Colección Ebro, 1966)

Low, Mary and Juan Breá, *Red Spanish Notebook: The First Six Months of the Revolution and the Civil War* (San Francisco: City Lights Books, 1979)

Miró, Fidel, *Vida intensa y revolucionaria* (Mexico City: Editores Mexicanos Unidos, 1989)

Negrete, Rosalio and Hugo Oehler, "Negrete and Oehler report back from Barcelona," *Revolutionary History*, 1, 2 (1988), http://www.revolutionary history.co.uk/index.php/155-articles/articles-of-rh0102/4243-negrete-and-oehler-report-from-barcelona [accessed 6 December 2017]

Nin, Andreu, *La revolución española* (Madrid: Diario Público, 2011)

Oliver, Edward H., *Sixth Anniversary of the Spanish Republic in Barcelona* (Chicago: Revolutionary Workers' League, 1937)

Orwell, George, *Orwell in Spain. The Full Text of* Homage to Catalonia *with Associated Articles, Reviews and Letters from* The Complete Works of George Orwell (London: Penguin, 2001)

Paz, Abel, *Chumberas y alacranes (1921–1936)* (Barcelona: Medusa, 1994)

Paz, Abel, *Viaje al Pasado* (Madrid: Fundación de Estudios Libertarios Anselmo Lorenzo, 2002)

Peirats Valls, Josep, *De mi paso por la vida* (Barcelona: Flor de Viento, 2009)

Pons Garlandí, Joan, *Un republicà enmig de faistes* (Barcelona: Edicions 62, 2008)

Prieto, Horacio M., *Secretario General de la CNT de España en 1936. Ex-ministro de la República en el exilio. Recuerdos* (Unpublished memoir, BPA: n.d.)

Prieto, Horacio M., *Secretario General de la CNT de España en 1936. Ex-ministro de la República en el exilio. Recuerdos. Tomo II, Utopistas (semblanzas de militantes libertarios)* (Unpublished memoir, BPA: n.d.)

Prieto, Horacio M., *Secretario General de la CNT de España en 1936. Ex-ministro de la República en el exilio. Recuerdos. Tomo III, ¡Ananké! Mi curriculum vitae: ilusión, aventura, frustración* (Unpublished memoir, BPA: n.d.)

Rebull, Josep, "Las Jornadas de mayo" (1937/1939), http://es.internationalism .org/book/export/html/3244 [accessed 1 December 2017]

Reparaz, Gonzalo de, *Lo que pudo hacer España en Marruecos y lo que ha hecho. Conferencia pronunciada en el cine Coliseum de Barcelona, el día 17 de enero de 1937* (Barcelona: Oficinas de propaganda CNT FAI, n.d. [1937?])

Rüdiger, Helmut, *Ensayo crítico sobre la revolución española* (Buenos Aires: Imán, 1940)

Sánchez Saornil, Lucía, *Horas de Revolución* (Barcelona: Publicaciones Mujeres Libres, n.d. [1937?])

Santillán, Diego Abad de, *Por qué perdimos la guerra. Una contribución a la historia de la tragedia española* (Madrid: Toro, 1975)

Schapiro, Alexander, "The USSR and the CNT: an unconscionable stance," trans. by Paul Sharkey, *Bulletin of the Kate Sharpley Library*, *14* (1998), http://www.katesharpleylibrary.net/pk0q0r [accessed 6 December 2017]

Sanz, Ricardo, *El sindicalismo y la política. Los "Solidarios" y "Nosotros"* (Barcelona: Copa y Difon, 2013)

Sirvent Romero, Manuel, *Un militante del anarquismo español (Memorias, 1889–1948)* (Madrid: Fundación de Estudios Libertarios Anselmo Lorenzo, 2011)

Weisbord, Albert, "Barricades in Barcelona", http://search.marxists.org/archive/weisbord/Barricades.htm [accessed 1 December 2017]

Zafón Bayo, Juan, *El Consejo Revolucionario de Aragón* (Barcelona: Editorial Planeta, 1979)

Pamphlets and published minutes

Alberola, José, *Interpretación anarquista de la revolución* (Lérida: Ediciónes Juventudes Libertarias, 1937)

C.N.T., *El Congreso Confederal de Zaragoza* (Bilbao: Zero, 1978)

"CNT-FAI Acta del Pleno de Columnas Confederales y Anarquistas celebrado en Valencia el día 5 de febrero de 1937", http://www.fondation-besnard.org//spip.php?article428 [accessed 1 December 2017]

Cornelissen, Christiaan et al., "The Manifesto of the Sixteen" (1916), trans. by Shawn P. Wilbur (2011), http://libertarian-labyrinth.blogspot.co.uk/2011/05/manifesto-of-sixteen-1916.html [accessed 7 June 2016]

El mitin del Olympia en Barcelona 21 de Julio de 1937 (Barcelona: Talleres Gráficos Bosch, 1937)

García Oliver, Juan, "Los organismos revolucionarios: El Comité Central de las Milicias Antifascistas de Cataluña," in *De julio a julio. Un año de lucha. Textos de los trabajos contenidos en el extraordinario de Fragua Social, de Valencia, del 19 de julio de 1937* (Barcelona: Ediciones Tierra y Libertad, 1937), 193–199

García Oliver, Juan, *Mi gestión al frente del ministerio de justicia, conferencia pronunciada en el Teatro Apolo de Valencia el 30 de Mayo de 1937* (Valencia: Ediciones de la Comisión de Propaganda y Prensa del Comité Nacional de la CNT, 1937)

Los Congresos del anarcosindicalismo. Tomo 1. Memoria del III Congreso extraordinario de la CNT. Madrid 1931 (Barcelona: Projecció Editorial, n.d.)

Memoria del Pleno Peninsular de Regionales celebrado en Valencia los días 4, 5, 6 y 7 de Julio 1937 (Valencia: FAI, 1937)

Santana Calero, J., *Afirmación en la marcha* (Barcelona: JJLL de Sanidad, n.d. [1937?])

"Three Resolutions" in *The Anarchists in the Russian Revolution*, ed. by Paul Avrich (London: Thames and Hudson, 1973), 117–120.

Press

Acracia. Órgano diario de la Confederación Nacional del Trabajo y de la F.A.I en Lérida (Lleida, época 2, 1936–1937)

Alerta…! Periódico al servicio de la revolución proletaria (Barcelona, 1937)

Amanecer. Órgano de la Escuela de Militantes de Cataluña (Barcelona, 1937)

Anarquía. FAI (Barcelona, 1937)

The Barcelona Bulletin (Glasgow, 1937)

Boletín de Información de la CNT-FAI (Barcelona, 1936–1938)

Boletín de la Agrupación Anarquista Los de Ayer y Los de Hoy (Barcelona, 1937)

El Amigo del Pueblo. Portavoz de Los Amigos de Durruti (Barcelona, 1937–1938)

El Quijote. Revista semanal de sociología, ciencia y arte (Barcelona, 1937)

Emancipación. Órgano quincenal del Secretariado Femenino del POUM (Barcelona, 1937)

Esfuerzo. Periódico mural de las Juventudes Libertarias de Cataluña (Barcelona, 1937)

Esfuerzo (Barcelona, 1937)

Evolución. Revista del Estudiante. Órgano regional de la Federación estudiantil conciencias libres (Barcelona, 1937)

Faro (Barcelona, 1937–1938)

Frente y Retaguardia. Portavoz de las Juventudes Libertarias de la provincia de Huesca y su frente (Huesca, 1937)

Hombres Libres. Órgano de la Federación Provincial de Sindicatos Únicos de Granada (Guadix and Baza, 1936–1938)

Ideas. Portavoz del movimiento libertario de la comarca del Bajo Llobregat (Barcelona, 1936–1937)

Juventud Comunista. Órgano central de la JCI (Barcelona, 1936–1937)

La Noche (Barcelona, 1924–1939)

La Revista Blanca. Sociología, ciencia, arte (Barcelona, época 2, 1923–1936)

La Vanguardia (Barcelona, 1881–present)

Le Combat Syndicaliste. Organe officiel de la Confédération Générale du Travail Syndicaliste Révolutionnaire, AIT (Paris, 1926–1939)

Más Lejos (Barcelona, 1936)

Mi Revista. Ilustración de Actualidades (Barcelona, 1936–1938)

Mujeres Libres (Madrid and Barcelona, 1936–1938)

Nosotros. Portavoz de la Federación Anarquista Ibérica (Valencia, 1936–1938)

Ruta. Órgano de las Juventudes Libertarias de Cataluña (Barcelona, 1936–1938)

Socialist Appeal: An Organ of Revolutionary Socialism (Chicago and New York, 1935–1941)

Solidaridad Obrera. Órgano de la Confederación Regional del Trabajo de Cataluña. Portavoz de la Confederación Nacional del Trabajo de España (Barcelona, época 6, 1930–1939)

Terre Libre. Organe de la Fédération anarchiste de langue française (Nîmes and Paris, 1934–1939)

Tierra y Libertad. Órgano de la FAI (Valencia and Barcelona, 1930–1939)

Secondary Sources

Ackelsberg, Martha A., *Free Women of Spain: Anarchism and the Struggle for the Emancipation of Women* (Oakland: AK Press, 2005)

Acton, Edward, "The libertarians vindicated? The libertarian view of the revolution in the light of recent Western research," in *Revolution in Russia: Reassessments of 1917*, ed. by Edith Rogovin Frankel, Jonathan Frankel and Baruch Knei-Paz (Cambridge: Cambridge University Press, 1992), 388–405

Aguilera, Manuel, *Compañeros y Camaradas. Las luchas entre antifascistas en la Guerra Civil Española* (Madrid: Editorial Actas, 2012)

Aguilera Povedano, Manuel, "Los hechos de mayo de 1937: efectivos y bajas de cada bando," *Hispania*, 73, 245 (2013), 789–816

Aguilera Povedano, Manuel, "Lista de víctimas de los Hechos de Mayo de 1937 en Barcelona," Miguel Aguilera Povedano blog (2013), http://wp.me/p2FTqL-8V [accessed 1December2017]

Aisa Pàmpols, Manel, *La huelga de alquileres y el Comité de Defensa Económica. Barcelona, abril–diciembre de 1931. Sindicato de la Construcción de CNT* (Barcelona: El Lokal, 2014)

Alba, Victor and Stephen Schwartz, *Spanish Marxism Versus Soviet Communism* (New Brunswick and London: Transaction Publishers, 2009)

Alpert, Michael, *A New International History of the Spanish Civil War* (Basingstoke: Palgrave Macmillan, 2004)

Alpert, Michael, *The Republican Army in the Spanish Civil War, 1936–1939* (Cambridge: Cambridge University Press, 2013)

Álvarez Junco, José, *La ideología política del anarquismo español (1868–1910)* (Madrid: Siglo XXI, 1991)

Álvarez Junco, José, Los 'amantes de la libertad': la cultura republicana española a principios del siglo xx," in *El republicanismo en España (1830–1977)*, ed. by Nigel Townson (Madrid: Alianza, 1994), 265–292

Álvarez, Ramón, *Avelino G. Mallada. Alcalde Anarquista* (Barcelona: Historia Libertaria de Asturias, 1987)

Amorós, Miquel, *La Revolución Traicionada: La verdadera historia de Balius y Los Amigos de Durruti* (Barcelona: Virus, 2003)

Amorós, Miquel, *José Pellicer: El Anarquista Integro* (Barcelona: Virus, 2009)

Amorós, Miquel, *Maroto, el héroe: Una biografía del anarquismo andaluz*

(Barcelona: Virus, 2011)

Amorós, Miquel, *Los Incontrolados de 1937. Memorias militantes de los Amigos de Durruti* (Barcelona: Aldarull, 2014)

Aróstegui, Julio, *Por qué el 18 de Julio... Y después* (Barcelona: Flor del Viento, 2006)

Aróstegui, Julio and Jesús A. Martínez, *La Junta de Defensa de Madrid, Noviembre 1936 – Abril 1937* (Madrid: Comunidad de Madrid, 1984)

Baer, James A., *Anarchist Immigrants in Spain and Argentina* (Chicago: University of Illinois Press, 2015)

Baxmeyer, Martin, "'Mother Spain, We Love You!': Nationalism and Racism in Anarchist Literature during the Spanish Civil War (1936–1939)," in *Reassessing the Transnational Turn: Scales of Analysis in Anarchist and Syndicalist Studies*, ed. by Constance Bantman and Bert Altena (New York: Routledge, 2015), 193–209

Beevor, Antony, *The Battle for Spain: The Spanish Civil War 1936–1939* (London: Phoenix, 2006)

Bernecker, Walther L., *Colectividades y revolución social. El anarquismo en la guerra civil Española, 1936–1939*, trans. by Gustau Muñoz (Barcelona: Crítica, 1982)

Berry, David, *A History of the French Anarchist Movement, 1917 to 1945* (Oakland: AK Press, 2009)

Bolloten, Burnett, *The Spanish Civil War: Revolution and Counterrevolution* (London: The University of North Carolina Press, 1991)

Borderias, Cristina and Mercedes Vilanova, "Memories of Hope and Defeat: Catalan miners and fishermen under the Second Spanish Republic, 1931–9," in *Our Common History: The Transformation of Europe*, ed. by Paul Thompson and Natasha Burchardt (London: Pluto Press, 1982), 38–53

Borkenau, Franz, *The Spanish Cockpit: An Eye-Witness Account of the Political and Social Conflicts of the Spanish Civil War* (Ann Arbor: University of Michigan Press, 1974)

Brademas, John, *Anarcosindicalismo y revolución en España (1930–1937)* (Barcelona: Ariel, 1974)

Broué, Pierre and Emile Témime, *The Revolution and the Civil War in Spain* (London: The MIT Press, 1972)

Buenacasa, Manuel, *El movimiento obrero español 1886–1926. Historia y crítica* (Madrid: Ediciones Júcar, 1977)

Cara Rincón, Josep, Jordi Jané Roca and Josep Quevedo García, "Introducció," in *Luz y Vida. Una publicació obrera de Gironella. Edició Facsímil, 4/11/1932–24/11/1933*, coord. by Centre d'Estudis Josep Ester Borràs (Barcelona: Ajuntament de Gironella i Centre d'Estudis Josep Ester

Borràs, 2003), 11–23

Casanova, Julián, "Socialismo y Colectividades en Aragón," in *Socialismo y Guerra Civil*, coord. by Santos Juliá (Madrid: Editorial Pablo Iglesias, 1987), 277–294

Casanova, Julián, "Rebelión y revolución" in *Víctimas de la guerra civil*, coord. by Santos Juliá (Madrid: Temas de Hoy, 2004)

Casanova, Julián, *Anarchism, the Republic and Civil War in Spain: 1931–1939*, trans. by Andrew Dowling and Graham Pollok (London: Routledge, 2005)

Casanova, Julián, *Anarquismo y Revolución en la Sociedad Rural Aragonesa, 1936–38* (Barcelona: Crítica, 2006)

Casanovas, Joan, "La Guerra Civil a Barcelona: les patrulles de control de Sants vistes per un del seus membres," *Historia y Fuente Oral, 11* (1994), 53–66

Cases, Remi et al., "La col·lectivització a Molins de Llobregat," in J. Lluís Adí net al., *Col·lectivitzacions al Baix Llobregat (1936–1939)* (Barcelona: Publicacions de l'Abadia de Montserrat, 1989), 191–258

Castells Duran, Antoni, *El proceso estatizador en la experiencia colectivista catalana (1936–1939)* (Madrid: Nossa y Jara Editores, 1996)

Castells Duran, Antoni, "Revolution and Collectivizations in Civil War Barcelona, 1936–9" in *Red Barcelona: Social Protest and Labour Mobilization in the Twentieth Century*, ed. by Angel Smith (London and New York: Routledge, 2002), 127–141

Cattini, Giovanni C., "La Dona entre la Guerra i la Revolució. L'ocupació de l'espai públic i la superació de les restriccions de gènere tradicionals," in *Breu Historia de la Guerra Civil*, ed. by Josep M. Solé Sabaté and Joan Villarroya (Barcelona: Edicions 62, 2005), 329–333

Christie, Stuart, *We, the Anarchists: A Study of the Iberian Anarchist Federation (FAI) 1927–1937* (Oakland: AK Press, 2008)

Corkett, Thomas, "Interactions between the Confederación Nacional del Trabajo and the Unión General de Trabajadores in Spain and Catalonia, 1931–1936," (Unpublished PhD thesis, University of Glasgow, 2011)

Cuadrat, Xavier, *Socialismo y anarquismo en Cataluña (1899–1911). Los orígenes de la CNT* (Madrid: Ediciones de la Revista de Trabajo, 1976)

De Madariaga, Javier, "Les Indústries de Guerra. La fabricacció, distribució, adquisició, control i experimentació de material bèl·lica," in *Breu Història de la Guerra Civil a Catalunya*, ed. by Josep M. Solé Sabaté and Joan Villarroya (Barcelona: Edicions 62, 2005), 317–328

Díaz, Carlos, *Víctor García, "el Marco Polo del anarquismo"* (Madrid: Madre Tierra, 1993)

Díez Torre, Alejandro R., *Trabajan para la eternidad. Colectividades de trabajo y ayuda mutua durante la Guerra Civil en Aragón* (Madrid and Zaragoza: La Malatesta Editorial and Prensas Universitarias de Zaragoza, 2009)

Ealham, Chris, "The myth of the maddened crowd: class, culture and space in the revolutionary urbanist project in Barcelona, 1936–1937" in *The Splintering of Spain: Cultural History and the Spanish Civil War, 1936–1939*, ed. by Chris Ealham and Michael Richards (Cambridge: Cambridge University Press, 2005), 111–132

Ealham, Chris, "Una revolución a medias: los orígenes de los hechos de mayo y la crisis del anarquismo," *Viento Sur*, (2007), 93–101

Ealham, Chris, *Anarchism and the City: Revolution and Counter-revolution in Barcelona, 1898–1937* (Oakland: AK Press, 2010)

Ealham, Chris, "De la unidad antifascista a la desunión libertaria," in *La España del Frente Popular*, coord. by Àngel Bahamonde Magro (Madrid: Casa de Velázquez, 2011), 121–142

Ealham, Chris, "Spanish Anarcho-Syndicalists in Toulouse: The Red-and-Black Counter-City in Exile," *Bulletin of Spanish Studies*, *91, 1–2* (2014), 95–114

Ealham, Chris, *Living Anarchism: José Peirats and the Spanish Anarcho-Syndicalist Movement* (Oakland: AK Press, 2015)

Elorza, Antonio and Marta Bizcarrondo, *Queridos Camaradas. La Internacional Comunista en España, 1919–1939* (Barcelona: Planeta, 1999)

Enzensberger, Hans Magnus, *El corto verano de la anarquía. Vida y muerte de Durruti*, trans. by Julio Forcat and Ulrike Hartmann (Barcelona: Editorial Anagrama, 2010)

Esenwein, George and Adrian Shubert, *Spain at War: The Spanish Civil War in Context, 1931–1939* (London: Longman, 1997)

Evans, Danny, "'Ultra-Left' Anarchists and Anti-Fascism in the Second Republic," *International Journal of Iberian Studies*, *29*, 3 (2016), 241–256

Fernández, Eliseo, "The FAI in Galicia," in *Anarchism in Galicia: Organisation, Resistance and Women in the Underground*, ed. and trans. by Paul Sharkey (London: Kate Sharpley Library, 2011), 1–20

Fernández Soria, Juan Manuel, *Cultura y libertad. La educación en las Juventudes Libertarias (1936–1939)* (Valencia: Universitat de Valencia, 1996)

Fontanillas, Antonia, "Nacimiento de la FIJL," in Felípe Alaíz, Víctor García and Antonia Fontanillas, *Vidas cortas pero llenas. 80 aniversario de la fundación de la FIJL* (Badalona: Centre d'Estudis Llibertaris Federica Montseny, 2012)

Fraser, Ronald, *Blood of Spain: The Experience of Civil War, 1936–1939* (London: Penguin, 1979)

Gabriel, Pere, "Un sindicalismo de Guerra: sindicatos y colectivizaciones industrials y agrarias en Cataluña, 1936–1939," *Actes II Seminari sobre la guerra cvil i el franquisme a Catalunya, Barberà del Vallès 14 i 15 de març de 1997* (Barberà del Vallès: Ajuntament de Barberà del Vallès, 1997), 55–77

Gabriel, Pere, *Historia de la UGT, Vol. 4. Un sindicalismo de guerra, 1936–1939* (Madrid: Siglo XXI, 2011)

Garangou, Sònia, *Les Joventuts Llibertàries de Catalunya (1932-1939)* (Maçanet de la Selva: Editorial Gregal, 2017)

García, Hugo, "Was there an Antifascist Culture in Spain during the 1930s?," in *Rethinking Antifascism: History, Memory and Politics, 1922 to the Present*, ed. by Hugo García, Mercedes Yusta, Xavier Tabet and Cristina Clímaco (New York: Berghahn, 2016), 92–113

García, Víctor, "José Xena Torrent: Aporte para una biografía necesaria," *Orto*, 54 (1989), 32-35

Gallego, Ferran, *La crisis del antifascismo. Barcelona, mayo de 1937* (Barcelona: Random House, 2008)

Gallordo Romero, Juan José and José Manuel Márquez Rodríguez, *Revolución y guerra en Gramenet del Besòs (1936–1939)* (Barcelona: Grupo de Estudios Históricos Gramenet del Besòs, 1997)

Gascón, Antonio and Agustín Guillamón, "Antonio Martín Escudero (1895–1937) 'The Durruti of the Cerdaña'," trans. by Paul Sharkey, Christie Books website (2015), http://www.christiebooks.com/ChristieBooksWP/2015/03/antonio-martin-escudero-1895-1937-the-durruti-of-the-cerdana-by-antonio-gascon-and-agustin-guillamon-translated-by-paul-sharkey [accessed 6December2017]

Gascón, Antonio and Agustín Guillamón, *Nacionalistas contra anarquistas en la Cerdaña (1936-1937)* (Barcelona: Descontrol, 2018)

Gimenólogos, Los, *En busca de los Hijos de la Noche. Notas sobre los Recuerdos de la guerra de España de Antoine Gimenez*, trans. by Francisco Madrid Santos, Carlos García Velasco and Los Gimenólogos (Logroño: Pepitas de calabaza ed., 2009)

Girón Sierra, Álvaro, "Una historia contada de otra manera: librepensamiento y 'darwinismos' anarquistas en Barcelona, 1869–1910," in *Cultura y política del anarquismo en España e Iberoamérica*, coord. by Clara E. Lida and Pablo Yankelevich (Mexico City: El Colegio de México, 2012), 95–133

Godicheau, François, "Los Hechos de Mayo de 1937 y los 'presos antifascistas': identificación de un fenómeno represivo," *Historia Social*, 3, 44 (2002), 39–63

Godicheau, François, *La Guerre d'Espagne. République et révolution en Catalogne (1936–1939)* (Paris: Odile Jacob, 2004)

Godicheau, François, "Periódicos clandestinos anarquistas en 1937–1938: ¿las voces de la base militante?," *Ayer*, 55 (2004), 175–205

Godicheau, François, *No callaron: las voces de los presos antifascistas de la República, 1937–1939* (Toulouse: Presses Universitaires du Mirail, 2012)

Gómez Casas, Juan, *Historia del anarcosindicalismo español* (Madrid: Zero, 1973)

Gómez Casas, Juan, *Anarchist Organisation: The History of the FAI*, trans. by Abe Bluestein (Montréal: Black Rose Books, 1986)

Graham, Helen, "The Socialist Youth in the JSU: the experience of organisational unity, 1936–8" in *Spain in Conflict 1931–1939, Democracy and Its Enemies*, ed. by Martin Blinkhorn (London: Sage Publications, 1986), 83–102

Graham, Helen, *Socialism and War: The Spanish Socialist Party in Power and Crisis, 1936–1939* (Cambridge University Press: Cambridge, 1991)

Graham, Helen, "'Against the State': A Genealogy of the Barcelona May Days (1937)," *European History Quarterly*, *29*, 4 (1999) 485–542

Graham, Helen, *The Spanish Republic at War* (Cambridge: Cambridge University Press, 2002)

Guillamón, Agustín, "Josep Rebull de 1937 a 1939: la crítica interna a la política del CE del POUM durante la Guerra de España," *Balance. Cuadernos de historia del movimiento obrero*, *19* and *20* (2000)

Guillamón, Agustín, *Barricadas en Barcelona. La CNT de la victoria de Julio de 1936 a la necesaria derrota de Mayo de 1937* (Barcelona: Ediciones Espartaco Internacional, 2007)

Guillamón, Agustín, *La Revolución de los Comités. Hambre y Violencia en la Barcelona Revolucionaria. De junio a diciembre de 1936* (Barcelona: Aldarull Edicions, 2012)

Guillamón, Agustín, *Los Amigos de Durruti. Historia y antología de textos* (Barcelona: Aldarull and Dskntrl-ed, 2013)

Guillamón, Agustín, *Los Comités de Defensa de la CNT en Barcelona, 1933–1938* (Barcelona: Aldarull, 2013)

Guillamón, Agustín, "Justo Bueno (1907–1944)" (2014), http://grupgerminal.org/?q=system/files/JustoBueno-1907-1944-Guillamon.pdf [accessed 1December2017]

Guillamón, Agustín, *La Guerra del pan. Hambre y violencia en la Barcelona revolucionaria. De diciembre de 1936 a mayo de 1937* (Barcelona: Aldarull and Dskntrl-ed, 2014)

Guillamón, Agustín, *La repression contra la CNT y los revolucionarios. Hambre y violencia en la Barcelona revolucionaria. De mayo a septiembre de 1937* (Barcelona: Descontrol, 2015)

Guillamón, Agustín, *Insurrección. Las sangrientas jornadas del 3 al 7 de mayo de 1937* (Barcelona: Descontrol, 2017)

Gutiérrez Molina, José Luís, *Crisis burguesa y unidad obrera. El sindicalismo en*

Cádiz durante la Segunda República (Madrid: Madre Tierra, 1994)

Gutiérrez Molina, José Luis, *Valeriano Orobón Fernández. Anarcosindicalismo y revolución en Europa* (Valladolid: Libre Pensamiento, 2002)

Hill, Christopher, *The Experience of Defeat: Milton and Some Contemporaries* (London: Faber and Faber, 1984)

Hobsbawm, E. J., "Religion and the Rise of Socialism," in E. J. Hobsbawm, *Worlds of Labour: Further Studies in the History of Labour* (London: Weidenfeld and Nicolson, 1984), 33–48

Ibárruri, Dolores, coord., *Guerra y Revolución en España 1936–1938, Vol. 3* (Moscow: Editorial Progreso, 1971)

Iñiguez, Miguel, *Esbozo de una enciclopedia histórica del anarquismo español* (Madrid: Fundación de Estudios Libertarios Anselmo Lorenzo, 2001)

Jackson, Gabriel, *The Spanish Republic and the Civil War 1931–1939* (New Jersey: Princeton University Press, 1965)

Kelsey, Graham, *Anarcho-syndicalism, Libertarian Communism and the State: The CNT in Zaragoza and Aragon, 1930–1937* (Amsterdam: International Institute of Social History, 1991)

Ledesma, José Luis, *Los días de llamas de la revolución. Violencia y política en la retaguardia republicana de Zaragoza durante la Guerra Civil* (Zaragoza: Institución "Fernando el Católico," 2003)

Ledesma, José Luis, "Una retaguardia al rojo. Las violencias en la zona republicana" in *Violencia Roja y Azul. España, 1936–1950*, ed. by Francisco Espinosa (Barcelona: Crítica, 2010), 146–247

Lines, Lisa, *Milicianas: Women in Combat in the Spanish Civil War* (Lanham: Lexington Books, 2012)

Linhard, Tabea Alexa, *Fearless Women in the Mexican Revolution and the Spanish Civil War* (Missouri: University of Missouri Press, 2005)

Lorenzo, César M., *Los anarquistas españoles y el poder* (Paris: Ruedo Ibérico, 1972)

Madrid Santos, Francisco, "Camillo Berneri, un anarquista italiano (1897–1937)," (Unpublished PhD thesis, Universidad de Barcelona, 1979)

Madrid, Francisco, "Los anarquistas internacionales en la Revolución Española" (n.d.), http://www.cedall.org/Documentacio/IHL/Anarquistas%20Revolucion%20Espanola.pdf [accessed 6December2017]

Marín Silvestre, Dolors, "Anarquistas y Sindicalistas en L'Hospitalet. La creación de un proyecto de autodidactismo obrero," in *El cinturón rojinegro: radicalismo cenetitsta y obrerismo en la periferia de Barcelona 1918–1939*, ed. by José Luís Oyón and Juan José Gallardo (Barcelona: Ediciones Carena, 2003), 125–146

Marín, Dolors, *Ministros Anarquistas. La CNT en el Gobierno de la II República (1936–1939)* (Barcelona: Random House, 2005)

Márquez Rodríguez, José Manuel and Juan José Gallardo Romero, *Ortiz, general sin Dios ni amo* (Barcelona: ed. Hacer, 1999)

Mintz, Frank, "Las influencias de Bakunin y Kropotkin sobre el movimiento libertario español," *Historia Actual Online*, 21 (2010), http://www.historia-actual.org/Publicaciones/index.php/haol/article/viewArticle/415 [accessed 6December2017]

Mintz, Frank, *Anarchism and Workers' Self-Management in Revolutionary Spain*, trans. by Paul Sharkey (Oakland: AK Press, 2013)

Mintz, Frank and Kelsey, Graham, "El Consejo Nacional de Defensa y el movimiento libertario," in *Cuadernos de la Guerra Civil. Consejo Nacional de Defensa* (Madrid: Fundación Salvador Seguí Ediciones, 1989), 7–20

Mintz, Jerome R., *The Anarchists of Casas Viejas* (Bloomington: Indiana University Press, 2004)

Monjo, Anna, *Militants. Participació i democràcia a la CNT als anys trenta* (Barcelona: Laertes, 2003)

Monjo, Anna and Carme Vega, *Els treballadors i la Guerra civil* (Barcelona: Editorial Empúries, 1986)

Moradiellos, Enrique, *Don Juan Negrín* (Barcelona: Ediciones Península, 2006)

Nadal, Antonio, *Guerra Civil en Málaga* (Málaga: Editorial Arguval, 1984)

Nash, Mary, *Defying Male Civilization: Women in the Spanish Civil War* (Denver: Arden Press, 1995)

Navarro Navarro, Javier, "Mundo obrero, cultura y asociacionismo: algunas reflexiones sobre modelos y pervivencias formales," *Hispania*, 63, 2 (2003), 467–484

Navarro Navarro, Javier, *A la revolución por la cultura. Prácticas culturales y sociabilidad libertarias en el País Valenciano (1931–1939)* (Valencia: Universitat de València, 2004)

Nelles, D.et al., *Antifascistas alemanes en Barcelona (1933–1939). El Grupo DAS: sus actividades contra la red nazi y en el frente de Aragón* (Barcelona: Editorial Sintra, 2010)

Newman, Saul, "The Horizon of Anarchy: Anarchism and Contemporary Radical Thought," *Theory & Event*, 13, 2 (2010), n.p.

Núñez Seixas, Xosé M., *¡Fuera el invasor! Nacionalismos y movilización bélica durante la Guerra civil Española (1936–1939)* (Madrid: Marcial Pons, 2006)

Ossorio y Gallardo, Ángel, *Vida y Sacrificio de Companys* (Barcelona: Nova Terra, 1976)

Oyón, José Luis, *La quiebra de la ciudad popular. Espacio urbano, inmigración y anarquismo en la Barcelona de entreguerras, 1914–1936* (Barcelona: Ediciones del Serbal, 2008)

Pagès, Pelai, *Andreu Nin: Su evolución política (1911–1937)* (Madrid: Zero, 1975)

Pagès i Blanch, Pelai, *La Guerra Civil espanyola a Catalunya (1936–1939)* (Barcelona: Els llibres de la Frontera, 1997)

Pagès i Blanch, Pelai, "La Fatarella: Una insurrecció pagesa a la reraguarda catalana durant la guerra civil," *Estudis D'Historia Agrària*, *17* (2004), 659–74

Pagès i Blanch, Pelai, "El asesinato de Andreu Nin, más datos para la polémica," *Ebre 38*, *4* (2010), 57–76

Pateman, Barry, "Anarchist History: Confessions of an awkward pupil," *Bulletin of the Kate Sharpley Library*, *84* (2015), 1–3

Payne, Stanley G., "A Critical Overview of the Second Spanish Republic," in *The Spanish Second Republic Revisited. From Democratic Hopes to Civil War (1931–1936)*, ed. by Manuel Álvarez Tardío and Fernando Del Rey Reguillo (Eastbourne: Sussex Academic Press, 2013), 9–19

Paz, Abel, *Durruti en la Revolucion Española* (Madrid: Fundación de Estudios Libertarios Anselmo Lorenzo, 1996)

Paz, Abel, *Durruti in the Spanish Revolution*, trans. by Chuck Morse (Oakland: AK Press, 2007)

Paz, Abel, *The Story of the Iron Column: Militant Anarchism in the Spanish Civil War*, trans. by Paul Sharkey (Oakland: Kate Sharpley Library and AK Press, 2011)

Peirats, José, *Los anarquistas en la crisis política española* (Editorial Alfa: Buenos Aires, 1964)

Peirats, José, *Figuras del movimiento libertario español* (Barcelona: Ediciones Picazo, 1977)

Peirats, José, *The CNT in the Spanish Revolution*, *Volume 2*, trans. by Paul Sharkey and Chris Ealham (Hastings: Christie Books, 2005)

Peirats, José, *The CNT in the Spanish Revolution*, *Volume 3*, trans. by Paul Sharkey and Chris Ealham (Hastings: Christie Books, 2006)

Peirats, José, *The CNT in the Spanish Revolution*, *Volume 1*, trans. by Chris Ealham (Hastings: PM Press, 2011)

Pirani, Simon, *The Russian Revolution in Retreat, 1920–24: Soviet Workers and the New Communist Elite* (London: Routledge, 2008)

Pons Prades, Eduardo, "Summer 1936: Why did we fail to take Zaragoza?," trans. by Paul Sharkey, Christie Books website (2011), http://www.christiebooks.com/wp-content/uploads/2011/07/Zaragoza.pdf [accessed 6 December2017]

Pozo González, Josep Antoni, *La Catalunya antifeixista, El govern Tarradellas enfront de la crisi política i el conflicte social (setembre de 1936 – abril de 1937)* (Barcelona: Edicions DAU, 2012)

Pozo González, Josep Antoni, *Poder legal y poder real en la Cataluña revolucionaria de 1936* (Sevilla: Espuela de Plata, 2012)

Prece, María Eugenia, "Barcelona y Guerra Civil," part of a series of works related to Gustavo Cochet held at the Museo Gustavo Cochet, http://ccpe.org.ar/textos.pdf [accessed 6December2017]

Preston, Paul, "The Creation of the Popular Front in Spain," in *The Popular Front in Europe*, ed. by Helen Graham and Paul Preston (New York: St. Martin's Press, 1987)

Preston, Paul, *The Coming of the Spanish Civil War: Reform, Reaction and Revolution in the Second Republic* (London and New York: Routledge, 1994)

Preston, Paul, *The Spanish Civil War: Reaction, Revolution and Revenge* (New York: W. W. Norton & Company, 2007)

Preston, Paul, *The Spanish Holocaust: Inquisition and Extermination in Twentieth-Century Spain* (London: Harper Press, 2012)

Preston, Paul, *The Last Days of the Spanish Republic* (London: William Collins, 2016)

Purkiss, Richard, *Democracy, Trade Unions and Political Violence in Spain: The Valencian Anarchist Movement, 1918–1936* (Brighton: Sussex Academic Press, 2015)

Quirosa-Cheyrouze y Muñoz, Rafael, *Almería, 1936–37. Sublevación militar y alteraciones en la retaguardia republicana* (Almería: Universidad de Almería, 1996)

Rabinowitch, Alexander, *The Bolsheviks in Power: The First Year of Soviet Rule in Petrograd* (Bloomington: Indiana University Press, 2008)

Radcliff, Pamela Beth, *From Mobilization to Civil War: The Politics of Polarization in the Spanish City of Gijón, 1900–1937* (Cambridge: Cambridge University Press, 1996)

Radosh, Ronald, Mary R. Habeck and Grigory Evostianov, eds, *Spain Betrayed: The Soviet Union in the Spanish Civil War* (London: Yale University Press, 2001)

Raguer, Hilari, *La pólvora y el incienso. La iglesia y la Guerra civil Española (1936–1939)* (Barcelona: Ediciones Península, 2001)

Richards, Vernon, *Lessons of the Spanish Revolution (1936-1939)* (London: Freedom Press, 1995)

Rider, Nicholas, "Anarchism, Urbanisation and Social Conflict in Barcelona, 1930–1932" (Unpublished PhD thesis, University of Lancaster, 1987)

Rider, Nick, "The practice of direct action: The Barcelona rent strike of 1931," in *For Anarchism: History, Theory and Practice*, ed. by David Goodway (London: Routledge, 1989), 79–105

Ridley, F. F., *Revolutionary Syndicalism in France: The Direct Action of its Time* (London: Cambridge University Press, 1970)

Rocker, Rudolf, *Anarcho-Syndicalism* (London: Pluto Press, 1989)

Roediger, David, *Seizing Freedom: Slave Emancipation and Liberty for All* (London: Verso, 2015).

Ruiz, Juan, "José Grunfeld (1907–2005)" (2006), *Kate Sharpley Library*, http://www.katesharpleylibrary.net/tqjrbp [accessed 6 December2017]

Sagués, Joan, "'Lleida la Roja.' El poder obrer a la capital de la Terra Ferma," in *Breu Història de la Guerra Civil a Catalunya*, ed. by Josep M. Solé Sabaté and Joan Villarroya (Barcelona: Edicions 62, 2005), 175–182

Santamaría, Jesús L., "Juventudes Libertarias y Guerra Civil (1936–1939)," *Studia Histórica*, 1 (1983), 215–222

Sanz, Carles, *La CNT en pie. Fundación y consolidación anarcosindicalista 1910–1931* (Barcelona: Anomia, 2010)

Scott, James C., "Foreword," in *Everyday Forms of State Formation: Revolution and the Negotiation of Rule in Modern Mexico*, ed. by Gilbert M. Joseph and Daniel Nugent (Durham and London: Duke University Press, 1994), vii–xii

Seidman, Michael, *Workers Against Work: Labor in Paris and Barcelona During the Popular Fronts* (Oxford: University of California Press, 1991)

Shubert, Adrian, "The epic failure: The Asturian revolution of October 1934," in *Revolution and War in Spain*, ed. by Paul Preston (London: Methuen, 1984)

Smith, Angel, *Anarchism, Revolution and Reaction: Catalan Labour and the Crisis of the Spanish State, 1898–1923* (New York: Berghahn Books, 2007)

Smith, Angel, "Los anarquistas y anarcosindicalistas ante la cuestión nacional," in *Izquierdas y nacionalismos en la España contemporánea*, ed. by Javier Moreno Luzón (Madrid: Editorial Pablo Iglesias, 2011), 141–156

Smith, S. A., *Red Petrograd: Revolution in the Factories 1917–1918* (Cambridge: Cambridge University Press, 1983)

Tavera, Susanna, "Anarchism or Anarchisms? The history of a heterogeneous revolutionary deployment, 1930–1938," *Catalan Historical Review*, 5 (2012), 101–116

Termes, Josep, *Anarquismo y sindicalismo en España. La Primera Internacional (1864–1881)* (Barcelona: Ariel, 1972)

Thomas, Maria, *The Faith and the Fury: Popular Anticlerical Violence and Iconoclasm in Spain, 1931–1936* (Brighton: Sussex Academic Press, 2013)

Tosstorff, Reiner, *El POUM en la revolució Espanyola* (Barcelona: Editorial Base, 2009)

Vadillo, Julián, "Desarollo y debates en los grupos anarquistas de la FAI en el Madrid Republicano," *Germinal*, 4 (2007), 27–65

Vega, Carme, Anna Monjo and Mercedes Vilanova, "Socialización y hechos de mayo: una nueva aportación a partir del proceso a Mauricio Stevens

(2 de junio de 1937)," *Historia y Fuente Oral, 3* (1990), 93–103

Vega, Eulàlia, *El trentisme a Catalunya. Divergències ideològiques en la CNT (1930–1933)* (Barcelona: Curial, 1980)

Vega, Eulàlia, *Entre revolució i reforma. La CNT a Catalunya (1930–1936)* (Lleida: Pagès, 2004)

Vega, Eulàlia, *Pioneras y revolucionarias. Mujeres libertarias durante la República, la Guerra Civil y el Franquismo* (Barcelona: Icaria, 2010)

Villa García, Roberto, "'Obreros, no votéis.' La CNT y el Frente Popular en las elecciones de 1936," *Pasado y Memoria. Revista de Historia Contemporánea, 13* (2014), 173–196

Wade, Rex A., *Red Guards and Workers' Militias in the Russian Revolution* (Stanford: Stanford University Press, 1984)

Weber, Max, "Politics as a Vocation," in *From Max Weber: Essays in Sociology*, ed. by H. H. Gerth and C. Wright Mills (London: Routledge, 1995), 77–128

Woodcock, George, *Anarchism* (Plymouth: Broadview Press, 2004)

Yeoman, James Michael, "Print Culture and the Formation of the Anarchist Movement in Spain" (Unpublished PhD thesis, University of Sheffield, 2016)

Anonymously authored online articles

"Anarcoefemèrides del 20 de febrer," http://www.estelnegre.org/anarcoefem erides/2002.html [accessed 6 December 2017]

"Antonio Bonilla Albadalejo – anarquista de la columna durruti," http:// puertoreal.cnt.es/bilbiografias-anarquistas/4329-antonio-bonilla-albadalejo-anarquista-de-la-columna-durruti.html [accessed 6 December 2017]

"Juan Giménez Arenas – anarquista conocido como el Quijote de Banat," http://puertoreal.cnt.es/bilbiografias-anarquistas/4337-juan-gimenez-arenas-anarquista-conocido-como-el-quijote-de-banat.html [accessed 6 December 2017]

"Juan Turtós Vallès – Anarquista del Grupo Orto," http://puertoreal.cnt.es/ bilbiografias-anarquistas/3415-juan-turtos-valles-anarquista-del-grupo-orto.html [accessed 6 December 2017]

"Mesas, Baldomero," http://militants-anarchistes.info/spip.php?article10656 [accessed 6 December 2017]

"Suñer Vidal, Matias" (2016), http://militants-anarchistes.info/spip .php?article13135 [accessed 1 December 2017]

Index

Page numbers in *italic* refer to illustrations. "Passim" (literally "scattered") indicates intermittent discussion of a topic over a cluster of pages.

Danny Evans is a Lecturer in Modern European History at Liverpool Hope University. He has published on anarchism and anti-fascism in a special issue of the *International Journal of Iberian Studies* that he co-edited with James Michael Yeoman on "New Approaches to Spanish Anarchism" (2016). His interests include the anarchist commitment to internationalism and gender equality in Spain, and the post-revolutionary experiences of defeat and exile.